Rational Expectations in Macroeconomics

Rational Expectations in Macroeconomics

An Introduction to Theory and Evidence

Second Edition
C. L. F. Attfield, D. Demery
and N. W. Duck

BLACKWELL
Oxford UK & Cambridge USA

Copyright © Clifford Attfield, David Demery, Nigel Duck, 1985, 1991

First published 1985
Reprinted 1986, 1987, 1989
Second edition 1991

Basil Blackwell Ltd
108 Cowley Road, Oxford, OX4 1JF, UK

Basil Blackwell, Inc.
3 Cambridge Center
Cambridge, Massachusetts 02142, USA

British Library Cataloguing in Publication Data

A CIP catalogue record for this book is available from the British Library.

Library of Congress Cataloging in Publication Data

Attfield, C. L. F. (Clifford L. F.)
Rational expectations in macroeconomics : an introduction to
theory and evidence / C. L. F. Attfield, D. Demery, and N. W. Duck. —
2nd ed.
p. cm.
Includes bibliographical references and index.
ISBN 0-631-17344-7 — ISBN 0-631-17947-X
1. Rational expectations (Economic theory) 2. Macroeconomics.
I. Demery, David. II. Duck, N. W. (Nigel W.) III. Title.
HB172.5.A79 1991
339'.0724—dc20 90-43291 CIP

Typeset in 11 on 13 pt Times
by Colset Private Limited, Singapore

Contents

Tables and Figures

Preface

In the years since the first edition of this book, the rational expectations hypothesis has become the standard, in fact almost the only,
general method of modelling expectations in macroeconomics and
in economics generally. The exploration and testing of the implications of the rational expectations hypothesis for complete macroeconomic models and for the individual components of those
models have been the main features of macroeconomic research.
The hypothesis has in effect radically transformed macroeconomic
research and modelling. However, the evidence relating to the
hypothesis is very mixed. The dominant role assumed by rational
expectations is more because of its theoretical appeal, and the
absence of an equally attractive alternative, than because of an
overwhelming weight of evidence in its favour.

In this book we attempt to explain in detail the rational expectations hypothesis and its role in macroeconomics. The book is
primarily intended for students who have studied macroeconomics
for at least a year and who, therefore, have some idea of the importance of expectations within macroeconomics, but who have not
yet studied the rational expectations hypothesis in any depth. The
book is very much an introduction to the topic; we have not set
out to explain all the implications of the rational expectations
hypothesis for macroeconomics (even if that were to be possible).
To attempt to do so would involve the introduction of material
which is technically very demanding, much of which is covered in
other books, notably Begg (1982), Minford and Peel (1983) and
Pesaran (1987).

Because the book is an introduction, we shall assume only
average mathematical skills and, where possible, use verbal and

diagrammatic techniques. However, this is not always possible, for the rational expectations hypothesis leads inevitably at times to complications which can only be dealt with efficiently by the use of mathematics. The mathematics employed rarely requires knowledge of more than simple algebra.

The book is organized as follows. In chapter 1 we illustrate the pervasive importance of expectations in macroeconomics. In chapter 2 we present a general statement of the rational expectations hypothesis, which forms the basis of the rest of the book. We also consider some of the general criticisms which have been directed against the hypothesis. In chapter 3 we explain most of the basic ideas involved in the testing of rational expectations models and give some illustrations. Chapter 4 presents a simple prototype 'island' model and considers its policy implications. In chapter 5 we examine criticisms of that model and consider some important theoretical counter-examples. In chapters 6 and 7 we consider the empirical evidence relevant to the models discussed in the previous two chapters. We discuss in chapter 8 the theoretical and empirical foundations for what has become known as 'real business cycle models'. Chapter 9 reviews the literature on rational expectations and the consumption function which has been a major area of applied research in recent years. We end the book with a brief summary in chapter 10.

During the preparation of the first edition of this book, the authors were in receipt of a grant from the Leverhulme Trust for research into rational expectations and macroeconomics, which they gratefully acknowledge. They are particularly grateful to Willem Buiter, Angus Deaton, Giancarlo Marini and Caroline Joll for helpful discussions on many of the ideas expressed in this book. The authors also appreciated helpful criticisms from many of our undergraduate students and from members of the Leverhulme Workshop in the University of Bristol, especially from Simon Burgess, John Beath, Paul Bowles, Martin Browning, Richard Dunn, Susan Harvey, Simon Musgrave, Martin Shell, David Webb, David Winter and Alan Winters.

C. L. F. Attfield
D. Demery
N. W. Duck
University of Bristol

1

Expectations in Macroeconomics

1.1 THE IMPORTANCE OF EXPECTATIONS IN MACROECONOMICS

It would be difficult to exaggerate the importance of the role that
expectations play throughout macroeconomics. Few, if any, of the
important macroeconomic relationships such as the consumption
function or the demand for money function are likely to be free
from the influence of *expected* variables, such as expected income
or the expected interest rate. And when such relationships are
combined to form a full macroeconomic model the general characteristics and policy implications of that model will depend upon
precisely how expectations are formed. This book is primarily
about one theory of how expectations are formed, the theory of
rational expectations. We begin it by illustrating the pervasive
importance of expectations in macroeconomics by considering in
turn the simple Keynesian IS–LM model, the permanent-income
hypothesis and the natural rate hypothesis.

(a) Expectations in the Keynesian IS–LM model

Consider the elementary Keynesian view of the economy expressed
in conventional IS–LM terms. According to this view the IS curve
is volatile: it is likely to shift by quite large amounts as firms change
the amount of investment expenditure that they wish to undertake.
Such volatility in the IS curve would be of no great importance
for the level of aggregate demand in the economy if the LM
curve were very steep: it would merely lead to sharp changes in
the rate of interest. But another important feature of elementary
Keynesian analysis is that the LM curve is not steep; indeed it is
likely, at times, to be nearly horizontal. It follows then that sharp

fluctuations in aggregate demand will occur whenever sharp shifts in the position of the IS curve interact with a near-horizontal LM curve. Indeed, this can be seen as the essential message of Keynes's (1936) *General Theory*: sharp fluctuations in aggregate demand .can originate in the private sector, and because they are likely to lead to sharp, undesirable fluctuations in the level of output and employment the government should vary its own expenditures to offset them.

But why do Keynesians believe that the IS curve is volatile and the LM curve horizontal? Parts of the answers to both questions are the same: because of their beliefs about how expectations of certain variables are formed. The volatile IS curve arises in Keynes's view because firms' expectations about the future profitability of their investment projects are themselves highly volatile; they are subject to what Keynes called in the following passage 'animal spirits':

> Most . . . of our decisions to do something positive . . . can only be taken as a result of animal spirits – of a spontaneous urge to action rather than inaction and not as the outcome of a weighted average of quantitative benefits multiplied by quantitative probabilities. Enterprise only pretends to itself to be mainly actuated by the statements in its own prospectus, however candid and sincere. Only a little more than an expedition to the South Pole is it based on an exact calculation of benefits to come. Thus if animal spirits are dimmed and the spontaneous optimism falters . . . enterprise will fade and die – though fears of loss may have a basis no more reasonable than hopes of profit had before. (J.M. Keynes, 1936, pp. 161–2)

Thus a belief about expectations is behind the Keynesian view that the IS curve is volatile. Another belief about expectations plays the key role in determining the slope of the LM curve, although what is important here are expectations about the future interest rate. According to Keynes's view of the demand for money, the typical individual holds a view or an expectation of what the future interest rate is likely to be. If the actual interest rate is below its expected value the individual expects the interest rate to rise and hence the price of bonds to fall. There will, for each individual, be some actual rate of interest so low that the expected losses from holding bonds just outweigh the interest earned on them. At this interest rate – sometimes called the critical rate of interest – the individual's demand for money becomes extremely responsive to a change in the rate of interest: if the interest rate falls below the critical rate, the individual, fearing large capital losses on bond holdings, will wish to hold no bonds and her demand for money will increase sharply. On certain assumptions there will be some interest rate so low that the *aggregate* demand for money will likewise become very responsive to interest rate changes. It is this extreme responsiveness of the demand for money to changes in the rate of interest – the so-called liquidity trap – which makes the LM curve horizontal and implies that sharp fluctuations in aggregate demand will occur in response to movements of the IS curve. If expectations about the future interest rate change quickly in response to changes in the actual interest rate these sharp fluctuations in aggregate demand might be short-lived and, for policy purposes, unimportant. But Keynes and his followers believed expectations about the future rate of interest to be very slow moving; indeed, in effect they treated the expected or normal interest rate as a constant for each individual. Thus the LM curve was horizontal at a more or less constant rate of interest.

Expectations therefore play a key dual role in the elementary Keynesian analysis: volatile expectations about the profitability of future investment projects are the source of sharp shifts in the IS curve; near-constant expectations about the future rate of interest are part of the mechanism by which such shifts produce sharp movements in aggregate demand.

The precise assumptions made in each case are crucial to the policy implications of the Keynesian model. If expectations about the future profitability of investment projects were *constant* but expectations about the future level of interest rates were highly sensitive to the *current* value of the interest rate, the IS curve might not be volatile and the LM curve not be flat at a constant rate of interest. As a result, fluctuations in the private sector's spending plans would not be so severe and government measures to offset them would not be so necessary. Thus a major policy implication of the *General Theory* would no longer follow.

(b) Expectations and the consumption function

One development in the post-Keynesian theory of the consumption function has been the permanent-income hypothesis. We shall discuss this more fully in chapter 9. The essential idea is that when deciding the level of their consumption expenditure people will take into account a fairly long-term view of their income prospects. Thus, when deciding how much to spend in any month or year they will not consider merely their actual income in that month or year; instead, their consumption will be related to what is termed their permanent income. The precise definition of permanent income need not yet concern us but it is clearly related to expectations about income prospects. Indeed, its originator, Milton Friedman (1957), describes the permanent component of income as 'analogous to the "expected" value of a probability distribution' (p. 21).

The actual value of consumption expenditure in any period – which is a key component of total spending in an economy – depends then on an expected variable, in this case expected or permanent income. So here too expectations play an important role: if a rise in actual income causes a rise in expected income, consumption expenditure will rise; but if, when actual income rises, expected income remains unchanged then so will consumption expenditure. This result has wider macroeconomic implications. If the government increases its own expenditure in an effort to stimulate the economy and if this causes a rise in actual income, there will, according to the Keynesian view of consumption, be further increases in spending because consumption expenditure rises as actual income rises. This is the basic idea behind Keynes's multiplier. But if consumption expenditure is determined by permanent or expected income, and if the rise in government expenditure leaves expected income unchanged, then there may not be the type of multiplier process which Keynes predicted. So the method by which people form their expectations about their income may be important not only for the purposes of predicting consumption expenditure, but also for the ability of government policies to affect aggregate demand.

(c) Expectations and the natural rate hypothesis

As a final illustration of the importance of expectations consider the so-called natural rate of unemployment hypothesis as put forward by Friedman (1968). Again, we shall have more to say about this in later chapters, but its central point can be made quite simply. Workers are interested not in the *nominal* value of their wage rate, W, but in its *real* value – the quantity of goods it will buy – W/P, where P is the general level of prices. But while workers know the value of the nominal wage rate they are receiving they cannot know for certain what the prices of all goods will be when they come to buy them. They will, therefore, have to form an *expectation* of what the general level of prices will be. If their nominal wage and their expectation of the general level of prices together make them think that their real wage is high they will supply more labour, whereas if their real wage looks low to them they will not. Now imagine an increase in aggregate spending which is tending to raise prices and is encouraging firms to raise the nominal wage rate that they are offering to workers in order to attract more labour. If workers correctly foresee the rise in prices they will realize that the higher nominal wages that they are being offered do not imply higher real wages and will therefore not supply any more labour: thus the rise in aggregate spending will have little or no effect on employment. But if workers do not foresee the rise in prices then the higher nominal wage offers will appear to them to imply higher real wages and they will therefore supply more labour. In this case the rise in aggregate spending will have stimulated employment.

The precise method by which workers form their expectations of future prices therefore influences the effect that changes in aggregate spending have on employment. And since one way in which governments attempt to influence employment is by influencing aggregate spending it follows that the way in which workers form their expectations is important for the power of government policy to influence employment.

1.2 THE NEED FOR A THEORY OF EXPECTATIONS

The pervasive importance of expectations is at the same time a frustration and a challenge to macroeconomics. It is frustrating because so little data are available on expectations. Data are readily available on *actual* prices, *actual* interest rates, *actual* income and many other *actual* series, but very few data on their *expected* counterparts. And the reason is not hard to see: it would be an enormously costly business to ask everyone in an economy what they expected the interest rate, or their income or the level of prices to be in the future. Of course, modern methods of sampling make it unnecessary to ask *everyone* what their expectations are, but it would be costly to obtain even a single, continuous and accurate expectations series. What is more, even if the collection of such data were to begin now it would be several years before a sufficiently large amount of data became available. And even if such series were available, there is an additional problem. Beliefs about the future are not easily interpretable. One individual, asked about his future price expectations, may have thought little about it if his own welfare does not depend on his being right. Another, say a trade union official negotiating a wage bargain for his workers, may well have thought much more carefully. The expectations series may include both these individuals, weighting them equally. But for the purposes, say, of explaining the behaviour of wages the trade union official's expectation might be much more important. Thus the usefulness of the series on expectations might be severely limited.

The challenge posed by the shortage of data on expectations is that of devising a theory of how expectations are formed which is *general* in its applicability, which can be *tested*, and which allows us to estimate macroeconomic relationships which include apparently unobservable expectations terms. The theory of rational expectations can be seen as an attempt to provide such a general theory of expectations formation. We begin our explanation of that theory in the next chapter. As a prelude to that chapter we consider in the remainder of this chapter an important, earlier theory of expectations formation which, while its originators would not claim it to be a general theory of expectations formation, has nevertheless frequently been used in empirical studies of inflation (e.g. Cagan, 1956), permanent income (e.g. Friedman, 1957) and in many other macroeconomic contexts. It is known as the *adaptive expectations hypothesis*.

1.3   THE ADAPTIVE EXPECTATIONS HYPOTHESIS

The essential idea of adaptive expectations is simple. It is that a person will change his expectation of any variable by some fraction of the difference between the variable's actual value last period and what he was expecting it to be last period. To illustrate, imagine that you are forming an expectation of what the rate of inflation will be this year. And imagine that the inflation rate you were expecting for last year was 10 per cent. If last year the actual rate of inflation *was* 10 per cent the adaptive expectations hypothesis predicts that you will not change your expectation about the inflation rate for this year: you will expect 10 per cent for this year too. But if last year the inflation rate was higher than 10 per cent, say 20 per cent, the hypothesis suggests that you will change your expectation of inflation for this year; more precisely, it suggests that you will raise your expectation above 10 per cent, although not necessarily all the way up to 20 per cent. And if the inflation rate last year was below 10 per cent, at say 4 per cent, it suggests that you will lower your expectation for this year to somewhere between 10 and 4 per cent. The hypothesis does not predict the exact amount by which you raise or lower your expectation: that will differ from case to case and can only be determined empirically. But the general idea is clear enough. People will change their expectation of any variable if there is a difference between what they were expecting it to be last period and what it actually was last period.

Specifically, they will raise their expectation if the actual value last period was higher than they were expecting, and they will lower their expectation if the actual value last period was below what they were expecting. If their expectation last period turned out to be correct they will not change their expectation.

This idea that people will adapt or change their expectations in response to last period's forecast error has a number of attractive features. First, it implies that if, for example, the inflation rate rises from 5 to 20 per cent and remains there, people's expectations of inflation will gradually rise (if, that is, they were initially expecting inflation to be less than 20 per cent), until they have 'homed in' on the new rate of 20 per cent. Similarly, if actual inflation falls back again to 5 per cent and remains there then, once again, people's expectations will gradually fall until they have homed in on the new rate of 5 per cent. So the adaptive expectations hypothesis has the appealing feature that while people can be fooled temporarily by the type of changes that we have assumed in the inflation rate, they will not be fooled in the longer run. It may, of course, take some time for people to adapt their expectations fully, but eventually they will catch on.

In addition to its intuitive appeal the hypothesis is apparently fairly general: we could easily have substituted unemployment, or the interest rate, or the rate of growth of real income for the inflation rate in the previous paragraph and the hypothesis would be just as reasonable.

A third attractive feature of the hypothesis is that it allows us to relate expected, *unobservable* variables to actual, *observable* variables. To see this we must first put the adaptive expectations hypothesis into a simple algebraic form. Imagine that we want to use the concept of expected income, perhaps to test the idea that consumption depends on expected rather than actual income. Of course, we do not have a direct measure of expected income – it is unobservable – but if the adaptive expectations hypothesis is correct then the following will be true:

$$Y_t^e - Y_{t-1}^e = \alpha(Y_{t-1} - Y_{t-1}^e) \tag{1.1}$$

where Y_t^e is the expected income in period t, Y_{t-1} is the actual income in period $t - 1$, and α is a positive coefficient which is less than one.

This equation can be simply rewritten as

$$Y_t^e = \alpha Y_{t-1} + (1 - \alpha)Y_{t-1}^e \tag{1.2}$$

But if equation (1.2) is generally true then it must be true for last period as well, and the period before that, and so on. Algebraically, we can derive from equation (1.2) equations (1.3)–(1.5):

$$Y_{t-1}^e = \alpha Y_{t-2} + (1 - \alpha)Y_{t-2}^e \tag{1.3}$$

$$Y_{t-2}^e = \alpha Y_{t-3} + (1 - \alpha)Y_{t-3}^e \tag{1.4}$$

$$Y_{t-3}^e = \alpha Y_{t-4} + (1 - \alpha)Y_{t-4}^e \tag{1.5}$$

and so on ad infinitum.

Using equations (1.3)–(1.5) we can substitute for Y_{t-1}^e in equation (1.2) and obtain

$$Y_t^e = \alpha Y_{t-1} + \alpha(1 - \alpha)Y_{t-2} + \alpha(1 - \alpha)^2 Y_{t-3}$$
$$+ \alpha(1 - \alpha)^3 Y_{t-4} + \ldots \tag{1.6}$$

This links the unobservable variable – expected income – to the observable variables – actual income in previous periods. In fact, this is an alternative way of viewing the adaptive expectations hypothesis. It suggests that the expectation of any variable can be written purely as a function of the past values of the actual variable: the coefficients attached to each lag are all less than one and decline as the length of the lag increases. Of course, one remaining problem is that, taken literally, equation (1.6) implies that to measure expected income this period we need observations on actual income which go back to the beginning of our time period. But if α is less than one, which the adaptive expectations hypothesis suggests it will be, then actual income in any period has less effect on current expected income the further back in time that period is. In other words, the most recent observations on actual income dominate the formation of expectations about future income. As a result, if we link the unobservable expected income to the observable values of actual income in, say, only the last five periods we will not be far wrong.

However, it is quite possible to think of many situations in which the adaptive expectations hypothesis is implausible. The reason for this implausibility is really the same in all the cases we look at below; it is that the hypothesis in effect assumes that agents ignore information which would enable them to improve the accuracy of their expectations. First, imagine an economy in which the inflation rate oscillates each period between 0 and 10 per cent. The adaptive expectations hypothesis implies that people will always expect something between 0 and 10 per cent. But is this likely when the pattern of the inflation rate is so obvious? Why should people expect an inflation rate that never occurs and never expect the inflation rates that do occur?

Another, perhaps more empirically relevant, illustration is the case in which the variable about which an expectation is being formed is continually rising or continually falling. For in this case the adaptive expectations hypothesis predicts that the expectation of the variable will always be less than the variable itself if the variable is rising, or always greater than it if it is falling. For example, start off with everyone expecting an inflation rate of 0 per cent and let the actual inflation rate be 0 per cent. And let people form expectations adaptively in accordance with the following:

$$\dot{P}_t^e = 0.5\dot{P}_{t-1} + 0.5\dot{P}_{t-1}^e \tag{1.7}$$

where $\dot{P}_t$ is the actual rate of inflation in period t, and $\dot{P}_t^e$ is the expected rate of inflation in period t.

Now let inflation start to rise by one percentage point each year: so in year one inflation is 1 per cent; in year two 2 per cent; in year three 3 per cent and so on. In year one expected inflation is 0 because last year's expectations of 0 per cent were correct. In year two expectations of inflation will rise to half the difference between actual inflation in year one, 1 per cent, and what was expected for last year, 0 per cent. So for year two expectations of inflation will be 0.5 per cent. For year three expectations of inflation will again be revised to 1.25 per cent; in year four to 2.125 per cent and so on. But each year the actual inflation rate is higher than expected. Is it plausible that people will continue to form expectations in a way which leads them to underpredict the inflation rate every period? Will they not realize that their method of forming expectations is leading to an obvious, systematic pattern in their forecasting errors, and will they not therefore change the method they are using to forecast the inflation rate? One way in which they might do this, suggested by Flemming (1976), is by 'shifting gear': they might begin to form expectations about the rate of change of inflation rather than the level of inflation. But if they do change the method by which they form expectations, whether by shifting gear or in some other way, the adaptive expectations hypothesis as formulated above is inadequate because it does not give any guide about when or under what conditions such a change in the method of expectations formation will take place, nor about the precise form of that change.

For another illustration imagine that the government has announced that it intends to increase the money supply over the coming year by 10 per cent. At the beginning of the year you might reasonably expect that the money supply at the end of the first six months will be roughly 5 per cent higher than it was at the beginning of the year. But what if it turns out to be 10 per cent higher? Does this make you expect that in the next six months the rate of growth of the money supply will be higher than 5 per cent, as the adaptive expectations hypothesis suggests? Or does it make you expect a rate of growth of 0 per cent, so that over the year as a whole the money supply will have grown in line with the government's stated policy? It is not immediately obvious what you should expect. One certainly cannot rule out the second possibility *a priori*, and so the adaptive expectations hypothesis may be misleading.

As a final example of the implausibility of the adaptive expectations hypothesis consider the ending of fixed exchange rates in the early 1970s. In the case of the UK this move to a more flexible exchange rate regime was accompanied by a large stimulus to the economy in the form of higher government spending and an increased rate of monetary growth. The fixed exchange rate was abandoned explicitly because it was felt that pressures for the exchange rate to depreciate were bound to occur as a result of the sharp boost being given to aggregate demand, and the government did not want these pressures to interfere with its aggregate demand policies. In these circumstances it would surely have been foolish to base an expectation of the future course of the exchange rate on past values of the exchange rate alone. People were practically being told that the exchange rate was going to fall. Why should they not use that more or less freely available information in forming their expectations about the exchange rate? Why should they consider only the past values of the exchange rate when predicting its future value?

All of these examples illustrate the same point: the adaptive expectations hypothesis assumes that people ignore information which would help them form better expectations. This information may be about the way in which the current value of the variable to be forecast is linked to its own past values, or about the link between the forecast variable and entirely different variables. In either case the adaptive expectations hypothesis appears to assume suboptimal behaviour on the part of agents forming expectations.

From a slightly different perspective – that of the economic model-builder – these criticisms can be seen as examples of a general criticism which could, with equal force, be applied to certain other theories of expectations formation. This criticism might be termed that of model-inconsistency. To understand what this means imagine that the variable which the economist is trying to model is the inflation rate, $\dot{P}$; and imagine that within that model expected inflation, $\dot{P}^e$, plays a role, along with other variables, in determining actual inflation, as it would, for example, if the model were designed within a natural-rate framework. We might write the model in general terms as

$$\dot{P}_t = f(X_1, X_2, \ldots, X_n, \dot{P}^e) \tag{1.8}$$

where X_1, X_2 and so on represent all of the other variables which the model suggests will affect inflation; and $f(\ )$ expresses the form in which inflation is related to the X variables and to $\dot{P}^e$.

To make this model operational a method by which people form their expectations of inflation has to be specified, linking the unobservable $\dot{P}^e$ to observable variables in some precise way. This expectations formation mechanism together with equation (1.8) then form the complete model. Given that the model itself states that actual inflation is determined in line with equation (1.8), to assume that agents within that model form their expectations of inflation according to some other, unrelated method would amount to admitting an internal inconsistency. Actual inflation is determined in one way while expectations of it are being formed in another. If the model is to be a guide to the behaviour of inflation over the longer run, one would want the method of expectation formation to be consistent with the way in which the model itself suggests that inflation is actually being determined. If there is not this consistency then there will always be scope for economic agents to change and (if the model is correct) thereby improve their method of forming expectations. But if they do then the complete model – equation (1.8) plus the specification of how $\dot{P}^e$ is formed – will change. Hence the earlier model will be inaccurate.

Therefore, for a model to be at least potentially satisfactory over the longer run it must have the characteristic that the method by which agents are assumed to form expectations about any variable within it is consistent with the way the model itself suggests that variable is determined. This will not in general be true of models which incorporate the adaptive expectations hypothesis since that hypothesis, as equations (1.1)–(1.6) illustrate, essentially links the expected variable only to lagged actual values of the variable with successively smaller (decaying) coefficients attached to higher lags, all of them less than one. There is no reason in general why a model of any variable should predict that its actual value will be linked only to its own past values or, if it is, that the coefficients decay and are less than one.

To take the examples mentioned earlier, any model which is capable of predicting oscillating or continually rising inflation, or the time path of the money supply or the behaviour of the exchange rate post-1972, is unlikely to be able to assume that agents form their expectations adaptively and in an internally consistent manner. Such an expectations formation mechanism simply could not be consistent with the model's own explanation of how the variable is being determined.

The adaptive expectations hypothesis is therefore best seen as a simple approximation which may be useful in certain conditions, for example when a variable is being determined largely by its own lagged values, but it should be not be applied without consideration of whether those conditions are likely to hold. And this is how its more sophisticated users have viewed it (see, for example, Friedman, 1968).

SUGGESTIONS FOR FURTHER READING

For a general discussion of uncertainty in economics see Shackle (1958). Keynes (1936, ch. 12) contains an interesting discussion of the formation of expectations, with particular reference to expectations about the prospective yields of a capital asset. Pesaran (1987, ch. 2 especially) argues that the search for an all-encompassing theory of expectations may be futile in view of the different types of uncertainty individuals face. Muth (1960) and Walters (1971) are early attempts to apply something like the rational expectations hypothesis to a macroeconomic model. B.M. Friedman (1979) presents an example in which adaptive expectations are optimal.

2

The Theory of Rational Expectations

This chapter provides the foundations for the rest of the book. It explains the theory of rational expectations and examines some of the criticisms of it. In this chapter both the explanation of the theory and the examination of the criticisms are general in nature. This is to emphasize the general applicability of the theory: it is not a theory which applies *only* to expectations about, say, inflation or income; it is intended as a theory of how expectations of a wide range of economic variables are formed. In later chapters we shall use the theory in specific contexts and thereby derive some more precise results, but here we just establish the basic ideas behind rational expectations. The first, and fundamental one is that many economic variables should be seen as being determined by *processes*. The process determining a variable can be seen as limiting the potential values of that variable, and in doing so it provides a basis for a rational expectation. It is this fundamental idea that we now explain.

2.1 VARIABLES AS THE OUTCOME OF PROCESSES

Imagine that you are trying to forecast the behaviour of a variable Y and that all you have to go on are the past values or 'history' of Y. And imagine that Y's history can be depicted as the bold line labelled Y in figure 2.1. At the beginning of the current period, t, you are trying to forecast the value of Y over the next five periods. Consider the figure and work out what you would forecast.

Clearly, the value of Y has fluctuated between 10 and 20 and so it would be strange if you were to forecast a value for Y which was

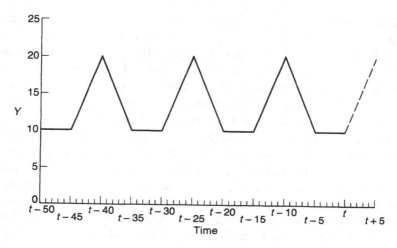

FIGURE 2.1 The behaviour of *Y* through time.

greater than 20 or less than 10. Why should such values occur if they have never occurred before? You cannot know for certain that they will not occur, but you have no real reason for believing that they are about to. So, at the very least, we would expect most people to guess five values of *Y* which lie between 10 and 20.

But we can go further than that, for it is clear from figure 2.1 that up to now *Y* has followed an obvious and simple pattern. For five periods it takes on a value of 10. For the next five periods it steadily increases by two units per period; and for the five periods after that it steadily decreases by two units per period. It is then constant at 10 for five periods and the process is repeated. Because there appears to be a process governing the behaviour of *Y*, and because it is possible to see what that process is, it seems natural to use one's knowledge of that process to forecast the next five values of *Y* – in which case one would make the predictions shown as the dotted line in figure 2.1. If the process governing the behaviour of *Y* does not change, then the actual value of *Y* will equal the prediction or expectation of *Y*.

This example is, of course, very simple but it does illustrate a fundamentally important idea. If variables are determined by systematic *processes* – if there is a pattern to a variable's behaviour – then knowledge of that pattern will be a great advantage to anyone who is trying to forecast it. The processes and links will in general be more complex than the very simple process illustrated in figure 2.1, but even when they are, it will nevertheless still be true that if the process determining a variable can be identified, expectations about the variable will be more accurately formed. To illustrate this point we draw in figure 2.2 the 'history' of a variable X up to the beginning of period t, and label the line X. What would you predict for the next five values of X?

This case is clearly more difficult since the pattern or process is harder to identify. X appears never to rise above 20 or fall below 10; it is often constant at 10; and when disturbed from this value it rises by two units for five periods and then falls by two units for five periods. But it is not easy to predict exactly when X is about to be disturbed. So on the basis of its 'history', X is more difficult to predict than Y. But what if there is a plausible economic theory which says that the value of X in any period is determined by the value of another variable Z in the previous period? In figure 2.2 we also plot the 'history' of this other variable Z as the line labelled Z. And it is clear from this line that the behaviour of Z provides the key to the pattern or process determining the behaviour of X.

The variable Z is usually constant at 5, but occasionally it rises to 7.5 for one period and then drops back again. Whenever Z rises above 5 the value of X next period is disturbed from its 'usual' value of 10 and behaves in the way described in the previous paragraph.

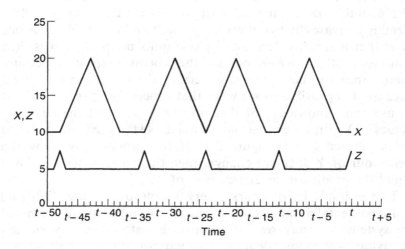

FIGURE 2.2   The behaviour of X and Z through time.

So the timing of the disturbance to X is now predictable. If Z in the previous period was 7.5 it will trigger a drawn-out disturbance in X beginning in the current period. Since in the period immediately before the current period, Z did rise above its 'usual' value it would be sensible to predict that a drawn-out disturbance in X was about to occur. Any other prediction would imply either a failure to use all the information available about the process determining X or the use of 'false' information; for example, that the process governing the behaviour of X had suddenly changed.

This example takes the fundamental idea about variables being determined by identifiable processes one stage further. In the first illustration the process determining Y is very simple and involves no variable other than Y. In this second example another variable is involved in the process. But the fundamental result is the same and can be stated quite generally: if the process determining a variable can be identified then the prediction of the variable's future value can be improved. This will be true whether the process is very simple, as in the case illustrated in figure 2.1, or more complex, as in the case shown in figure 2.2.

An implication of this general result is that predictions of any variable will be improved as more information relating to the process determining the variable is used in forming the prediction. Therefore a sensible forecaster will always use the information on the relevant process when making a forecast of any variable. A forecaster who does not use the available information on the process is acting inefficiently, and his forecast errors will be unnecessarily large.

The inefficiency of forecasts which do not use all the available information relating to the process determining the variable concerned has already been illustrated in chapter 1. There we described three cases in which adaptive expectations were inefficient. In the first, inflation oscillated each period between 0 and 10 per cent; in the second, inflation increased each period by one percentage point; and in the third, drawn from the actual behaviour of the UK government in the 1970s, the previously fixed exchange rate was to be depreciated as a result of expansionary monetary and fiscal policy. In all three cases expectations about the relevant variable would be more accurate if the process determining the variable concerned was identified and used as the basis for prediction. The pattern or processes in the first two illustrations are very simple.

Once identified they allow forecasters to make perfectly accurate predictions. In the third case the process is much more vague, but clearly forecasts of the future values of the exchange rate which take account of the available information on the government's aggregate demand policies will be more accurate than those that do not.

2.2 PROCESSES AND RATIONAL FORECASTS

It is on the basis of these considerations that the theory of rational expectations argues the following. Sensible people will use all the available information relating to the process determining a variable when forming their forecast or expectation of that variable. In economics it is usual to assume that people act sensibly or rationally. Therefore, when modelling how people form their expectations about any variable, economists should assume that expectations are formed on the basis of all the available information relating to the true or actual process governing the behaviour of the variable.

To make this central idea of the rational expectations hypothesis less vague imagine an economic variable Y, the value of which in any period t is *actually* determined by its own lagged values and by lagged values of other variables X and Z in accordance with the following process:

$$Y_t = \alpha_0 + \alpha_1 Y_{t-1} + \alpha_2 X_{t-1} + \alpha_3 Z_{t-1} \tag{2.1}$$

where X, Y and Z are all variables and α_0, α_1, and so on are constant coefficients.

It is worth emphasizing that this equation is merely an algebraic representation of a *process*, though apparently a more complex one than those shown in figures 2.1 and 2.2. It is also at this stage a very general representation: we have not said precisely what X, Y and Z represent, nor what the precise values of the α coefficients are. The reason for this generality is that the rational expectations hypothesis is a general hypothesis about expectations formation: it is not meant to apply *solely* to expectations of inflation, or to expectations of income or expectations of anything else. It is put forward as having *general* applicability to a wide range of expectations about economic phenomena. In fact, the hypothesis of rational expectations was originally applied to the problem of forecasting the future price of a good which took time to produce: its originator was John Muth (1961).

Imagine now that the process described in equation (2.1) has repeated itself sufficiently often for those forming an expectation about Y to be aware of its nature (just as when asked to guess the next values of Y in figure 2.1 you were shown a sufficiently long 'history' of Y to be able to identify the process determining Y). This means that they know which variables are affecting Y; that is, its own lagged values and the lagged values of X and Z as shown in equation (2.1). It also means that they know the actual values of the α coefficients, because these determine or are part of the process determining Y.

Consider a person who, at the end of period $t - 1$, is trying to form an expectation about the value that Y is going to take in period t. She knows that the process determining Y is given by equation (2.1): knowledge of this process is therefore said to be part of her *information set* at the end of period $t - 1$. If, as we shall assume, by the end of period $t - 1$ she also knows the values of all the lagged values of X, Y and Z, that is all the variables on the right-hand side of equation (2.1), these too are part of her information set at the end of period $t - 1$. If she is rational her expectation of what Y is going to be in period t, the expectation being formed on the basis of her information set at the end of period $t - 1$, will be formed in line with the process determining Y as follows:

$$E_{t-1} Y_t = \alpha_0 + \alpha_1 Y_{t-1} + \alpha_2 X_{t-1} + \alpha_3 Z_{t-1} \qquad (2.2)$$

where $E_{t-1} Y_t$ is the expectation of Y_t formed on the basis of the information available at the end of period $t - 1$.

More formally, $E_{t-1} Y_t$ is equal to $E(Y_t | I_{t-1})$, where E is the mathematical expectations operator and I_{t-1} is the set of information available at period $t - 1$. The rational expectation of Y_t formed at period $t - 1$ is the mathematical expectation of Y_t *conditional on the available information*. In the remainder of this book, E_i is generally the rational expectations operator for expectations formed on the basis of information dated period i.

It is an obvious implication of equation (2.2) that if Y does indeed continue to follow the process shown in equation (2.1) then this person's expectation will be perfectly accurate or, in other words, the person's *forecasting* or *expectational error* is zero. The expectational error is defined as the difference between the actual value a variable takes and the value the person was expecting it to take.

This result, that the expectational error will be zero every period, is not a general result. It is not generally the case that the rational expectations hypothesis implies that forecasters and expectations are always right. We have obtained that result in this case because we have assumed something very special about the process determining Y. We have assumed that it is *deterministic*. Most economic processes are not thought of as deterministic but as *stochastic*; that is, they include an inherently unpredictable element. The usual rationalization of this is that economics is about the behaviour of human beings, and that there is a basic and unpredictable element of randomness in human responses. One way to incorporate this element of randomness in a process such as that shown in equation (2.1) is to add to it a random variable term. This we do as follows.

$$Y_t = \alpha_0 + \alpha_1 Y_{t-1} + \alpha_2 X_{t-1} + \alpha_3 Z_{t-1} + \nu_t \qquad (2.3)$$

Here, the term ν_t is a random variable which may be positive or negative. Since this variable is seen as the result of a large number of random factors affecting human behaviour, many pulling in opposite directions, it is natural to think of small values of ν occurring more frequently than large values. In fact, it is usual to think of ν as a variable with a probability distribution centred at zero and having a constant and finite variance (σ_ν^2).

The really important feature of ν is that its value in period t is unknown at the end of period t; it is not part of the information set at period $t - 1$. But it is clear from equation (2.3) that a rational forecaster, who is using the process which actually determines Y to forecast at the end of period $t - 1$ the value of Y in the current period, has to form some expectation of the value that ν is going to take in period t. That is, the rational expectation of Y in period t based on the information set at the end of period $t - 1$ must be formed in accordance with equation (2.3) as:

$$E_{t-1} Y_t = \alpha_0 + \alpha_1 Y_{t-1} + \alpha_2 X_{t-1} + \alpha_3 Z_{t-1} + E_{t-1}\nu_t \qquad (2.4)$$

where $E_{t-1}\nu_t$ is the expectation of ν_t formed on the basis of all the information available at the end of period $t - 1$.

To be consistent, the rational expectations hypothesis must

assume that the expectation formed by the rational person of this period's value of v is made on the basis of the process determining v, given the available information at period $t - 1$. If, as we shall assume, the process determining v is such that v is a random term with a mean of zero, the value of which cannot be predicted on the basis of any information available in period $t - 1$, it follows that the best guess a rational agent can make of the current value of v is that it will equal its *mean* value. In other words the rational expectation of v in period t, based on the information set available in period $t - 1$, is that v will equal zero. Formally,

$$E_{t-1} v_t = 0 \qquad (2.5)$$

It follows from this that the rational expectation of Y in period t, based on the information available at period $t - 1$, can be written as follows:

$$E_{t-1} Y_t = \alpha_0 + \alpha_1 Y_{t-1} + \alpha_2 X_{t-1} + \alpha_3 Z_{t-1} \qquad (2.6)$$

If the actual value of Y is determined in accordance with equation (2.3), it follows that the expectational error will be given by:

$$Y_t - E_{t-1} Y_t = v_t \qquad (2.7)$$

2.3 THE GENERAL CHARACTERISTICS OF RATIONAL EXPECTATIONS

Equations (2.1)–(2.7) are of fundamental importance to the rest of this book, so it is worth repeating what they imply. Equation (2.3) shows that the variable Y is determined by a particular process, as described by the right-hand side of that equation. If people who are trying to form an expectation about Y have knowledge of that process it will make sense for them to form their expectation of Y using that knowledge. If at the end of period $t - 1$ they know the value of Y_{t-1}, X_{t-1} and Z_{t-1} their expectation of Y for period t will be given by equation (2.6). It follows that if the process determining Y remains unchanged, their forecast or expectational error will be the random component of Y, that is v. A number of important implications follow from the fact that, if the process determining Y is understood, the error of a rational expectation of Y is the same as the random component of the process determining Y. They are as follows: (a) the mean or average error is zero;

(b) there will be no discernible pattern to the expectational error;
(c) the rational expectation is in general the most accurate expectation it is possible to form. We discuss each of these characteristics in turn.

(a) The errors of rational expectations are on average zero

It is clear from equation (2.7) that once the process determining Y is allowed to be stochastic, that is to include the random component ν, the rational expectation of Y will not always be perfectly accurate, for the random component ν is inherently unpredictable. Its value only becomes known after it has occurred – it cannot be accurately guessed beforehand. So even if the process determining Y is known and even if the values of Y_{t-1}, X_{t-1} and Z_{t-1} are known in time to predict Y_t, the value of ν_t would not be known. The best the rational forecaster could do is expect the mean or average value of ν. But the mean value of ν is assumed to be zero. (In fact, the mean value of ν is really *defined* to be zero; for if the average value of ν was not zero but, say, 5 then the constant term on the right-hand side of equation (2.3) would be defined to be 5 units higher and the random error term redefined as the old one minus 5, so that its mean value was zero.) It follows that the error made each period by the rational forecaster will equal the actual value of ν in that period. Sometimes the error will be positive, sometimes negative, sometimes zero. But on average or over a large number of periods the negative errors will cancel out with the positive ones, leaving an average error of zero.

Therefore, once the process determining Y is allowed to be stochastic, rational expectations no longer have the implausible characteristic of being perfectly accurate each period. Instead they have the 'weaker' feature of being correct *on average*. This is quite consistent with large or even very large errors in any individual period. The size of the expectational error depends upon the size of the unpredictable component of the process itself. If the absolute value of ν (remember that ν can be positive or negative) tends to be large, then so will the error of a rational forecast, but that will be because Y is inherently difficult to predict, not because of an unintelligent forecasting method. And since ν can be large and negative as well as large and positive the mean value of ν and hence the average expectational error will still be zero.

(b) The errors of rational expectations exhibit no pattern

In discussing the theory of adaptive expectations we argued that if the variable being forecast was always rising, an adaptive expectation of it would always be below the actual value of the variable. There would, in other words, always be a positive error. The method by which expectations are made is hardly likely to remain unchanged in the face of such an obvious pattern to mistakes. But the adaptive expectations hypothesis does not indicate when the method of forecasting will change or how. It thus admits the possibility of a pattern to forecasting errors but is silent about the likely response to the recognition of such a pattern.

The theory of rational expectations is less vulnerable to this criticism in that it rules out any pattern in forecasting errors and is more precise about when the method of forming expectations will change. For if expectations are rationally formed, the forecasting or expectational error will equal the random element in the process determining the variable being forecast. And by assumption this random element itself exhibits no pattern: it cannot be predicted on the basis of any information available at the time the forecast is being made. Since the random element, v, exhibits no pattern then neither does the forecasting error if expectations are rational. But what if the random element v *does* exhibit a pattern? What if, for example, the current value of v is linked to the previous period's value of v in the following way:

$$v_t = \beta_1 v_{t-1} + \epsilon_t \tag{2.8}$$

where ϵ_t is a random error with zero mean which cannot be predicted on the basis of any information available at the end of period $t - 1$; and β_1 is a coefficient, the value of which lies between -1 and $+1$.

The answer given by the rational expectations hypothesis is simply this. If v is being determined by the process described in equation (2.8) then rational people will form their expectation of the current period's value of v in accordance with that process. And since the value of v in the previous period, $t - 1$, will be part of the available information at the end of period $t - 1$, it follows that the forecast of v will diverge from the actual value of v by the unknown, unpredictable element ϵ_t. This latter element, of course, exhibits no pattern and has a mean value of zero. Thus even if v did exhibit a pattern, the rational forecast of Y would, on average, still be correct and the forecasting error would exhibit no pattern. As for the timing of a change in the method of forming expectations, the rational expectations hypothesis suggests that so long as the process determining a variable does not change, neither will the method of forming expectations. But if the actual process determining a variable is known to have changed, then the method by which expectations are formed will change in line with it.

(c) Rational expectations are the most accurate expectations

Forecasts of a variable Y made using all the available information on the *true* process determining Y are bound to be at least as accurate as, and usually more accurate than, forecasts of Y made on some other basis. By 'more accurate' we do not mean that in every particular instance the rational expectation will be closer to the actual value of Y than a non-rational expectation. It is perfectly possible to form an expectation stupidly and by chance be right: it would be a fluke, but flukes can happen. However, by their very nature they do not occur regularly. More often than not, the rational expectation – the expectation formed in accordance with the process actually determining the variable – will be a more accurate expectation than one formed on another basis. To put this point another way, however expectations are formed, the unpredictable part of Y cannot regularly be predicted. So any method of expectations formation will be inaccurate to a degree determined by the likely range of values that v can take. But it is possible to be even more inaccurate by forecasting without reference or with only partial reference to the process determining the variable. Thus there is no scope to be more accurate than the rational expectations method, but there is plenty of scope to be less.

This point can be expressed formally as follows. The unpredictability of the variable Y arises because of the presence of the random element v. The latter variable has a mean of zero but in any period can take on a positive or negative value. However, there are certain limits to the possible values of v; that is, v can be seen as having a finite variance, σ_v^2. From this variance we can tell how likely it is that any given value of v will occur. If the variance of v is very high then very high (absolute) values of v are quite likely to occur. If the variance of v is very low then only low (absolute) values of v are likely to occur. The variance of v can therefore be seen as measuring the inherent unpredictability of Y. The higher the variance of v the more unpredictable Y is, and so the more inaccurate any forecast of Y is likely to be. In the limit, if the variance of v is zero Y is perfectly predictable: v is always zero, it never varies and so we are back to the case illustrated in equations (2.1) and (2.2). At the opposite extreme, if the variance of v is infinite then Y is a perfectly unpredictable variable: its value could be anything between plus and minus infinity. In general we shall be dealing with the more plausible case in which v has a non-zero but finite variance.

The actual size of the variance of v sets an upper limit on the accuracy of any method of forecasting Y. But if expectations are formed rationally the expectational error in any period is identified as the random element v in that period. The likely range of the forecasting errors is therefore the same as the likely range of the unpredictable component of the process determining Y. In this case, then, the upper limit of accuracy is reached. With any other method of forecasting the level of accuracy over any significant length of time can only be lower – it cannot be higher. In this formal sense, then, rational expectations are the most *efficient* method of forecasting: the variance of the forecasting errors will be lower under rational expectations than under any other method of forecasting or forming expectations.

2.4 GENERAL CRITICISMS OF THE THEORY OF RATIONAL EXPECTATIONS

Now that we have stated what a rational expectation is – one formed in accordance with the actual process determining a variable conditional on the available information – and now that we have examined the main characteristics of the forecasting errors from rationally formed expectations – a mean of zero, no pattern to them, and the lowest variance of any forecasting method – we turn to some criticisms of the rational expectations hypothesis *per se*. In subsequent chapters we discuss the implications of the rational expectations hypothesis for macroeconomics, and the criticism directed against it in that context.

(a) The plausibility of rationality

One criticism of the rational expectations hypothesis takes the following form. Is it really plausible to assume that when forming expectations the typical individual is sufficiently sensible to use all the information about the process determining a variable? Is it not rather the case that in reality people are often very ignorant about economic matters? How many people, for example, would be able to give a reasonably precise definition of what the money supply is, let alone tell you at what rate it has been growing? Yet information on the growth of the money supply is fairly easy to come by, and many economists believe that the rate of growth of the money supply plays a key role in the process by which the rate of inflation is determined. So if people are forming rational expectations about the rate of inflation they ought to know what the money supply is and how it has been growing. Essentially, this criticism is that a major assumption behind rational expectations is implausible.

There are a number of responses that can be made to this criticism. First of all the idea that the typical individual is capable of making the best of the opportunities open to him is a common one in economics. For example, in demand theory it is assumed that the typical person chooses to consume goods at a point given by the tangency of an indifference curve and a budget constraint. The mathematics behind this choice strategy is highly sophisticated and for the vast majority of people completely unintelligible. Yet it is assumed that people act *as if* they understand it. Similarly, firms are assumed to act *as if* they understand the complicated mathematics behind the requirement that they select that level of output at which marginal cost equals marginal revenue.

No-one believes that the typical consumer or firm really could explain the mathematical complexities involved in making the best of the opportunities open to them. But the important question is whether the theories which incorporate such apparently unrealistic assumptions are nevertheless successful in predicting the data on what consumers buy or what output levels firms decide on. If the assumption that firms and consumers act as if they do understand these complexities leads to theories which make accurate predictions, then the assumption of mathematical awareness is thereby shown to be a useful one.

The idea that people make the best of the opportunities open to them when forming expectations can be justified along the same lines. In other words, the ultimate test of the usefulness of the assumption that people act rationally when forming their expectations is the accuracy of the predictions made by the theory of rational expectations. However, it may be felt unwise to consider such tests of rationality in expectations formation without first providing some arguments for the intuitive plausibility of the assumption. One such argument is that in many instances the typical *individual* does not have to form an expectation on his own: other people will do it for him. These other people may be firms who specialize in or provide the service of making economic forecasts; or they may be government bodies who make their forecasts public. All of these will have an incentive to provide the best forecasts they can of any variable and, as we have seen, this implies an incentive to form expectations rationally. On this argument then, the fact that the typical *individual* cannot define the money supply is irrelevant: he obtains forecasts from people who can, and is, if you like, rational at one remove. A second argument in favour of the intuitive plausibility of the assumption of rationality is that irrational expectations can lead to overprediction or underprediction. It is not at all clear that irrationality should consistently lead to one or the other. Some individuals might irrationally overpredict and others irrationally underpredict. This is quite consistent with expectations being rational on average.

A more subtle criticism of the role of rationality in the rational expectations hypothesis is this. Usually in economic theory rationality implies that the typical person weighs up the costs and benefits of any activity and carries out that activity up to the point where the marginal cost of it equals the marginal benefits. So, for example, a firm increases its level of output up to the point where the marginal revenue gained from producing and selling an additional unit of output is equal to the marginal cost of so doing. When applied to expectations formation this principle implies that forecasters should weigh up the marginal costs of acquiring more information about the process determining a variable and the marginal benefits of making more accurate forecasts. When the two are equal forecasters should not attempt to acquire any more information to improve their forecasts – it is not worth it. But the point at which the marginal costs and marginal benefits are equal does not necessarily correspond to the point at which the forecasting error is equal to the purely random component of the determining process. It may be that knowledge about some determining variable could be obtained and extra accuracy thereby achieved, but only at a price which it is not worth paying. In that case the forecasting error will tend to be absolutely greater than the random element in the determining process.

This criticism is a valid one, but for most purposes it is not one of great significance. The reason for this is that forecasting errors themselves are observed at no cost. For example, any error in your forecast about the level of prices is observed as a costless side-effect of shopping. In other words, the marginal cost of information about one's forecasting errors is negligible. It must therefore be worthwhile to exploit this information fully, until its marginal benefit is zero. Two implications of this are that the average error of expectations will be zero and the errors themselves will exhibit no pattern; for if either of these is not the case the information on past errors is not being fully exploited. Hence two of the characteristics of rational expectations would remain even where expectations are formed after a weighing up of the costs and benefits of acquiring information. All that would be different is that expectations would be less efficient than they could be if all the available information was used. But they would still be more accurate than expectations formed by any other method.

(b) The availability of information

In outlining the theory of rational expectations we assumed that the process determining Y is known and that the values of the variables in that process are known at the end of period $t - 1$. But what if the process determining Y contains variables the values of which are not known at the end of period $t - 1$? How will a rational agent forecast the value of Y in period t then? And how exactly do people learn the nature of the process determining Y?

The first of these questions has a straightforward answer. If, at the end of period $t - 1$ the rational agent does not know the true value of X in period $t - 1$, and if the value of X in period $t - 1$ determines the value of Y in this period, the agent will have to form an expectation of the value of X in period $t - 1$. And, of course, this expectation of the value X took in period $t - 1$ will be a rational one; it will use all the information on the process determining X that is available when the expectation is being made. For example, let the process determining Y be as follows:

$$Y_t = \alpha_0 + \alpha_1 Y_{t-1} + \alpha_2 X_{t-1} + \alpha_3 Z_{t-1} + v_t \tag{2.9}$$

where the notation is as before.

However, let the value of X_{t-1} be unknown at the end of period $t-1$; it may be a variable such as industrial production which is difficult to calculate and takes time to be published. And let the process determining X in any period t be as follows:

$$X_t = \beta_0 + \beta_1 V_{t-1} + \beta_2 W_{t-1} + \epsilon_t \tag{2.10}$$

where V and W are other variables, the β's are coefficients, and ϵ is a random error term with mean zero.

If the process determining X is known, and if at the end of period $t-1$ the forecaster knows the value of all the variables which influenced X in period $t-1$ except the random term, ϵ_{t-1}, then the rational forecast of the unknown value of X in period $t-1$ will be as follows:

$$E_{t-1} X_{t-1} = \beta_0 + \beta_1 V_{t-2} + \beta_2 W_{t-2} \tag{2.11}$$

This expectation of the value of X in period $t-1$ will be used in place of the actual value of X in period $t-1$ in the forecast of the value of Y for period t. Thus if the value of X in period $t-1$ is unknown, the rational expectation of Y in period t, using all the information available at the end of period $t-1$, will be:

$$E_{t-1} Y_t = \alpha_0 + \alpha_1 Y_{t-1} + \alpha_2 [\beta_0 + \beta_1 V_{t-2} + \beta_2 W_{t-2}] + \alpha_3 Z_{t-1} \tag{2.12}$$

The forecasting error will therefore be given by:

$$Y_t - E_{t-1} Y_t = v_t + \alpha_2 \epsilon_{t-1} \tag{2.13}$$

Since both v_t *and* ϵ_{t-1} are random errors with means of zero, neither of which can be even partly predicted on the basis of any information available at the end of period $t-1$ (remember X_{t-1} and therefore ϵ_{t-1} are assumed here to be unknown at the end of period $t-1$), it follows that the forecasting error has a mean of zero and cannot be predicted on the basis of any information available at the end of period $t-1$. Furthermore, if the actual value taken by X in period $t-1$ is unknown at the end of period $t-1$, for whatever reason, the forecast of Y shown in equation

(2.12) and identified as the rational forecast or expectation will in general be the most accurate forecast. No other forecasting method will reach this upper limit of accuracy imposed by the random element in the process determining Y and the random element in the process determining X in period $t - 1$.

Therefore the question 'What are the implications for rational expectations if the process determining Y contains a variable the value of which is unknown at the time the forecast is to be made?' is a relatively easy one to answer. Much more difficult is the question of how people become aware of the process determining a variable. How do they know which variables are important influences on Y, and how do they know the actual size of the coefficients in the process determining Y, that is the values of the α's in equation (2.9)?

The usual answer is in line with the approach to rational expectations adopted at the beginning of this chapter. The rational expectations hypothesis is seen as applying to processes which recur and are therefore at least capable of being identified. And, of course, there is an incentive to improve the accuracy of one's forecasts by discovering the process determining a variable. But the fact that there is an incentive to improve accuracy does not guarantee that the process determining a variable will be discovered. After all, there is an incentive to forecast inflation accurately, but there is still quite fierce disagreement amongst professional economists about what the actual process determining inflation is.

This point is a serious one but there are a number of arguments that can be put forward in favour of retaining the assumption that rational forecasters know the process determining a variable. First, as more evidence becomes available about the process, the process should become more, rather than less, precisely known. Knowledge of the process is therefore likely to be growing, and the assumption that people know the process is therefore becoming more true rather than less true. This argument illustrates an important feature of the rational expectations hypothesis. Rational expectations are an *equilibrium* concept: models of any economic variable in which expectations play a part but which do not assume rational expectations cannot be full equilibrium models. For if more information is becoming available about the process determining the variable and if this is leading to changes in the method by which expectations are formed then clearly the method of expectations formation is not 'at rest', and so the model itself is not in full long-run equilibrium. The assumption of rational expectations can in this sense be seen as helping to define the full equilibrium.

A second, related argument is that the imposition of any other assumption is likely to be just as arbitrary as the assumption of knowledge of the process. What determines which part of the process is known and which is not? At the very least some reason ought to be given for believing that the process is not known, and some justification given for imposing a particular non-rational method of expectation formation. This is especially true when expectations of a variable are used as part of a model in which the actual value of that variable is determined.

These last arguments can be illustrated by the liquidity trap version of Keynes's IS–LM model, in which expectations of the rate of interest help to determine the actual value of the rate of interest. The Keynesian IS–LM model can, of course, be viewed as a theory of the process by which the rate of interest is determined. And if that model or theory is being put forward as the correct one, it is at the same time being identified as the true process determining the rate of interest. In that case rational people should forecast the rate of interest in line with that process. Yet in the standard textbook version of Keynes's model the expected rate of interest is not the same as the rate of interest that the model predicts: rather, the normal or expected rate of interest is arbitrarily assumed to be a constant which is slightly above the actual rate of interest. Thus expectations are not being formed in accordance with the process identified by Keynes as determining the rate of interest. To have within the same model one process determining the expectation of a variable and quite another determining its actual value is highly unsatisfactory. At the very least it suggests that the process identified as determining the actual variable is unstable; it will change as people change their method of forming expectations, until that method and the process determining the actual variable become consistent. It is for this reason that rational expectations are sometimes referred to as a consistency axiom for economic models (see Lucas, 1987, p. 13).

A final justification of the assumption that the process determining a variable is known is the empirical one mentioned above. The ultimate test of the assumption is the accuracy of the predictions to which it leads. If it leads to predictions which are consistently inaccurate it should be discarded; if it does not then it can be usefully retained.

Of course, even if the process determining a variable is not known there is no obvious reason why this should lead to forecasting errors which do not have a mean of zero and which exhibit some discernible pattern.

Thus there are still reasons for believing that typical forecasts will exhibit two of the key features of rational forecasts – an average error of zero and no pattern to the errors. For if they do not it implies that forecasters are not fully exploiting the costless information provided by their own errors.

(c) The limits to the applicability of rational expectations

As we have emphasized, the rational expectations hypothesis is seen as applying to variables which are determined by recurring processes which are stochastic. The characteristic features of the errors of rational forecasters were derived above from an analysis of just such a process. But in many instances in economics the variable about which expectations are being formed may not be of this type.

A recent example is provided by the Thatcher government in the UK in the early 1980s. This government was committed to 'tight' monetary and fiscal policy. Yet many people doubted that government's ability to maintain such policies for very long, and there was much speculation about whether, indeed when, Mrs Thatcher herself or a replacement would abandon them. And there were very good reasons for believing that such a 'U-turn' was not far away. A significant number of Conservative MP's and even cabinet ministers were known to be unsympathetic to the policies being pursued; unemployment was rising at what was a spectacularly high rate for the period after the Second World War; and the government was performing badly in by-elections. After the Falklands crisis in 1982 speculation about a 'U-turn' largely vanished. But before then it would have been perfectly reasonable for an intelligent observer to expect higher monetary growth in the future than actually occurred. And, moreover, it would have been perfectly reasonable to go on expecting it even though it kept not occurring. So over the period until the Falklands crisis a perfectly rational person might have persistently overestimated future monetary growth because he attached a non-zero probability to a 'U-turn'. His expectational error over this period at least would not have averaged zero.

A much earlier example is provided in the following quotation:

> One incidental by-product of our analysis is to illustrate a limitation of much recent work on rational expectations. One way that concept has been made operational is by regarding rationality of expectations as requiring that on the average expectations are correct and hence by testing rationality of expectations by direct or indirect comparisons of expectations with the subsequent values of the variables about which expectations were formed. But consider the period from 1880 to 1896. It was surely not irrational according to a commonsense interpretation of that term for participants in the financial markets to fear that growing political support for free silver would lead the United States to depart from the gold standard and to experience subsequent inflation. Indeed, the longer the deflation proceeded, the more pressure built up for free silver, and the higher an intelligent observer might well have set his personal probability of inflation within, say, three years.
>
> As it happened, the departure from gold was avoided. That does not prove that the persons who bet the other way were wrong – any more than losing a two to one wager that a fair coin will turn up heads proves that it was wrong to take the short end of the wager. Given a sufficiently long sequence of observations, of course, it could be maintained that all such events will ultimately average out, that in the century of experience our data cover, for example, there are enough independent episodes so that it is appropriate to test rationality of expectations by their average accuracy. But that is cold comfort, since few studies cover so long a period, and our aim is surely to derive propositions that can be applied to shorter periods . . . (Friedman and Schwartz, 1982, pp. 556–7)

The general point which these two specific examples illustrate is that many events about which expectations have to be formed cannot easily be seen as the result of a recurring process which it is possible to discern and exploit. On the contrary, many important economic events can genuinely be seen as unique, or at least exceptional or unusual. In what sense can the rational expectations hypothesis be said to apply to these exceptional cases?

The first point to make here is that it is perfectly true that the rational expectations hypothesis can best be applied to variables or events which can be seen as part of a recurring process. However, this class of events may be a larger one than is commonly thought. For example, in the past 30 years in the UK government policy has tended to oscillate between tight and loose fiscal and monetary policy. At the beginning of each expansionary phase the switch of policy has often been presented as unique, as a new and bold experiment, a 'dash for growth'. And, of course, it is always possible to analyse it in terms of the personalities of the politicians involved in its design, the particular political circumstances of the day and so on. Such analysis would emphasize its unique or exceptional nature. But at a deeper level such switches of policy could be seen as part of a fairly regular and reasonably predictable process, one element in which is the desire by governments to have a high level of economic activity at the time of a general election. So an event which could be portrayed as unique may well, from another viewpoint, be part of an underlying recurring process.

Even where events cannot be seen in this way there is no obvious reason for abandoning the assumption that all the relevant, available information will be used in forming expectations. The belief, mentioned above, that the Thatcher government was likely to perform a 'U-turn' was presumably prompted by an examination of the political circumstances of the day, plus some 'feel' for the likely force they would exert and the resistance they would meet. This 'feel' was almost certainly partly determined by previous experience of the same sort of circumstances, in the case of the Thatcher government the experience of the previous Conservative administration which *had* performed a 'U-turn' in its economic policy. Even in these cases then, expectations are likely to be formed from an intelligent appraisal of circumstances (after all, no-one was seriously predicting a drastic *tightening* of the policies being pursued by the Thatcher government), although the process behind such circumstances may be a lot harder to discern.

(d) The testability of the rational expectations hypothesis

Some have criticized the rational expectations hypothesis on the grounds that it is not testable. There are a number of layers to this criticism. First, if the rational expectations hypothesis is taken rather loosely to imply that people make the best of their available information, then it may always be possible to define the available information so that the hypothesis becomes immune to falsification. This criticism would be perfectly valid if tests of the rational expectations hypothesis tended to employ the loose form of the hypothesis. But they do not. On the contrary, they tend to employ very strong versions of the hypothesis in which people's knowledge of the process determining a variable is assumed to be the same as the best estimate that can be made of that process by standard econometric techniques. A theme of this book is that this frequently made assumption leads to predictions which are both clear and different from the predictions derived from other theories about expectations. To put that another way, the imposition in a wide variety of contexts of the strong version of rational expectations leads to significant restrictions on what we should and should not observe. One can therefore test the rational expectations hypothesis in a wide variety of contexts by seeing whether we do observe what the rational expectations hypothesis predicts we should not, and whether we do not observe what the rational expectations hypothesis predicts we should. This first criticism of the testability of the rational expectations hypothesis is hardly a strong one.

A more subtle criticism is that expectations about a variable are almost always only *part* of a model. Tests of models which incorporate the rational expectations hypothesis are therefore always *joint* tests of the rational expectations hypothesis itself *and* the rest of the model. If the model fails the tests to which it is subjected one can always 'rescue' the rational expectations hypothesis by arguing that it is the rest of the model which is wrong. For example, as we shall see in a later chapter, when combined with the assumption that consumption expenditure is a constant proportion of permanent or expected income, the rational expectations hypothesis produces some quite distinctive predictions. If the data prove that these predictions are very wrong then it would always be possible to argue that the form of the relationship between consumption and permanent income was misspecified and that it was this misspecification which was causing the model to be rejected.

This criticism has some force, although of course it applies equally to other theories about how expectations are formed. However, it is at times possible, as we shall see later in the book, to distinguish between the restrictions imposed on the data by the rational expectations hypothesis itself and the restrictions imposed by the rest of the model. It is then possible to go some way towards testing the rational expectations hypothesis itself. However, this may not always be possible and the usefulness of the rational expectations hypothesis can then only be tested informally and less satisfactorily. For example, as we have said, the rational expectations hypothesis can be applied in a wide variety of contexts: if, time after time, the models incorporating rational expectations were rejected then this would almost certainly force a rejection of the rational expectations hypothesis.

A related, and even more subtle, criticism of the testability of rational expectations models is what is known as 'observational equivalence'. We shall discuss this more fully in later chapters, but it is worth giving a brief description of it here. In fact, it is a general problem, not restricted to economics, but it has been much discussed in the context of rational expectations where it takes the following form. For any rational expectations model which 'fits the data' there will always be a non-rational expectations model which fits the data equally well. For it is always possible to devise a non-rational expectations model which has exactly the same implications for any given set of data as the rational expectations model but which has different policy implications. The data themselves cannot discriminate between the two theories, which are said therefore to be observationally equivalent. The obvious implication of this is that even if a rational expectations model 'passes' conventional empirical tests that does not necessarily imply that one should accept the hypothesis. Whether you do or do not depends upon whether you find it more 'plausible' on some other unspecified grounds than the non-rational expectations model.

2.5 SUMMARY

At the end of this chapter it is worth emphasizing its main themes, since their development or application in different contexts constitutes the rest of the book. Many economic variables can be thought of as being determined by processes. A rational expectation of a variable is one which is formed in accordance with the process determining that variable and which uses all the available information relating to that process. It is more natural to think of such expectations being formed about variables which are determined by recurring processes rather than variables which are unique or 'unusual' events, since the recurrent nature of the process is what allows it to be discerned. Rational expectations are in this sense an equilibrium concept in that they are best seen as applying to processes which have recurred sufficiently often to have been discerned. Rationality of expectations thus helps to define full equilibrium.

The characteristic features of the errors of rational forecasts are that their mean is zero, that they exhibit no pattern and that their variance is at least as low as the variance of errors produced by any other method of expectations formation. Because of the pervasive role of expectations in macroeconomics it is possible to apply the theory of rational expectations in a wide variety of macroeconomic contexts. Such application reveals that the theory of rational expectations has some very strong implications for the general characteristics of macroeconomic models, for the individual components of those models and for government economic policy. And because of its strong and distinctive predictions it is possible to test it and thereby come to some conclusions about its usefulness. In the next chapter we consider the general problem of testing the rational expectations hypothesis, and give some examples. We then consider the rational expectations hypothesis in a number of specific macroeconomic contexts.

SUGGESTIONS FOR FURTHER READING

Shiller (1978), Fellner (1980) and Friedman (1979) contain various criticisms of the rational expectations hypothesis. The Friedman reference is particularly relevant to the first two chapters of this book, in that it suggests that under certain assumptions about the sensible use of available information rational expectations and adaptive expectations become very similar. Lucas (1977) presents a very simple application of the idea of rational expectations to the problem of the business cycle. Duck (1983) considers the implications within a rational expectations model of an uncertain process for monetary policy.

3

Testing the Rational Expectations Hypothesis

In this chapter we consider some of the basic issues involved in testing the rational expectations hypothesis. As in the previous chapter we shall at this stage keep the discussion fairly general, leaving more precise discussion to later chapters, in which we consider tests of rational expectations in specific contexts. We first consider tests of the rational expectations hypothesis in those relatively few cases when the expected variable is directly measured. We then consider the more usual problem facing us: how to test the rational expectations hypothesis when the expected variable is not directly observed or measured. The central, distinctive idea here is that the rational expectations hypothesis can be seen as imposing restrictions on what we should observe in the world, and so the validity of rational expectations can be tested by testing for the validity of those restrictions.

3.1 DIRECT TESTS OF RATIONALITY

Imagine that we could *directly* observe a particular person's or group's expectation formed last period of the current period's value of an economic variable. We might think of this variable as the retail price index and label its current value P_t, but it could be any economic variable. Possession of such direct observations on expectations would allow us to test the validity of the rational expectations hypothesis in two ways. The first, and weaker test, would exploit one of the central predictions of the rational expectations hypothesis which we explained in chapter 2: that forecast errors arise from the inherent unpredictability or stochastic nature of the variable and should exhibit no pattern; that is, they should not be predictable on the basis of any information available at the time the forecast is made; and the forecast errors should, on average, be zero. For the variable we are considering, this prediction implies that the difference between the current value of the retail price index and the expectation of that index formed last period will be a serially uncorrelated random variable with mean zero, that is:

$$P_t - E_{t-1}P_t = \nu_t \tag{3.1}$$

where P_t is the actual value of the current retail price index, $E_{t-1}P_t$ is the expectation of P_t formed in period $t - 1$, and ν_t is the random forecast error, which is uncorrelated with any information available in period $t - 1$ or earlier.

If we could directly observe $E_{t-1}P_t$ then we could use the data on P_t and $E_{t-1}P_t$ in the regression:

$$P_t = \alpha_0 + \alpha_1 E_{t-1}P_t + \eta_t \tag{3.2}$$

where α_0 and α_1 are coefficients to be estimated and η_t is a random error with zero mean and constant variance.

If the prediction of the rational expectations hypothesis embodied in equation (3.1) is correct then the regression in equation (3.2) should yield an estimate of α_0 which implies that α_0 is zero, and an estimate of α_1 which implies that α_1 is unity. More formally, the regression should yield results such that the joint null hypothesis H_0: $\alpha_0 = 0$, $\alpha_1 = 1$ cannot be rejected. (In the next section we discuss how 'restrictions' such as $\alpha_0 = 0$ and $\alpha_1 = 1$ can be tested.) We should also observe that the error term in the regression, η_t, is a serially uncorrelated random error; that is, it should exhibit no pattern since, under the hypothesis of rational expectations, it is the forecasting error. The test of the null hypothesis, H_0, is called a test of the 'unbiasedness property' of rational expectations. It is also referred to as a 'weak test'.

Direct observations on what people are expecting allow a second and stronger test of the rational expectations hypothesis. This test is based on the following implications of the hypothesis: if expectations of a variable are rational, they are formed in accordance with the process determining that variable and therefore they will depend upon any set of past variables in exactly the same way as the variable itself depends upon that set of past variables.

This property of rational expectations is known as the 'efficiency property'. As an illustration take the link between P_t and its own past values, $P_{t-1}, P_{t-2}, \ldots$. Imagine that we regress the actual price index on its own past values:

$$P_t = \beta_1 P_{t-1} + \beta_2 P_{t-2} + \ldots + \beta_k P_{t-k} + v_{1t} \qquad (3.3)$$

where the β_i's are the coefficients to be estimated and v_{1t} is a zero mean, constant variance, random error.

Since we are assuming that we have direct observations on $E_{t-1}P_t$, we can carry out a regression of $E_{t-1}P_t$ on exactly the same variables as those on the right-hand side of equation (3.3). That is, we can estimate the following equation:

$$E_{t-1}P_t = \gamma_1 P_{t-1} + \gamma_2 P_{t-2} + \ldots + \gamma_k P_{t-k} + v_{2t} \qquad (3.4)$$

where the γ_i's are the coefficients to be estimated and v_{2t} is a zero mean, constant variance, random error.

If the rational expectations hypothesis is correct we should find, provided that we have a large enough sample, that the coefficient estimated on each variable in equation (3.3) is approximately the same as the coefficient estimated on the same variable in equation (3.4); that is, β_1 should equal γ_1, β_2 should equal γ_2, and so on. More formally, we can test the rational expectations hypothesis by testing the joint null hypothesis, H_0: $\beta_i = \gamma_i$ for $i = 1, \ldots, k$. Rejection of H_0 would imply a rejection of the rational expectations hypothesis. The reason why the two sets of coefficients in equations (3.3) and (3.4) should be the same under rational expectations can be seen clearly if we subtract equation (3.4) from equation (3.3) to obtain:

$$P_t - E_{t-1}P_t = (\beta_1 - \gamma_1)P_{t-1} + (\beta_2 - \gamma_2)P_{t-2} + \ldots$$
$$+ (\beta_k - \gamma_k)P_{t-k} + v_{1t} - v_{2t} \qquad (3.5)$$

The left-hand side of equation (3.5) must equal a random variable, as shown in equation (3.1), which it will if $\beta_i = \gamma_i$ for all i. Another way of putting this is that under rational expectations the forecast error, $P_t - E_{t-1}P_t$, is independent of all lagged information, in this case lagged prices.

Both of the tests we have examined require direct observations of the expected variable. As we explained in chapter 1, for most variables we do not have such direct observations and cannot therefore carry out the tests. But for some variables we do, and some economists have used the available data to carry out these tests of the rational expectations hypothesis.

One of the first studies to test the unbiasedness property was by Turnovsky (1970). He used data from a survey which had asked 'informed business economists' their predictions for six and twelve months ahead for a number of economic series which included the consumers' price index for the period 1954–69 in the US. He found that the only period to be consistent with rational expectations was from 1962 to 1969. That is, for the period 1954–64, using the six month ahead predictions, in the regression shown above in equation (3.2) he obtained an estimate of α_0 of 1.137 with an estimated standard error of 0.306 and an estimate of α_1 of 0.184 with an estimated standard error of 0.17. Therefore α_0 appears to be non-zero and α_1 appears to be less that unity, which refutes the hypothesis that these expectations were rationally formed. For the period 1962–9, however, Turnovsky obtained an estimate of α_0 which was not significantly different from zero and an estimate of α_1 of 1.039 with an estimated standard error of 0.083, which implies that the hypothesis that α_1 is equal to unity cannot be rejected. So, for this period, the expectations did satisfy the unbiasedness property of rational expectations. The twelve month ahead forecasts gave similar results. A number of other researchers have investigated this same data set (see, e.g., Pesando, 1975; Carlson, 1977; Pearce, 1979; Figlewski and Wachtel, 1981), but their conclusions are mixed and no decisive case for or against rational expectations emerges.

Another data set of interest rate expectations of a panel of money-market professionals has been extensively analysed by Benjamin Friedman (1980). He found that survey respondents did not make unbiased predictions and that they did not efficiently exploit the information contained in past interest rate movements, and concludes that his results are 'mixed to unfavourable' to the hypothesis that expectations are rational.

One other implication of the rational expectations hypothesis is apparent from an examination of equation (3.1). Because the term $E_{t-1}P_t$ is uncorrelated with the forecast error, v_t (if they were correlated superior forecasts could be obtained, thus violating the rational expectations hypothesis), if we rewrite equation (3.1) as:

$$P_t = E_{t-1}P_t + v_t$$

and take the variance of both sides of the equation, we obtain:

$$var\ (P_t) = var(E_{t-1}P_t) + var(v_t)$$

There is no covariance on the right-hand side of the above equation because the terms $E_{t-1}P_t$ and v_t are uncorrelated. A prediction of the rational expectations hypothesis is therefore that the variation in the actual series, var (P_t), should *exceed* the variation in the anticipated series, var $(E_{t-1}P_t)$, if var $(v_t) > 0$. Lovell (1986) reviews around a dozen papers which have carried out tests of the rational expectations hypothesis using direct survey data. Among them is one by Muth (1985) which applies the above variance inequality test to some data on anticipated and realized production levels for some firms in Pittsburgh between 1957 and 1970. The findings were that for a majority of the firms the variance of anticipations exceeded the variance of the realizations, which is inconsistent with the rational expectations hypothesis. Lovell's overall conclusion on the results of the tests he surveyed is pessimistic: he writes '. . . it seems to me that the weight of empirical evidence is sufficiently strong to compel us to suspend belief in the hypothesis of rational expectations, pending the accumulation of additional empirical evidence' (Lovell, 1986, p. 12).

On the face of it then, the direct evidence from sample surveys of businessmen's expectations seems to provide very little, if any, support for the rational expectations hypothesis.

There are, however, a number of reasons why we should be cautious about interpreting the results of tests which use this type of data. First, when the questions asked in the surveys are qualitative in nature (for example: Do you expect the inflation rate to rise, fall, stay the same?), any quantitative index we use to measure the response is likely to be a crude indicator of the magnitude of the true underlying expectation and is likely to contain measurement errors. Such errors, as we show in the next section, induce biases into least-squares estimators. For example, α_1 in equation (3.2) may be biased downwards from its true value of one if the variable $E_{t-1}P_t$ is measured with error. Second, even if the questions posed in the surveys are quantitative in nature (for example: What do you expect the inflation rate to be in the next year?) and the average expectations elicited from the surveys in a particular market appear biased and inefficient, only a few 'sophisticated' individuals operating in that market *could* make the market function *as if* rational expectations were operating, even though many of the individuals operating in the market are not behaving rationally. When attempting to explain *market behaviour*, the rational expectations hypothesis will be valid in such cases.

3.2 MEASURING A RATIONAL EXPECTATION OF A VARIABLE BY ITS ACTUAL VALUE

In this section we shall begin to consider how we might estimate a macroeconomic model of the economy which includes rational expectations, but where the expectation of the variable is not directly observed. We shall show first that what might appear to be an obvious way to proceed is not in fact likely to be valid and that a more subtle approach is required. Then we shall show that this more subtle procedure is a valid way of estimating a macro-economic model which incorporates rational expectations and that it allows us to test rational expectations *conditional* on the economic model with which it is combined.

To see why an obvious procedure may not be valid we will consider a simple example. Suppose that the macroeconomic model we are estimating states that consumption expenditure in period t depends upon what people in period $t - 1$ expect their income will be in period t, that is:

$$C_t = \alpha_0 + \alpha_1 E_{t-1} Y_t + \eta_t \tag{3.6}$$

where C_t is desired consumption expenditure, $E_{t-1} Y_t$ is expected income, η_t is a random error with zero mean and constant variance, α_0 is a constant, and α_1 is the marginal propensity to consume (MPC) out of expected income.

Now suppose that we wish to estimate the value of α_1, the MPC out of expected income. If we believe that expectations about Y_t are formed rationally then we must also believe that the actual value of Y_t diverges from the value that people expect, $E_{t-1} Y_t$, by a random error which we label v_t. Thus the rationality of expectations implies that:

$$Y_t = E_{t-1} Y_t + v_t \tag{3.7}$$

Since the actual value of income diverges from the expected value
by only a random error it is tempting to replace the expected
income term in equation (3.6) with actual income and rewrite
equation (3.6) as:

$$C_t = \alpha_0 + \alpha_1 Y_t + \eta_t - \alpha_1 \nu_t \qquad (3.8)$$

To estimate the MPC, α_1, it might be thought that we could carry
out the following regression:

$$C_t = \alpha_0^* + \alpha_1^* Y_t + \nu_t^* \qquad (3.9)$$

where ν_t^* is an error term, and treat the value obtained for α_1^* as
an estimate of the MPC, α_1. It might appear to be an attractive
feature of the rational expectations hypothesis that it suggests
such a simple method of incorporating expectations into macroeconomic models; that is, use of the actual value of a variable to
measure the expectation of it. Unfortunately, this method is *not*
valid. If expectations are rational than equation (3.7) implies that
Y_t is (positively) correlated with ν_t. Furthermore, if equation (3.8)
is true, then ν_t^* in equation (3.9) must in fact equal $\eta_t - \alpha_1 \nu_t$.
Therefore, in equation (3.9) Y_t and ν_t^* must be correlated since
they both depend upon ν_t. The consequence of this correlation
between the explanatory variable and the equation error in equation (3.9) will be to bias the estimator of α_1^* away from the true
MPC, α_1, and towards zero.

The intuitive reason for this result is as follows. High (or low)
values for ν_t imply, through equation (3.7), high (or low) values
for actual income, but no change in expected income and therefore,
from equation (3.6), no change in consumption expenditure. But,
we are using actual income to measure expected income, and
so a positive value for ν_t will suggest that there has been a rise
in expected income with no accompanying rise in consumption
expenditure.

Similarly, a negative value for ν_t will suggest a fall in expected
income but no accompanying fall in consumption expenditure.
So, to the extent that changes in Y_t are due to such changes in ν_t
rather than $E_{t-1} Y_t$, C_t will appear to be unaffected by expected
income as we measure it, and therefore we shall obtain an estimate
of α_1 which will tend to be less than the true value of α_1. This
downward bias will be more severe the more that changes in actual
income are due to changes in ν_t rather than changes in expected

income; in other words, the more inaccurate our measure of expected income is, the greater is the severity of the bias.

More formally, if equations (3.6)–(3.8) are the 'truth' and we carry out an ordinary least-squares regression of C_t on Y_t, as shown in equation (3.9), then, assuming that we have a very large sample so that we can use population variances in place of sample variances, our estimator of α_1^* will tend to the conventional formula:

$$\alpha_1^* = \frac{\text{covar } (C, Y)}{\text{var } (Y)} \tag{3.10}$$

where covar (C, Y) is the covariance between C and Y and var (Y) is the variance of Y.

We can derive the term covar (C, Y) as the covariance between Y and the terms on the right-hand side of equation (3.8) since these terms in sum equal C. Thus, assuming that Y_t and η_t are uncorrelated we have:

$$\text{covar } (C, Y) = \alpha_1 \text{ var } (Y) - \alpha_1 \text{ covar } (Y, \nu) \tag{3.11}$$

Now, assuming that $E_{t-1} Y_t$ and ν_t are uncorrelated we can derive, from equation (3.7), an expression for covar (Y, ν) as:

$$\text{covar } (Y, \nu) = \text{var } (\nu) \tag{3.12}$$

Thus, our estimator of α_1^* will tend to:

$$\alpha_1^* = \frac{\alpha_1 \text{ var } (Y) - \alpha_1 \text{ var } (\nu)}{\text{var } (Y)}$$

$$= \alpha_1 - \frac{\alpha_1 \text{ var } (\nu)}{\text{var } (Y)} \tag{3.13}$$

So, α_1^* will equal α_1 only if the variance of ν is zero. This will be the case if ν_t is always zero and hence, from equation (3.7), our measure of expected income is perfectly accurate. If our measure of expected income is perfectly inaccurate in the sense that all changes in Y_t reflect variations in ν_t, not $E_{t-1} Y_t$, then α_1^* will tend to zero because var $(\nu)/$var (Y) will tend to unity. The problem essentially is that instead of estimating the true MPC, α_1, in equation (3.6) we are in fact estimating the composite function in equation (3.13). To be able to obtain a separate estimate of α_1 we need more information. One source of information could be knowledge of the variance of ν, var (ν), for then we could obtain the variance of Y, var (Y), from our sample and hence an estimate of α_1 from equation (3.13).

An alternative procedure is to find 'instrumental variables' for Y, which are uncorrelated with ν^*, and obtain an instrumental variable estimate of α_1. (For a discussion of instrumental variable estimation see Johnston (1984), and for its application in rational expectations models see Wickens (1982).)

Notice that the error ν_t in equation (3.7) can be interpreted as a 'measurement error' in the variable Y. We are trying to measure expectations, but can only obtain an indicator which is the true variable $E_{t-1} Y_t$ plus a random measurement error. The analysis leading to equation (3.13) is sometimes known as 'errors in variables' or measurement error analysis.

3.3   TESTING THE RESTRICTIONS IMPLIED BY RATIONAL EXPECTATIONS

A more fruitful method of incorporating rational expectations into a macroeconomic model makes use of the central idea of rational expectations that economic variables are determined by processes. Suppose that the process determining Y_t in the above example is:

$$Y_t = \theta_0 + \theta_1 Y_{t-1} + \theta_2 X_{t-1} + \theta_3 Z_{t-1} + \nu_t \qquad (3.14)$$

where X and Z are unspecified variables that determine Y, the θ's are coefficients and ν_t is a random error with zero mean and constant variance.

It follows that if expectations are rational we can write:

$$E_{t-1} Y_t = \theta_0 + \theta_1 Y_{t-1} + \theta_2 X_{t-1} + \theta_3 Z_{t-1} \qquad (3.15)$$

Substituting this expression for $E_{t-1} Y_t$ into the consumption expenditure equation (3.6) we obtain:

$$C_t = \alpha_0 + \alpha_1 \theta_0 + \alpha_1 \theta_1 Y_{t-1} + \alpha_1 \theta_2 X_{t-1} + \alpha_1 \theta_3 Z_{t-1} + \eta_t$$
$$(3.16)$$

It is clear from equations (3.14) and (3.16) that we could employ a two-stage procedure to obtain estimators of α_0, α_1 and the θ's, which are 'consistent' in the formal statistical sense. This means that as we use more and more observations we would expect the means of our estimators to tend towards their true values while the variability of the estimators decreases.

The first step of the two-stage procedure is to regress Y_t on the set of variables Y_{t-1}, X_{t-1} and Z_{t-1}, as in equation (3.14), and thereby secure estimates of the θ's. These estimated θ's can then be used to estimate $E_{t-1}Y_t$ from equation (3.15), that is:

$$\hat{E}_{t-1}Y_t = \hat{\theta}_0 + \hat{\theta}_1 Y_{t-1} + \hat{\theta}_2 X_{t-1} + \hat{\theta}_3 Z_{t-1} \tag{3.17}$$

where a '^' over a variable or coefficient denotes our estimate of the variable or coefficient.

The second stage of the procedure would then be to regress C_t on our estimate of $E_{t-1}Y_t$ given in equation (3.17). Notice that only one variable, $\hat{E}_{t-1}Y_t$, is being used in this regression. The four elements which together add up to $\hat{E}_{t-1}Y_t$ have been combined to form the single variable $\hat{E}_{t-1}Y_t$, and C_t is regressed on this single variable. The resulting estimators of the constant term and the MPC out of expected income would be consistent estimators of α_0 and α_1 respectively. The problem experienced when using actual income to measure expected income would disappear under this two-stage procedure, since the source of the problem was the correlation between v_t and the measure used for $E_{t-1}Y_t$. As equation (3.17) indicates, our measure of expected income is no longer correlated with the error term v_t, since v_t does not appear in equation (3.17), and so the problem no longer occurs.

Therefore the rational expectations hypothesis suggests a valid method of incorporating additional information when estimating macroeconomic models which contain expectation terms. The key element in it is that the process determining the variable about which variables are being formed has to be estimated alongside the rest of the model. A further and very important advantage of this method is that it suggests a way of testing the validity of the rational expectations hypothesis itself. To see this consider again the consumption expenditure model we have been discussing. If we measure expected income in accordance with our estimate of the process determining income, that is by equation (3.17); and if consumption expenditure is determined in accordance with equation (3.6) then, as we have shown, it follows that we can write C_t as:

$$C_t = \alpha_0 + \alpha_1 \hat{\theta}_0 + \alpha_1 \hat{\theta}_1 Y_{t-1} + \alpha_1 \hat{\theta}_2 X_{t-1} + \alpha_1 \hat{\theta}_3 Z_{t-1} + \eta_t$$

$$(3.18)$$

But this implies that if we regressed C_t on the three variables $\hat{\theta}_1 Y_{t-1}$, $\hat{\theta}_2 X_{t-1}$ and $\hat{\theta}_3 Z_{t-1}$ entered separately, rather than as a sum as in equation (3.18), we should observe that the coefficients estimated on these three variables are approximately all the same, as they are all estimates of α_1, provided that we have specified the model correctly. Thus the rationality of expectations imposes *restrictions* on what we should find when we estimate equation (3.18). This is a common feature of the rational expectations hypothesis and it provides an obvious way of testing the hypothesis, for if on estimating equation (3.18) we found 'widely different' coefficients on $\hat{\theta}_1 Y_{t-1}$, $\hat{\theta}_2 X_{t-1}$ and $\hat{\theta}_3 Z_{t-1}$, widely different estimates of α_1, then it would suggest that either equation (3.6) is untrue or expectations are not formed rationally. So, to test the rational expectations hypothesis, on the assumption that the rest of the model (in our example (3.6) and (3.14)) is specified correctly, we can test the validity of the restrictions imposed by the assumption of rational expectations. To do this, of course, we have to be more precise about the meaning of the phrase 'widely different'.

The precise statistical formulae for testing the validity of restrictions may appear complex but the essential idea behind them is simple. If a restriction is imposed on a model of a particular variable's behaviour, then if that restriction is valid its imposition should not affect the model's success in explaining the variable's behaviour, whereas if the restriction is invalid it should. To make clear how we can formally test for the validity of restrictions we shall consider first of all the following simple linear regression model:

$$Y_t = \beta_0 + \beta_1 X_t + \beta_2 Z_t + v_t \qquad (3.19)$$

where Y, X and Z are variables, the β's are coefficients and v_t is an error with a zero mean and a constant variance.

Suppose that we have a theory which predicts that $\beta_1 = \beta_2$ in equation (3.19). If we had a large enough sample of observations on Y_t, X_t and Z_t we would expect a linear regression of Y_t on X_t and Z_t to yield the result that the estimates of β_1 and β_2 were the same – except for sampling variation – if it really is true that

$\beta_1 = \beta_2$. Another way of putting this is that if we impose the restriction that $\beta_1 = \beta_2$ by adding X and Z together to form a single variable $(X + Z)$, and carry out the regression:

$$Y_t = \beta_0 + \beta_1(X_t + Z_t) + \eta_t \qquad (3.20)$$

if β_1 really is equal to β_2 in the process generating Y_t then the estimates of β_0 and β_1 from equation (3.20), in a large sample, should not differ very much from the estimates from equation (3.19). Furthermore, the ability of the regression equation (3.20) to explain the behaviour of Y_t should not be any worse than the ability of equation (3.19) to do the same. If, on the other hand, our hypothesis $\beta_1 = \beta_2$ is false, the estimates of β_0 and β_1 from equation (3.20) are likely to be very different from those obtained from equation (3.19), and the ability of equation (3.20) to explain the behaviour of Y is likely to be very much worse than that of equation (3.19).

But what precisely do 'very different' and 'ability to explain behaviour' mean in this context? What precise statistical procedure can be applied to test whether the coefficients and explanatory power of equation (3.19), the unrestricted model, are significantly different from those in equation (3.20), the restricted model? A sensible way to proceed is to compare the estimated sum of square residuals from equation (3.19), $\Sigma \hat{v}^2$, say, with those obtained from equation (3.20) where the restrictions have been imposed, $\Sigma \hat{\eta}^2$, where the '^' denotes an estimated value of the variable. Intuitively, if the hypothesis that $\beta_1 = \beta_2$ is true we would expect $\Sigma \hat{v}^2$ and $\Sigma \hat{\eta}^2$ to be approximately equal in a large sample, since that implies that both models explain the behaviour of Y equally well. Imposing a restriction which is *true* should not worsen the ability of the explanatory variables to explain the dependent variable or, alternatively, relaxing the restriction and allowing the estimators of β_1 and β_2 to be different should not lead to a much better fitting equation if β_1 and β_2 are in fact not different.

If it is assumed that v_t and η_t are normally distributed, it can be shown that the ratio $[(n - k)/g][(\Sigma \hat{\eta}^2 - \Sigma \hat{v}^2)/\Sigma \hat{v}^2]$ is distributed as an F-variate with g and $n - k$ degrees of freedom, where g is the number of restrictions, n is the number of observations and k is the total number of coefficients being estimated in the unrestricted model. In our example there is only one restriction, $\beta_1 = \beta_2$, so $g = 1$ and the unrestricted coefficients are β_0, β_1 and

β_2, so $k = 3$. For a proof that the above distribution is distributed as F, see Maddala (1977). Thus, to test the restrictions in our simple example we would estimate equations (3.19) and (3.20) separately and, from the sum of square residuals for each regression, compute the F-test statistic given above; then, compare the result with the critical F value, given the appropriate degrees of freedom, and reject the hypothesis that the restrictions are valid if the computed F statistic is higher than the critical value from tables of the F distribution. The test is equally valid for a *set* of restrictions. For example, in equation (3.19) we might wish to test the null hypothesis that $\beta_0 = 4\beta_1$ and, simultaneously, that $\beta_1 = \beta_2$. Provided that the restrictions are all independent, none of them are just rearrangements or multiples of other restrictions, we proceed as before. Imposing the restrictions on equation (3.19) we obtain:

$$Y_t = 4\beta_1 + \beta_1(X_t + Z_t) + \eta_t = \beta_1(4 + X_t + Z_t) + \eta_t \quad (3.21)$$

Once again we compute the formula $[(n - k)/g][(\Sigma\,\hat{\eta}^2 - \Sigma\,\hat{v}^2)/\Sigma\,\hat{v}^2]$, where the $\hat{v}$'s come from the unrestricted model in equation (3.19) and the $\hat{\eta}$'s now come from the regression of Y_t on the variable $(4 + X_t + Z_t)$. In this case we have two restrictions so $g = 2$, while k, the number of coefficients estimated in the unrestricted model, remains at a value of 3.

One problem with the above test of a set of restrictions is that, strictly, it can only be applied when the model is linear and the restrictions themselves are linear. Thus, if in our example we had the *non-linear* restriction $\beta_1 = 1/\beta_2$ it would not really be valid to use the F distribution.

Another test which, like the F-test, is based on the sum of square residuals, but which can be used in much more general situations, is the likelihood ratio test. It can be shown that for large samples the statistic $n[\log(\Sigma\,\hat{\eta}^2) - \log(\Sigma\,\hat{v}^2)]$, called the likelihood ratio test statistic, is distributed as a chi-square variate with g degrees of freedom where, as before, g is the number of restrictions and 'log' stands for natural logarithm. Once again the $\hat{\eta}$'s are computed from the model with restrictions imposed and the $\hat{v}$'s from the unrestricted model. The crucial difference with the likelihood ratio test is that the models that provide the $\hat{\eta}$'s and $\hat{v}$'s can be highly nonlinear. The drawback is that the likelihood ratio test statistic is only distributed as a chi-square when n is very large, and misleading results may be obtained in small samples. The intuition behind the test is once again that if the restrictions are valid we would expect the sum of square residuals, and hence their logarithms, to be approximately the same in both the restricted and the unrestricted models. Notice that for small differences the expression $[\log(\Sigma \hat{\eta}^2) - \log(\Sigma \hat{v}^2)]$ is approximately equal to the formula $(\Sigma \hat{\eta}^2 - \Sigma \hat{v}^2)/\Sigma \hat{v}^2$ which appears in the F statistic.

With linear restrictions on a linear model, then, the F-test is to be preferred for it is valid for any sample size: in most other cases the likelihood ratio test could be used. The restrictions generated by rational expectations models are very often non-linear and are also imposed across equations rather than in a single equation. As an example, take the consumption function model discussed in sections 3.2 and 3.3. There, from the following two equations:

$$C_t = \alpha_0 + \alpha_1 E_{t-1} Y_t + \eta_t \tag{3.6}$$

$$Y_t = \theta_0 + \theta_1 Y_{t-1} + \theta_2 X_{t-1} + \theta_3 Z_{t-1} + v_t \tag{3.14}$$

and the assumption of rationality we derived the following two-equation model:

$$C_t = \alpha_0 + \alpha_1 \theta_0 + \alpha_1 \theta_1 Y_{t-1} + \alpha_1 \theta_2 X_{t-1} + \alpha_1 \theta_3 Z_{t-1} + \eta_t \tag{3.16}$$

$$Y_t = \theta_0 + \theta_1 Y_{t-1} + \theta_2 X_{t-1} + \theta_3 Z_{t-1} + v_t \tag{3.14}$$

As we noted earlier, the coefficients on each variable in the consumption relationship are restricted to equal the coefficients on the same variable in the process determining income multiplied by the MPC, α_1. Because of the non-linearity of the cross-equation restrictions we cannot use the F-test in this case, but we can use the likelihood ratio. As the restrictions arise in a two-equation model (rather than the single equation we considered before), we now require a method of summarizing the variation in both equation errors so that we can compare an unrestricted with a restricted model. We begin by defining the variance–covariance matrix of the equation errors as:

$$E\begin{bmatrix} \eta_t \\ v_t \end{bmatrix} [\eta_t, v_t] = \begin{bmatrix} E(\eta_t^2) & E(\eta_t v_t) \\ E(v_t \eta_t) & E(v_t^2) \end{bmatrix} = \begin{bmatrix} \sigma_\eta^2 & \sigma_{\eta v} \\ \sigma_{\eta v} & \sigma_v^2 \end{bmatrix} = \Sigma$$

Next, we define the generalized variance as the determinant of the variance–covariance matrix Σ, which, for the two-equation case, is defined as:

$$\det(\Sigma) = \sigma_\eta^2 \sigma_\nu^2 - \sigma_{\nu\eta} \sigma_{\eta\nu}$$

Now, consider the completely unrestricted model, by which we mean a model in which C_t and Y_t are regressed on the same variables as in equations (3.16) and (3.14) but the coefficients attached to each variable are not restricted in any way:

$$C_t = \pi_0 + \pi_1 Y_{t-1} + \pi_2 X_{t-1} + \pi_3 Z_{t-1} + \omega_{1t} \qquad (3.22)$$
$$Y_t = \pi_4 + \pi_5 Y_{t-1} + \pi_6 X_{t-1} + \pi_7 Z_{t-1} + \omega_{2t}$$

where the π's are coefficients and the ω's are serially uncorrelated random errors.

We define the variance–covariance matrix for this unrestricted model's equation errors as:

$$E \begin{bmatrix} \omega_{1t} \\ \omega_{2t} \end{bmatrix} [\omega_{1t}, \ \omega_{2t}] = \Omega$$

Then, the generalized variance of the equation errors for the unrestricted model is given by $\det \Omega$. In general, it can be shown that for a large sample of size, n, and where all the elements of the matrices Σ and Ω are unrestricted, the statistic:

$$n[\log(\det \hat{\Sigma}) - \log(\det \hat{\Omega})]$$

is distributed as a chi-square variate with g degrees of freedom where, once again, g is the number of restrictions on the model. The estimates of Σ and Ω, $\hat{\Sigma}$ and $\hat{\Omega}$, are formed from the sample variances and covariances of the estimated residuals from the relevant equations. The intuition behind this result is much the same as before. If the restrictions are valid we would expect the generalized variance from the restricted and unrestricted models to be approximately the same. The likelihood ratio test statistic shown above is a formalization of this. The test can easily be generalized to the case of more than two equations.

3.4 OBSERVATIONAL EQUIVALENCE, EXCLUSION RESTRICTIONS AND REGIME BREAKS

The simple consumption function model used above to illustrate the idea of restrictions can also be used to illustrate certain other issues in the econometrics of rational expectations. The first of these is the problem of *observational equivalence*, a problem first discussed in the context of rational expectations models by Sargent (1976a). The problem, simply stated, is that for any rational expectations model one can always specify a non-rational expectations model which has exactly the same implications for a given set of data, even though it may have other implications which are quite different. Because the two models have exactly the same implications for the data one cannot use the data to discriminate between them: the two models are *observationally equivalent*.

As an illustration of this problem take equation (3.6) as our model of consumption, C_t, and equation (3.14) as the process determining Y_t. The assumption of rational expectations implies that we can write $E_{t-1} Y_t = \theta_0 + \theta_1 Y_{t-1} + \theta_2 X_{t-1} + \theta_3 Z_{t-1}$, and thereby derive equations (3.16) and (3.14) as the rational expectation consumption model.

Now consider an *alternative* model in which equation (3.14) is still the true process determining Y_t, but in which expectations are formed in the following irrational way:

$$E_{t-1}^* Y_t = \gamma_0 + \gamma_1 Y_{t-1} + \gamma_2 X_{t-1} + \gamma_3 Z_{t-1} \tag{3.23}$$

where the γ's are coefficients, and $E_{t-1}^* Y_t$ is an *irrational* expectation of Y_t formed in period $t - 1$.

Provided that the γ's are not identical to the θ's, equation (3.23) represents an irrational way of forming expectations, since it implies that expectations are being formed in a way which is inconsistent with the true process; that is, equation (3.14). Assume next an *alternative* model of consumption:

$$C_t = \alpha_0^* + \alpha_1^* E_{t-1}^* Y_t + \alpha_2^* Y_{t-1} + \alpha_3^* X_{t-1} + \alpha_4^* Z_{t-1} + \eta_t \tag{3.24}$$

where the α^*'s are coefficients.

Substituting for $E_{t-1}^* Y_t$ in equation (3.24) using equation (3.23), we can deríve:

$$C_t = \alpha_0^* + \alpha_1^* \gamma_0 + (\alpha_1^* \gamma_1 + \alpha_2^*) Y_{t-1} + (\alpha_1^* \gamma_2 + \alpha_3^*) X_{t-1}$$
$$+ (\alpha_1^* \gamma_3 + \alpha_4^*) Z_{t-1} + \eta_t \tag{3.25}$$

Now under certain conditions equation (3.25) is identical to equation (3.16). These conditions are:

(i) $\quad \alpha_0^* = \alpha_0 + \alpha_1 \theta_0 - \alpha_1^* \gamma_0$ $\qquad$ (ii) $\alpha_2^* = \alpha_1 \theta_1 - \alpha_1^* \gamma_1$

(iii) $\alpha_3^* = \alpha_1 \theta_2 - \alpha_1^* \gamma_2$ (iv) $\alpha_4^* = \alpha_1 \theta_3 - \alpha_1^* \gamma_3$

Since the imposition of these conditions on equation (3.25) gives an equation which is identical to equation (3.16) we have derived a model of consumption which has a different underlying theory of consumption and assumes irrational expectations, but which has exactly the same implications for the data as our rational expectations consumption model. No examination of the data could discriminate between them.

Despite this observational equivalence of the two models they are different models and have different implications. For example, imagine that for whatever reason the coefficient attached to X_{t-1} in equation (3.14) increased to $\theta_2 + \theta_4$. If the rational expectations model of consumption is correct then this change in the process through which Y_t is determined should affect the behaviour of C_t; that is, consumption should now behave according to:

$$C_t = \alpha_0 + \alpha_1 \theta_0 + \alpha_1 \theta_1 Y_{t-1} + \alpha_1 (\theta_2 + \theta_4) X_{t-1} + \alpha_1 \theta_3 Z_{t-1} + \eta_t$$

$$(3.26)$$

The very fact that the process about which expectations are being formed has altered should, under the rational expectations model, alter the response of consumption to X_{t-1}. The same is *not* true of the non-rational expectations model. There is nothing within that model to imply a change in the response of consumption to X_{t-1} as a result of a change in the Y_t process: expectations in this model are not being formed in accordance with the process driving Y_t, so a change in that process does not imply any change in the expectations forming process. So although the two models are observationally equivalent they *are* different in that they make different predictions about what would happen if the economic environment changed.

Of course, if the economic environment–in this case the process driving Y_t – *did* change in the way we have assumed, then the two models would cease to be observationally equivalent. Clearly it cannot be the case that $\alpha_3^* = \alpha_1 \theta_2 - \alpha_1^* \gamma_2$ and that $\alpha_3^* = \alpha_1 (\theta_2 + \theta_4) - \alpha_1^* \gamma_2$ if θ_4 is non-zero, and so condition (iii) above cannot hold in both environments. The possibility exists then to discriminate between the two models if there is a break in the process determining Y_t; that is, if there is what is called a *regime* *break*, a break in the process about which expectations are being formed.

In rational expectations models such regime breaks should result in a change in the way expectations are formed and hence in the behaviour of the variable influenced by expectations. In other models no such response is implied. In our example the behaviour of consumption should show an observable change as a result of the regime break, whereas under the alternative model it should not.

If one can identify regime breaks then one can discriminate between models which were previously observationally equivalent. In our example if the assumed regime break occurs we can discriminate between the two models by testing the implication that the coefficient on X_{t-1} in equation (3.16) has increased to $\alpha_1(\theta_2 + \theta_4)$ after the regime break. Examples of such tests of rational expectations models using regime breaks are given in Attfield and Duck (1986) and Bean (1984).

An alternative way of dealing with the problem of observational equivalence is to impose *a priori* what are called *exclusion restrictions*. What this amounts to is that on theoretical grounds one excludes certain possibilities and hence excludes the possibility of an observationally equivalent model. For example, it may be that there is no theoretical reason whatsoever why the variables X_{t-1} and Z_{t-1} should affect consumption except through their influence on Y_t. That is, there may be no theoretical reason for the coefficients α_3^* and α_4^* being other than zero. If zero values for α_3^* and α_4^* can be imposed on theoretical grounds then the conditions necessary for the non-rational expectations observationally equivalent model can be ruled out as implausible. Thus if the data satisfy the restrictions implied by equations (3.14) and (3.16) it can be taken as support for the rational expectations model of consumption: the observationally equivalent non-rational expectations model is ruled out on theoretical grounds.

Exclusion restrictions are a frequent feature of empirical studies involving rational expectations. The major difficulty with them is that in most contexts it is not in general possible on theoretical grounds alone to exclude the influence of one variable on another. The typical economic variables used in empirical studies, variables such as output, prices and interest rates, are such that it is usually possible to think of some reason why any one of them might exert an independent influence on another. As a result the imposition of exclusion restrictions is often a controversial matter.

3.5   EXAMPLE 1: SPOT AND FORWARD EXCHANGE RATES

We now provide two examples of ways in which rational expectations has introduced restrictions which can be tested using the methods we have just described. In the first, which we cover in this section, we examine the relationship between spot and forward exchange rates, and in the second we examine the relationship between the rates of return on assets with differing terms. These are not meant to be comprehensive surveys of the literature, but are simply designed to illustrate the application of rational expectations to specific areas. Later we devote a full chapter to the application of rational expectations to the theory and estimation of the aggregate consumption function. The material that follows in this chapter made be skipped by the reader, if desired, without interfering with the book's continuity.

The first example in particular illustrates two features of many tests of rational expectations models. First, it is not always possible to test rational expectations *per se*, but only jointly with other, supplementary assumptions. Second, rational expectations often introduces restrictions which may be tested against the data. The expectation of the future value of a currency is, strictly speaking, unobservable. Yet the foreign exchange market (like many other asset markets) has one feature which may provide a good indicator of what agents' expectations are. It is possible to buy and sell foreign exchange in 'futures' markets: that is, it is possible to conclude a contract now to buy foreign exchange at some specific future date at a price specified now. These markets are known as forward exchange markets. Thus, someone who knows that he or she will want to buy dollars (with pounds) in three months time could either agree a price for that transaction now (that is, buy in the forward market) or wait three months and buy in the 'spot' market (the market in which foreign exchange is bought and sold immediately, or 'on the spot'). What will the rational agent do? If he expects the price of dollars – the exchange rate – in the spot market to be the same as the current forward price, then a rational agent would be indifferent between the transactions under certain conditions.

What are these conditions? The first is that the agent is risk-neutral. The advantage of the forward market is that the transaction is risk-free: the price is specified now, with certainty. In contrast, the future spot price cannot be known with certainty precisely because it is a future price. A risk-averse individual would only be indifferent between transacting on the forward market and transacting on the future spot market if the terms he expects on the uncertain future spot market were sufficiently more favourable than the forward market to encourage him to take the risk. But the risk-neutral trader in foreign exchange will not need more favourable terms: he will be indifferent between transacting in the forward and future spot markets, provided that the expected future spot rate is the same as the forward rate offered currently.

There is a second condition required for a rational agent to be indifferent between equal forward and expected future spot rates. Suppose that there are costs associated with transactions in the foreign exchange markets (brokers' fees and so on). If the costs of transactions in forward and spot markets are the same, then risk-neutral traders will again be indifferent between the same forward and expected future spot rates. But imagine that transactions costs are greater in the forward market (and there is some evidence to suggest that they might be) than they are in the spot market. Here again a rational trader will want sufficiently advantageous terms in the forward market to compensate for the extra costs of transacting. The forward rate may not be equal to the expected future spot rate.

There may be other reasons why forward and expected future spot rates may not be equal (for example, Frenkel and Razin (1980) show that stochastic prices may result in a divergence between the two, but admit that this effect is of little significance in practice). It is therefore important to distinguish two hypotheses. The first is referred to as the efficient markets hypothesis. This says that agents use all the available information to forecast the future spot rate; that is, they form rational expectations of the future exchange rate. The market efficiency hypothesis states that the market behaves as if traders possessed rational expectations. Thus market efficiency implies:

$$s_{t+1} = E_t s_{t+1} + \epsilon_{t+1} \tag{3.27}$$

where ϵ_{t+1} is a serially independent forecast error with mean zero, and s is the logarithm of the spot rate (we take logarithms to avoid a problem that arises with exchange rates because of Seigel's paradox – see Seigel (1972)). Moreover, the error term is uncorrelated with any lagged (and therefore known) variable. Clearly, market efficiency on its own is not testable as the expectations term on the right-hand side of equation (3.27) is not observable. The second hypothesis, referred to by Bilson (1981) as the 'speculative efficiency' hypothesis, requires that the forward rate is equal to the expected future spot rate:

$$f_t = E_t s_{t+1} \qquad (3.28)$$

Here f_t denotes the logarithm of the forward rate at time t for foreign exchange transactions which will take place at time $t + 1$. Equation (3.28) depends for its validity on risk-neutrality and identical transactions costs in forward and spot markets. Combining equations (3.27) and (3.28) we obtain the speculative efficiency hypothesis as:

$$s_{t+1} = f_t + \epsilon_{t+1} \qquad (3.29)$$

It is now clear that tests of equation (3.29) are not tests of 'market efficiency' or rational expectations on its own, for equation (3.29) could only be derived with the auxiliary assumptions of risk-neutrality and identical transaction costs. For this reason, Bilson's term 'speculative efficiency' helps to emphasize that we have two hypotheses in equation (3.29): rational expectations and the equality of forward and expected future spot rates. Nevertheless, equation (3.29) (or something very like it) has formed the basis of a large number of tests of rational expectations in the foreign exchange market.

(a) Weak tests

A weak test of speculative efficiency involves estimation of the following:

$$s_{t+1} = \alpha + \beta f_t + v_{t+1} \qquad (3.30)$$

where α and β are parameters and v_{t+1} is an error term.

If speculative efficiency is valid in the foreign exchange market, then we would expect to find the null hypothesis $H_0: \alpha = 0, \beta = 1$

to be true. Estimation of equation (3.30) may give parameter estimates such that α is non-zero and β is not unity, and the null hypothesis is rejected. If such tests have been correctly carried out (statistically speaking) market efficiency (as opposed to speculative efficiency) may still be valid.

Suppose, for example, that *risk-averse traders* will only trade in the future spot market if the terms being offered there are sufficiently attractive to compensate for the extra risks incurred in delay. A trader seeking to buy dollars (for example) in the forward market will buy at a forward rate which is less advantageous to him (that is, if the exchange rate is defined as the sterling price of a dollar, f_t may be greater than $E_t s_{t+1}$). On the other hand, traders buying sterling with dollars will be prepared to trade in the forward market at a rate that is also less attractive to them when compared with the expected future spot rate (in this case f_t will be less than Es_{t+1}). If the values of UK purchases of dollars and of US purchases of stering are roughly equal, dealers in the foreign exchange market will be able to balance their books at a forward rate that is equal to the expected future spot rate. UK and US traders will happily buy in the forward market at a rate that is equal to the future spot rate, but without the latter's uncertainty. However, if the forward market is 'unbalanced' in some way (for example, if the value of UK purchases of dollars forward is greater than the value of US purchases of sterling) then the market forward rate may depart from the expected future spot rate. If then follows that the sign of the risk premium cannot be decided *a priori*.

Suppose that risk considerations mean that $f_t = \alpha + E_t s_{t+1}$, where α is a constant. This would be true if there are more purchases of dollars by risk-averse buyers in the forward market than sales by risk-averse sellers. Market efficiency now implies:

$$s_{t+1} = E_t s_{t+1} + \epsilon_{t+1} = -\alpha + f_t + \epsilon_{t+1} \qquad (3.31)$$

In this case estimation of equation (3.30) will lead to a non-zero intercept. Note that the market is still efficient and is using all current information in its forecast of the exchange rate. Speculative efficiency does not hold because of the presence of a risk premium.

It still appears to be possible to test for market efficiency, for equation (3.31) predicts that the coefficient of f_t will be 1. If equation (3.30) were estimated by ordinary least-squares techniques (which assume that the error term, ν_{t+1}, is uncorrelated with f_t) then an estimator of the coefficient β may still be biased downwards. Why may this arise? The answer lies in the fact that the risk premium may not be a simple constant (α in the example) but is likely to fluctuate from period to period. Thus we may write $f_t = \alpha + E_t s_{t+1} + \eta_t$, where η_t is a random, serially independent variable designed to pick up the random movements in the risk premium. The forward rate is now a 'noisy' predictor of the future spot rate. Cosset (1984) provides evidence that the risk premium is highly volatile and random, and Cornell (1977) has shown that the risk premium changes sign over time but has a mean of zero. The spot rate equation is now:

$$s_{t+1} = -\alpha + f_t + \epsilon_{t+1} - \eta_t \tag{3.32}$$

If equation (3.32) were the true model, it may now be clear why ordinary least-squares estimators of the parameters in equation (3.30) will lead to biased estimators of the coefficients in equation (3.32). In particular, the estimator of β may be less than unity. This is because f_t and η_t are positively correlated, so that f_t and v_{t+1} will be negatively correlated. This will lead to a downward bias in the estimator of β. It is possible to employ statistical techniques that take into account the correlation between f_t and the error (instrumental variable estimation, for example), but some of these methods are not statistically efficient, so that the standard errors of the estimators may be inflated. This further complicates our task, which is to discover whether β is statistically different from one. The discussion in this section would suggest that one would be surpised if the joint hypothesis that $\alpha = 0$ and $\beta = 1$ were satisfied in the ordinary least-squares estimation of equation (3.30), even when market efficiency is true.

Many weak tests, that is tests of the coefficients in equation (3.30), have failed to reject the speculative efficiency hypothesis. The results of some recent studies for the pound–dollar, franc–dollar, mark–dollar and lira–dollar exchange rates are set out in table 3.1. The three studies reported in the table adopt different estimation methods. Edwards (1983) uses 'seemingly unrelated regression', a method which allows the errors in each of the equations for the four exchange rates to be correlated with one another. This arises from the fact that that all four exchange rates involve the dollar: an unexpected shock which affects the dollar – an unexpected change in the US money supply, for example – will affect all four currencies simultaneously. Frenkel (1981) uses instrumental variable estimation and Baillie et al. (1983) use ordinary least-squares. Despite the use of very different techniques, the results of each study are remarkably similar. For the pound–dollar, the mark–dollar and the lira–dollar the hypothesis that $\alpha = 0$ and $\beta = 1$ cannot be rejected at the 5 per cent level. The speculative efficiency hypothesis cannot be rejected for these currencies. In each of the three studies, speculative efficiency can be rejected for the French franc – dollar rate, both because the constant is non-zero and the coefficient on the forward rate is less than unity. These results are typical of the others: the speculative efficiency hypothesis is rejected for some but not for other exchange rates. The weak tests are inconclusive.

Of course where we fail to reject H_0: $\alpha = 0$, $\beta = 1$, it does not follow that speculative efficiency is true, only that these weak tests have failed to reject it. The tests reported in table 3.1 may be insufficiently powerful to allow rejection. One possible reason for this is that both forward and spot rates may be strongly time-trended. If s and f are both on a strong upward (or downward) trend, it may be difficult to obtain true estimates of the parameters α and β. For this reason Bilson (1981) wrote the speculative efficiency hypothesis as:

$$s_{t+1} - s_t = \alpha_0 + \beta_0(f_t - s_t) + v_{t+1} \qquad (3.33)$$

where the right-hand side is the rate of change of the exchange rate and $f_t - s_t$ is called the 'forward premium'. Again speculative efficiency implies that $\alpha_0 = 0$ and $\beta_0 = 1$. Using ordinary least-squares to estimate the parameters in equation (3.33), Bilson obtains mixed results. For the pound–dollar and mark–dollar rates the speculative efficiency hypothesis is not rejected (although the Durbin–Watson test statistic indicated the presence of serial correlation in the equation error for the pound–dollar). In the case of the franc–dollar and lira–dollar the speculative efficiency hypothesis was rejected both because the estimate of β_0 was different from unity and because the errors showed signs of serial correlation (in the case of the lira–dollar).

(b) Testing restrictions

In a rather different approach the assumption of speculative efficiency may be tested by exploiting the cross-equation restric-

TABLE 3.1 Weak tests of speculative efficiency ($s_{t+1} = a + \beta f_t + v_{t+1}$)

	Edwards (1983)		Frenkel (1981)			Baillie et al. (1983)		
	α	β	α	β	DW^a	α	β	DW
Pound–dollar	-0.033 (0.018)[b]	0.957 (0.025)	0.030 (0.018)	0.961 (0.025)	1.74	0.033 (0.016)	0.956 (0.022)	1.33
Franc–dollar	-0.568 (0.179)	0.816 (0.058)	-0.236 (0.080)	0.844 (0.053)	2.24	-0.174 (0.060)	0.884 (0.040)	1.85
DM–dollar	0.026 (0.027)	0.967 (0.032)	-0.021 (0.027)	0.973 (0.032)	2.10	-0.024 (0.020)	0.968 (0.024)	1.98
Lira–dollar	0.246 (0.155)	0.962 (0.023)	—	—	—	-0.235 (0.120)	0.964 (0.018)	1.67

[a] Terms in parentheses are estimated standard errors.
[b] DW is the Durbin–Watson statistic.

tions that it implies. This approach has been adopted by Baillie et al. (1983) and Hakkio (1981). In order to see how speculative efficiency imposes restrictions of this sort we shall present a simplified version of the Baillie et al. and Hakkio models. Suppose that s_t and f_t follow a simple first order autoregressive process of the form:

$$s_t = \gamma_1 s_{t-1} + \gamma_2 f_{t-1} + \omega_{1t}, \qquad f_t = \beta_1 s_{t-1} + \beta_2 f_{t-1} + \omega_{2t}$$

$$(3.34)$$

where γ_i and β_i are coefficients, and ω_{it} is a random error which is serially uncorrelated with mean zero. Speculative efficiency implies that $s_{t+2} - f_t = \epsilon_{t+2}$, where f_t is assumed to be the forward rate for trading two periods forward. Taking expectations of this expression conditional on information dated t, we can write:

$$E_t s_{t+2} - E_t f_t = 0$$

since $E_t \epsilon_{t+2} = 0$.

Leading the first equation in (3.34) by two periods and taking expectations of both equations in (3.34), conditional on information dated t, we can write:

$$E_t s_{t+2} = \gamma_1 E_t s_{t+1} + \gamma_2 E_t f_{t+1}, \qquad E_t f_t = f_t$$

Since speculative efficiency implies that the difference between $E_t s_{t+2}$ and f_t is zero, and noting that $E_t s_{t+1} = \gamma_1 s_t + \gamma_2 f_t$, we must have the following restriction on the model in equations (3.34):

$$(\gamma_1^2 + \gamma_2 \beta_1) s_t + (\gamma_2 \gamma_1 + \gamma_2 \beta_2 - 1) f_t = 0 \qquad (3.35)$$

This restriction is satisfied when:

$$\gamma_1^2 + \gamma_2 \beta_1 = 0 \qquad \text{and} \qquad \gamma_2 \gamma_1 + \gamma_2 \beta_2 = 1$$

These conditions can be rearranged to give:

$$\beta_1 = -\gamma_1^2 / \gamma_2 \qquad \text{and} \qquad \beta_2 = (1 - \gamma_1 \gamma_2)/\gamma_2$$

Imposing these restrictions, we can write equations (3.34) as:

$$s_t = \gamma_1 s_{t-1} + \gamma_2 f_{t-1} + \omega_{1t}$$

$$(3.36)$$

$$f_t = \left(\frac{-\gamma_1^2}{\gamma_2} \right) s_{t-1} + \left(\frac{1 - \gamma_1 \gamma_2}{\gamma_2} \right) f_{t-1} + \omega_{2t}$$

These two equations can be estimated imposing the non-linear restrictions between the coefficients that are implied by speculative efficiency. The likelihood of the model given by equations (3.36) may be compared with the likelihood of an unrestricted model which is given by:

$$s_t = \pi_1 s_{t-1} + \pi_2 f_{t-1} + \xi_{1t}, \qquad f_t = \pi_3 s_{t-1} + \pi_4 f_{t-1} + \xi_{2t}$$

where ξ_{it} is a random error which is serially uncorrelated with mean zero.

If speculative efficiency is true, we would expect the likelihood from the unrestricted model to differ insignificantly from that of the restricted model. This example illustrates the general point made earlier in this chapter; namely, that rational expectations introduces restrictions across equations which may be tested using the likelihood ratio test (or something similar).

In practice the processes for s and f described in equations (3.34) are unlikely to be this simple. Even if we restrict the process to include only lagged values of s and f, it is highly likely that longer lags in s and f will have an effect on their current values. A lengthening of the lags in equations (3.34) and the lengthening of the period covered in the forward rate will not change the type of restrictions imposed, but they will greatly complicate them. Indeed, the cross-equation restrictions may become so complicated as to make computation of the restricted model difficult or impossible in practice. For this reason Hakkio was obliged to limit himself to four lagged terms in equations (3.34) even when there was firm evidence of longer lags. The likelihood ratio tests of the restrictions conducted by Hakkio rejected the speculative efficiency hypothesis for five exchange rates (gilder–dollar, mark–dollar, Canadian dollar – US dollar, Swiss franc – dollar and pound–dollar).

Using similar methods, Baillie et al. (1983) investigated the speculative efficiency hypothesis using weekly data for six dollar-exchange rates (pound, mark, lira, French franc, Canadian dollar and Swiss franc). They avoided the necessity of computing the restricted model by estimating the unrestricted model and testing the restrictions using the Wald test. This test examines the validity of the restrictions without the need to estimate the restricted model. The Wald test is equivalent to the likelihood ratio test in large samples. Baillie et al. reject the speculative efficiency hypothesis in all cases.

The tests carried out by Hakkio and Baillie et al. are more powerful than the weak tests described at the beginning of this section. But there may be reasons to think that they may reject the null hypothesis of speculative efficiency even when the latter is in fact true. The tests they use are large-sample tests, and the distributions of the test statistics they use (such as the likelihood ratio) are not known exactly for small samples. The application of these tests may increase the probability of rejecting the null hypothesis when it is in fact true. There is no straightforward way, at present, of evaluating the quantitative importance of this problem.

3.6 EXAMPLE 2: THE TERM STRUCTURE OF INTEREST RATES

We turn now to the second example of the way in which rational expectations introduces restrictions which can be tested. In particular, we will see how the assumption of rational expectations places certain testable restrictions on the relationship between long-run and short-run interest rates.

The bond market at any time t consists of a number of outstanding bonds with differing maturity dates. At one end of the scale there are short-term bonds which are about to be redeemed, and at the other end long-term bonds – perpetuities – which will never be redeemed. The term structure of interest rates is the relationship between the rates of return on bonds with different maturity dates. In a world of perfect certainty and perfect foresight the traditional view of the term structure is that long-run interest rates are simply averages of future short-term rates, so that:

$$i_{nt} = (1/n)(i_{1t} + i_{1t+1} + i_{1t+2} + \ldots + i_{1t+n-1}) \qquad (3.37)$$

where i_{1t} denotes the 'one-period' rate, that is the market rate of interest at time t on bonds with one period to maturity; and i_{nt} denotes the 'n-period' rate, that is the market interest rate at time t on bonds with n periods to maturity. Equation (3.37) tells us that if short-term rates are constant at time t and for the following $n - 1$ periods the n-period rate will equal the one-period rate.

In a world of uncertainty it may be assumed that equation (3.37) becomes:

$$i_{nt} = (1/n)(i_{1t} + E_t i_{1t+1} + E_t i_{1t+2} + \ldots + E_t i_{1t+n-1}) \qquad (3.38)$$

That is, individuals at time t can observe the current market short rate, i_{1t}, and the current market rate on a bond which has maturity date n, i_{nt}. However, they have to form expectations about future short rates. This is where the theory of rational expectations emerges once again. We will see that if individuals are rational the manner in which they form the expectations in equation (3.38) places certain testable restrictions on the underlying model.

Following the work of Sargent (1979) we will work with a model in first differences, so we define:

$$i_{nt-1} = (1/n)(i_{1t-1} + E_{t-1} i_{1t} + \ldots + E_{t-1} i_{1t+n-2}) \qquad (3.39)$$

Then, subtracting equation (3.39) from equation (3.38) gives:

$$\begin{aligned}
\Delta i_{nt} &= i_{nt} - i_{nt-1} \\
&= (1/n)\{ \Delta i_{1t} + (E_t i_{1t+1} - E_{t-1} i_{1t}) + (E_t i_{1t+2} - E_{t-1} i_{1t+1}) \\
&\quad + \ldots + (E_t i_{1t+n-1} - E_{t-1} i_{1t+n-2})\} \qquad (3.40)
\end{aligned}$$

Now suppose that at time $t - 1$ the only information available to individuals is contained in the set I_{t-1}. For example, I_{t-1} may consist of just Δi_{1t-1} and Δi_{nt-1}, the most recent changes in the short and long rates. Then, taking expectations of the left-hand side of equation (3.40) conditional on I_{t-1} yields:

$$E(\Delta i_{nt} | I_{t-1}) = E_{t-1} \Delta i_{nt}$$

which is in accordance with our definition of rational expectations.

Likewise, taking expectations of the first term on the right-hand side of equation (3.40) gives $E(\Delta i_{1t} | I_{t-1}) = E_{t-1} \Delta i_{1t}$. The expectation of the second term on the right-hand side of equation (3.40) is:

$$E(E(i_{1t+1} | I_t) | I_{t-1}) = E(i_{1t+1} | I_{t-1}) = E_{t-1} i_{1t+1} \qquad (3.41)$$

Taking expectation of all the remaining terms in equation (3.40) produces:

$$\begin{aligned}
E_{t-1} \Delta i_{nt} &= (1/n)(E_{t-1} \Delta i_{1t} + E_{t-1} \Delta i_{1t+1} \\
&\quad + \ldots + E_{t-1} \Delta i_{1t+n-1}) \qquad (3.42)
\end{aligned}$$

Now assume that the only information available is Δi_{1t-1} and

Δi_{nt-1}, and suppose that we write the vector autoregression (VAR):

$$\Delta i_{1t} = \alpha \Delta i_{1t-1} + \beta \Delta i_{nt-1} + \nu_{1t},$$
$$\Delta i_{nt} = \gamma \Delta i_{1t-1} + \delta \Delta i_{nt-1} + \nu_{2t} \qquad (3.43a,b)$$

where ν_{1t} and ν_{2t} are random errors with zero means, and are uncorrelated with Δi_{1t-1} and Δi_{nt-1}.

Now, the important point about the rational expectations assumptions which lead to equation (3.42) is that they impose restrictions on equation (3.43b). To see the form of the restrictions we will work with the very simple case when $n = 2$. The relationship in equation (3.42) now becomes:

$$E_{t-1} \Delta i_{2t} = \tfrac{1}{2}(E_{t-1} \Delta i_{1t} + E_{t-1} \Delta i_{1t+1}) \qquad (3.44)$$

From the equations in (3.43) we can deduce that:

$$E_{t-1} \Delta i_{1t} = \alpha \Delta i_{1t-1} + \beta \Delta i_{2t-1},$$
$$E_{t-1} \Delta i_{2t} = \gamma \Delta i_{1t-1} + \delta \Delta i_{2t-1} \qquad (3.45a,b)$$

since $E_{t-1} \nu_{1t} = 0 = E_{t-1} \nu_{2t}$. These expressions enable us to obtain the expectations on the right-hand side of equation (3.44). That is, $E_{t-1} \Delta i_{1t}$ is obtained directly from equation (3.45a) and $E_{t-1} \Delta i_{1t+1}$ can be obtained by noting that:

$$E_{t-1} \Delta i_{1t+1} = E_{t-1}(\alpha \Delta i_{1t} + \beta \Delta i_{2t})$$

Then, using equations (3.45) we have:

$$E_{t-1} \Delta i_{1t+1} = \alpha(\alpha \Delta i_{1t-1} + \beta \Delta i_{2t-1}) + \beta(\gamma \Delta i_{1t-1} + \delta \Delta i_{2t-1})$$

so

$$E_{t-1} \Delta i_{1t+1} = (\alpha^2 + \beta\gamma) \Delta i_{1t-1} + (\alpha\beta + \beta\delta) \Delta i_{2t-1}$$

We can now rewrite equation (3.44) as:

$$\begin{aligned} E_{t-1} \Delta i_{2t} &= \tfrac{1}{2}[\alpha \Delta i_{1t-1} + \beta \Delta i_{2t-1} + (\alpha^2 + \beta\gamma) \Delta i_{1t-1} \\ &\quad + (\alpha\beta + \beta\delta) \Delta i_{2t-1}] \\ &= \tfrac{1}{2}[(\alpha + \alpha^2 + \beta\gamma) \Delta i_{1t-1} + (\beta + \alpha\beta + \beta\delta) \Delta i_{2t-1}] \end{aligned}$$
$$(3.46)$$

But, from the unrestricted equation in (3.43b) we have that:

$$E_{t-1} \Delta i_{2t} = \gamma \Delta i_{1t-1} + \delta \Delta i_{2t-1} \qquad (3.47)$$

Comparing equation (3.46) with equation (3.47) we see that rational expectations imposes the restrictions that:

$$\gamma = \frac{\alpha + \alpha^2 + \beta\gamma}{2} \quad \text{and} \quad \delta = \frac{\beta + \alpha\beta + \beta\delta}{2}$$

or, alternatively:

$$\gamma = \frac{\alpha(1 + \alpha)}{2 - \beta} \quad \text{and} \quad \delta = \frac{\beta(1 + \alpha)}{2 - \beta} \quad \text{(3.48a,b)}$$

In other words, if the assumption of rational expectations is correct we would expect that a regression of the two equations in equation (3.43), using a large sample of observations, would produce estimates of γ and δ approximately equal to the expressions on the right-hand sides of equations (3.48a) and (3.48b) evaluated at the estimates of α and β. Moreover, we could test the restrictions by comparing the likelihood for the unrestricted equations in (3.43) with the restricted version where the right-hand sides of equations (3.48) replace γ and δ in equation (3.43b). As we saw earlier in this chapter, the likelihood ratio test statistic could then be compared with a chi-square variate with, in this case, two degrees of freedom since there are two restrictions on the model.

Now suppose that we have data on a one-period rate and on a three-period rate, so that $n = 3$. The term structure in equation (3.38) now becomes:

$$i_{3t} = \tfrac{1}{3}(i_{1t} + E_t i_{1t+1} + E_t i_{1t+2})$$

and the unrestricted VAR in equation (3.43) becomes:

$$\Delta i_{1t} = \alpha \Delta i_{1t-1} + \beta \Delta i_{3t-1} + \nu_{1t},$$
$$\Delta i_{3t} = \gamma \Delta i_{1t-1} + \delta \Delta i_{3t-1} + \nu_{2t} \quad \text{(3.49a,b)}$$

Carrying out similar substitutions to the ones that led to equations (3.45) we obtain:

$$\gamma = \tfrac{1}{3}(\alpha + \alpha^2 + \alpha^3 + \beta\gamma + 2\alpha\beta\gamma + \beta\gamma\delta) \quad \text{(3.50a)}$$
$$\delta = \tfrac{1}{3}(\beta + \alpha\beta + \beta\delta + \alpha^2\beta + \alpha\beta\delta + \beta^2\gamma + \beta\delta^2) \quad \text{(3.50b)}$$

Clearly then, as n becomes larger the restrictions placed upon the γ and δ coefficients become more complex. Sargent (1979) generalizes the model to the case in which:

$$i_{nt} = (1/n)(i_{1t} + E_t i_{1t+1} + E_t i_{1t+2} + \ldots + E_t i_{1t+n-1})$$

with the unrestricted VAR:

$$\Delta i_{1t} = \alpha_1 \Delta i_{1t-1} + \ldots + \alpha_m \Delta i_{1t-m} + \beta_1 \Delta i_{nt-1}$$
$$+ \ldots + \beta_m \Delta i_{nt-m} + \nu_{1t} \tag{3.51a}$$

$$\Delta i_{nt} = \gamma_1 \Delta i_{1t-1} + \ldots + \gamma_m \Delta i_{1t-m} + \delta_1 \Delta i_{nt-1}$$
$$+ \ldots + \delta_m \Sigma i_{nt-m} + \nu_{2t} \tag{3.51b}$$

In this case the restrictions on the γ_i's and the δ_i's in equation (3.51b) are complicated non-linear functions of the α_i's and β_i's.

Sargent's derivation of the restrictions for the general case need not concern us here. What we do need to know, however, is how these complex restrictions can be imposed on the term structure model so that the rational expectations assumptions can be tested. Sargent's suggested solution to this problem can be seen by looking at the simple $n = 3$ case, which led to the restrictions of equation (3.50). He suggests that we first obtain estimates of α and β, say $\hat{\alpha}$ and $\hat{\beta}$, from an ordinary least-squares regression of equation (3.49a). We then set γ and δ on the right-hand side of equations (3.50) to zero and obtain:

$$\gamma^{(1)} = \frac{\hat{\alpha} + \hat{\alpha}^2 + \hat{\alpha}^3}{3}, \qquad \delta^{(1)} = \frac{\hat{\beta} + \hat{\alpha}\hat{\beta} + \hat{\alpha}^2\hat{\beta}}{3}$$

These estimated values of γ and δ, $\gamma^{(1)}$ and $\delta^{(1)}$, are then substituted into the right-hand side of the equations in (3.50) together with the original estimates of α and β to give:

$$\gamma^{(2)} = \frac{\hat{\alpha} + \hat{\alpha}^2 + \hat{\alpha}^3 + \hat{\beta}\gamma^{(1)} + 2\hat{\alpha}\hat{\beta}\gamma^{(1)} + \hat{\beta}\gamma^{(1)}\delta^{(1)}}{3}$$

$$\delta^{(2)} = \frac{\hat{\beta} + \hat{\alpha}\hat{\beta} + \hat{\beta}\delta^{(1)} + \hat{\alpha}^2\hat{\beta} + \hat{\alpha}\hat{\beta}\delta^{(1)} + \hat{\beta}^2\gamma^{(1)} + \hat{\beta}\delta^{(1)}\delta^{(1)}}{3}$$

The values of $\gamma^{(2)}$ and $\delta^{(2)}$ are then inserted into the right-hand side of equations (3.50) and so on until the method converges; that is, until the differences between $\gamma^{(k)}$ and $\gamma^{(k-1)}$ and between $\delta^{(k)}$ and $\delta^{(k-1)}$ from iteration k to $k-1$ become negligible. At this point we will have found values of γ and δ that satisfy the non-linear equations in (3.50). In fact, Sargent shows how the restrictions can be incorporated into a maximum likelihood procedure so that the restrictions can be tested using the likelihood ratio.

Sargent applies the above method to the model in equations (3.51) with $m = 4$ using quarterly data on the five-year government

TABLE 3.2   Term structure of interest rates: estimates for a five-year bond rate and 91-day Treasury bill rate

α	$j = 1$	$j = 2$	$j = 3$	$j = 4$
Unrestricted estimated				
α_j	−0.3663	−0.3235	0.1234	−0.0694
β_j	0.6373	0.4322	−0.3286	0.1703
γ_j	−0.2962	0.0203	0.2480	−0.1047
δ_j	0.2812	0.1200	−0.3934	0.0765
Maximum likelihood estimates				
α_j	−0.0717	−0.3660	−0.1465	0.0433
β_j	0.3700	0.3270	0.0995	0.0900
γ_j	−0.0183	−0.0154	−0.0033	0.0014
δ_j	0.0298	0.0172	0.0063	0.0029

bond rate and the 91-day Treasury bill rate for the period 1953(2) to 1971(4) in the US: we reproduce his results in table 3.2. The unrestricted estimates were obtained by ordinary least-squares while the maximum likelihood estimates were obtained with all the restrictions on the γ and δ coefficients imposed. The likelihood ratio test statistic for testing the null hypothesis that the restrictions are correct is 8.58, which has to be compared with a chi-square variate with eight degrees of freedom. At the 5 per cent significance level the critical value of chi-square is 15.5. Therefore, the rational expectations restrictions cannot be rejected.

The above procedure gives a flavour of how the assumption of rational expectations can be used to give a model of the term structure of interest rates which can be tested. It should be pointed out, however, that Sargent's empirical results have not gone unchallenged. Shiller (1980) argues, for example, that Sargent's method of first differencing his data imposes further restrictions on the stochastic properties of his model which he does not test. Attfield and Duck (1982) found that they could reject the rational expectations theory of the term structure of interest rates when they applied the above model to three-monthly, five-yearly and ten-yearly rates of interest in the UK.

3.7   SUMMARY

In this chapter we have considered alternative tests of rational expectations. Direct estimates of expected variables are relatively rare. Studies using those that do exist provide little support for the rational expectations hypothesis. In the more general case, in which there is no direct estimate of the expected variable, one cannot merely see the actual value of a variable as a measure of the rational expectation of that variable, despite the fact that the two should differ only by a random error. But it is possible to use the process determining a variable to generate a measure of the rational expectation of that variable, and this method has the attractive feature of allowing a formal statistical test of a model which includes rational expectations. This feature occurs because rational expectations generally implies restrictions on the coefficients of the model, and if the restrictions are valid then imposing them should not worsen the model's explanatory power.

We have also presented two examples of how rational expectations introduce testable restrictions: in the first we examined the relationship between the spot and the forward exchange rates and in the second we examined the implications for the term structure of interest rates.

SUGGESTIONS FOR FURTHER READING

Reviews of some of the literature on tests of the rational expectations hypothesis using direct survey data can be found in chapter 1 of Sheffrin (1983), chapter 3 of Hudson (1982) and part III of Pesaran (1987). Good reviews of the method of maximum likelihood estimation and testing are in chapters 3 and 5 of Harvey (1981) and in Cramer (1986). Methods of incorporating rational expectations assumptions into economic models and estimating and testing the models are discussed in Wallis (1980), Revankar (1980), Hoffman and Schmidt (1981), part II of Pesaran (1987) and in Lucas and Sargent (1981). Further discussions of the observational equivalence problem can be found in McCallum (1979), chapters 4 and 5 of Begg (1982), Buiter (1983), chapter 10 of Minford and Peel (1983), in Abel and Mishkin (1983) and in chapter 6 of Pesaran (1987).

4

Rational Expectations and a Flexible-price Macroeconomic Model

One of the first and most dramatic applications of rational expectations was to a flexible-price version of Friedman's (1968) natural rate hypothesis. The initial aim of this application was to show that in a model in which agents were fully rational, even to the extent of having rational expectations, movements in *nominal* spending could still affect aggregate real output or employment. Such an effect was hard to reconcile with classical microeconomic theory, which suggests that if agents act optimally then decisions about real variables such as output would be influenced only by other real variables, and not by nominal variables. Thus output might be altered by a technological breakthrough, or by changes in the structure of taxation which affected the choice between work and leisure, or by changes in other real variables, but should not be affected by a change in nominal spending: such changes should affect the price at which the available output is sold and not the quantity of output itself. But a lot of evidence appeared to suggest that variations in nominal spending had, at times, marked effects on real variables. The strongest single piece of such evidence was the Great Depression in the 1930s, when a large slump in nominal spending appeared to induce a large fall in output and a large rise in unemployment. Other influential evidence was provided by Phillips (1958) who showed that for the UK for almost 100 years before the late 1950s there appeared to exist a stable relationship – which became known as the Phillips curve – between a real variable, unemployment, and the rate of change of a nominal variable, nominal wages.

Friedman's statement of the natural rate hypothesis went a long way towards reconciling such evidence with basic classical theory.

His central assumption was that agents are not perfectly informed about prices in markets other than their own. From this he showed that they could be temporarily fooled into changing real output by nominal spending movements, the effects of which on prices they had not fully expected. However, Friedman did not explicitly introduce rationality of expectations into the natural rate hypothesis, and indeed appeared to favour the use of an adaptive expectations model, at least for the US at the time he was writing. It is clear that one of the aims of early rational expectations theorists, Lucas (1972) in particular, was to show that Friedman's apparent theoretical reconciliation of optimal behaviour with the broad facts could be extended to cover rationality of expectations. This chapter explains how that aim was achieved.

The model obtained by combining rational expectations and the simple natural rate hypothesis produces a particularly dramatic policy conclusion, and one which gave rational expectations some initial notoriety, for it suggested that the Keynesian approach to macroeconomic policy which governments in many countries had adopted after the Second World War was at best unnecessary and at worst harmful. We explain these policy implications in this chapter. In following chapters we discuss the criticisms levelled at the rational expectations – simple natural rate model and its empirical relevance.

4.1 THE AGGREGATE DEMAND CURVE

In figure 4.1 we have drawn a conventional IS–LM diagram. The IS curve shows combinations of the level of real income and the level of the nominal interest rate, i, for which it is true that the aggregate demand for output equals the actual quantity of output. It is drawn for given levels of certain key variables, such as the level of real government expenditure, tax rates and the level of autonomous expenditure. The LM curve shows combinations of the level of real income and the nominal interest rate for which it is true that the quantity of money demanded equals the quantity of money supplied. It too is drawn on the assumption that the values of certain key variables are given, in this case the quantity of money and, importantly, the general level of prices.

Let the relevant IS curve be the one labelled IS_0 and the

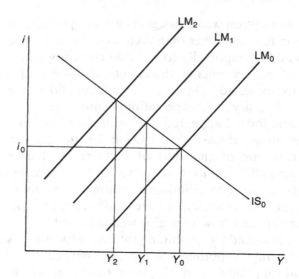

FIGURE 4.1   Equilibrium output at different prices.

relevant LM curve be initially the one drawn for the general level of prices, P_0, and labelled LM_0. The point at which these two curves intersect gives the equilibrium interest rate and the equilibrium level of aggregate demand, i_0 and Y_0 respectively. This level of aggregate demand, Y_0, is the equilibrium level in the sense that if that level of output, Y_0, is actually produced each period then all that output and no more will be willingly demanded each period. Clearly, the equilibrium level of aggregate demand is dependent on the positions of the IS and LM curves. In particular, if the general level of prices is higher at, say, P_1 the LM curve will be to the left of LM_0 at, say, LM_1 and the equilibrium level of aggregate demand will be lower at Y_1. And if the general level of prices is higher still at, say, P_2 the LM curve would be even further to the left at, say, LM_2 giving an even lower equilibrium level of aggregate demand, Y_2.

In figure 4.2 we draw the line which plots the different values of P, the general level of prices, against the equilibrium levels of aggregate demand which they generate, given the values of all the other variables which determine the positions of the IS and LM curves, such as the level of real government expenditure and the nominal quantity of money. We label this line AD_0 and shall refer

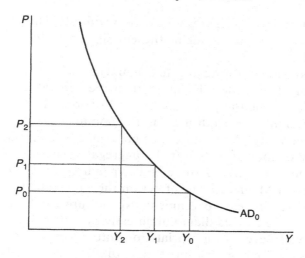

FIGURE 4.2   The aggregate demand curve.

to it as the aggregate demand curve. It shows for any general level
of prices what, *ceteris paribus*, the equilibrium level of aggregate
demand is. Clearly, $P_0 Y_0$, $P_1 Y_1$ and $P_2 Y_2$ are combinations of P
and Y lying on this line.

The intuitive explanation for the negative slope of the aggregate
demand curve is that a higher price implies, *ceteris paribus*, a lower
real quantity of money in the economy since the real quantity of
money is defined to be the nominal quantity of money, M, divided
by the general level of prices, P, that is M/P. One way in which
people may respond to finding themselves with less real money
than they had before is by selling off holdings of bonds to rebuild
their holdings of money. But this can only work at the individual
level: it cannot work for the economy as a whole since the quantity
of nominal money is fixed, and so one person obtains more money
by selling bonds only with the result that someone else – the person
who buys the bonds – finds himself with less. The general attempt
to sell bonds will tend to drive down the price of bonds and raise
their rate of interest, and this will help eliminate the excess demand
for money, since the higher the rate of interest the lower the
demand for money. But the rise in the rate of interest will do
something else too: it will depress investment expenditure and
thereby cause a fall in aggregate demand. As a consequence the

equilibrium level of aggregate demand will fall. Thus a rise in the price level leads to a fall in the equilibrium level of aggregate demand.

The position of the aggregate demand curve is determined by the values of all the variables other than the general level of prices which determine the positions of the IS and LM curves, such as real government expenditure and the nominal quantity of money in the economy. A rise in either government expenditure or the quantity of money will shift the aggregate demand curve to the right, the exact size of the effect depending upon the slopes of the IS and LM curves. The effect on the aggregate demand curve of a change in real government expenditure or the quantity of money can be derived diagrammatically by shifting the IS and LM curves, whichever is appropriate, or, intuitively, along the following lines. A rise in government expenditure adds directly to aggregate spending and hence will tend to increase the equilibrium level of aggregate demand. Of course, the financing of such an increase in government spending by the sale of an equivalent quantity of government bonds will tend to raise interest rates and thus choke off some private expenditure, but unless the interest elasticity of private expenditure is very high, or the interest elasticity of the demand for money very low, the net effect of an increase in government spending will be significantly to raise the equilibrium level of aggregate demand at any price level. Thus a rise in real government expenditure shifts the aggregate demand curve to the right.

A rise in the nominal quantity of money will have the same effect, although the route here is slightly different. The rise in the quantity of money leads, *ceteris paribus*, to a rise in the real quantity of money. One way people might respond to finding themselves with more real money than they want would be to use their excess holdings of money to buy bonds. The general attempt to do this will drive the interest rate on bonds down and thereby stimulate investment expenditure and hence aggregate demand. Provided that investment expenditure is significantly influenced by changes in the rate of interest, the rise in the quantity of money will significantly shift the aggregate demand curve to the right.

There are many differences of opinion amongst economists about the relative power of fiscal policy and monetary policy to influence the position of the aggregate demand curve, but these debates are of no great concern to the question we are dealing with here. What is more important for our purposes is the way in which the aggregate demand curve interacts with the aggregate supply curve to determine the equilibrium general level of prices and the equilibrium level of output; we are especially interested in the nature of that interaction when expectations are rational. To understand that interaction we must first analyse the flexible-price, natural rate version of the aggregate supply curve.

4.2 THE FLEXIBLE-PRICE – NATURAL RATE AGGREGATE SUPPLY CURVE

Imagine the economy as consisting of a large number of geographically separate markets. It may help to think of each of these markets as being located on its own island. On every island, that is in every market, the same type of good is bought and sold each period. It is a one-good economy, but that one good is traded in many separate markets. Furthermore, on each island the price of the good adjusts each period to equate the supply of the good *on that island* and the demand for the good *on that island*. In each period, on each island there are a large number of suppliers and demanders. They trade with each other and then, next period, may find themselves on different islands and the whole process is repeated. Prices throughout this economy are fully flexible and competitively determined, that is they move to equate supply and demand, and no individual exerts any significant influence on price. In the previous section we analysed the factors determining aggregate demand in this economy, in other words the aggregate demand curve. To derive an aggregate supply curve we shall assume that suppliers are primarily influenced by the *relative* price of the good on their island. If the price of the good in their market is, for whatever reason, known to be higher than its average price in the whole economy they will take advantage of this high relative price and supply a higher quantity of the good than they otherwise would. The total level of output supplied when the relative price of the good on all islands is correctly perceived we shall call the natural level of aggregate output. But why should the relative price of the good on any island ever change? Why should the price of the good established on one island ever be any different from the price of the good established on any other island? After all, it is the *same* good which is being traded on each island. The answer is because of the *relative demand* shifts between islands which, we shall assume, are a significant feature of the economy. One way of conceiving of this is that in any period there are in some islands a greater than average number of demanders, and in others a smaller number than average. This produces in some islands higher than average demand and in others lower than average demand. Of course, over the whole economy these relative demand changes sum to zero, and aggregate or average demand is given by the aggregate demand curve derived in section 4.1. But any individual market or island may experience somewhat higher or lower demand than average, those with lower than average demand cancelling out those with higher than average demand. (If these perturbations around the average do not cancel each other out, they cannot be reflecting purely relative demand changes because there would be some net *aggregate* effect.) In those islands where demand is relatively high the equilibrium price of the good will be relatively high and in those islands where demand is relatively low the price of the good will be relatively low. So, given the set-up of the model, in particular given that in any one period people can only buy or sell in the island on which they are located, different equilibrium prices can be established for the *same* good.

What would be the relationship between the general level of prices, or the average price of the good in this economy, and the total or aggregate quantity of output supplied? The answer to this question depends upon the amount of information that people have about what is happening in the economy. If suppliers know not only the current price in their own market but also the current price in all other markets the aggregate level of output will be *independent* of the average level of prices. For if their own equilibrium price rises by 10 per cent and the average of all other prices rises by 10 per cent too, then they will not increase output because they know that there has been no increase in the *relative* price of the good on their island. If their own price rises by 10 per cent and they know that on average other prices have risen by 5 per cent then they will increase their output. But in the nature of averages the price on some other island(s) must have risen by less than 5 per cent. For simplicity, imagine that on one island the price of the good has not risen at all. On this latter island output will be lower than normal because of the known fall in the relative price of the good on that island. Given symmetric behaviour aggregate output in this case too will remain at its natural level: the increase in output in one market cancelling out the fall in output on the other. So in both cases *aggregate* output will remain at its natural level in the face of a change in the general level of prices.

On the other hand, if we assume that there is imperfect information, in the sense that suppliers and demanders know the current price for the good on *their* island but only get to know the price in *other* markets with a one-period time lag, the relationship between aggregate supply and the general level of prices becomes much more subtle. For now if you, as a supplier, observe a rise in the price of the good on your island of 10 per cent you cannot be certain whether all other markets are experiencing the same rise on average. If they are you would not want to raise output above its natural level because there has been no rise in your relative price. But if they are experiencing on average a *smaller* rise, you would want to raise output, taking advantage of the high relative price on your island; and if they are experiencing a *larger* rise you would want to *reduce* supply. So in order to decide what quantity to supply you would have to form an *expectation* of the average, economy-wide price of the good. You would then compare this with the actual price on your island, and depending upon whether your actual price is higher, lower or the same as your expectation of the average price you would supply a quantity of output which is higher, lower or the same as your natural level. And what is true for you would be true for every other supplier: they too will supply more than the natural level if the price on their island is above what they expected the average price to be, and less if it is below. So the aggregate level of output will be above its natural level if the average price level is above the economy-wide expectation of it, below it if the average price level is below the economy-wide expectation of it, and equal to its natural level if the average level of prices equals the economy-wide expectation of it.

For an economy such as the one we have imagined in which there is imperfect information in the sense we have described, the relationship between aggregate supply and the general level of prices can be depicted as it is in figure 4.3. The aggregate natural level of output is labelled Y^n. The vertical line from Y^n shows the relationship between output and the price level *when the actual price level is correctly forecast* – the long-run aggregate supply

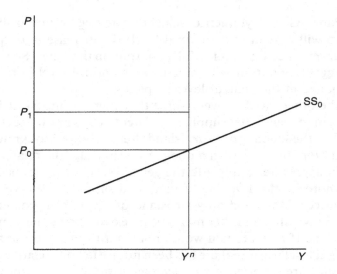

FIGURE 4.3   The long- and short-run aggregate supply curves.

curve. As we have shown, correct expectations imply that aggregate output will equal its natural level. (This is quite consistent with some suppliers who face a relatively low level of demand producing below normal, while those who face a relatively high level of demand produce above normal, the two groups offsetting each other.)

The line labelled SS_0 is drawn on the assumption that the general expectation of the average level of prices is P_0. If this expectation is correct and the average price level is P_0 then, of course, the aggregate level of output will equal its natural level – that is why this line cuts the vertical line from Y^n at P_0. But if the average level of prices is above the level generally expected, P_0, then, as we have shown, the quantity of output will be above its natural level, whereas if the general level of prices is below the level expected, then aggregate output will be below its natural level. Thus the relationship between the general level of prices and aggregate output when the expected price level is held constant at P_0 – the short-run aggregate supply curve – can be depicted as an upward-sloping line which cuts the vertical line from Y^n at price level P_0. If we had assumed that the expected level of prices was P_1 and had drawn the relationship between the general level of prices and aggregate output on that assumption we would have drawn the short-run aggregate supply curve as an upward-sloping line which cuts the vertical line from Y^n at P_1.

This aggregate supply curve is of fundamental importance to the macroeconomic policy conclusions often drawn from the rational expectations hypothesis. The crucially important aspect of it is that changes in the level of prices which are foreseen, or are expected, have no effect on the level of output. Only unforeseen or unexpected price changes will cause output to deviate from its natural level. To understand this result we have to combine the aggregate demand curve derived in section 4.1 with our aggregate supply curve and consider how the equilibrium level of prices and the equilibrium level of real output are determined.

4.3 AGGREGATE DEMAND AND EQUILIBRIUM OUTPUT

Imagine that an economy's aggregate demand curve is AD_0 in figure 4.4 and that its natural level of output is Y^n. If the expectation of the general level of prices in this economy is P_0, the relevant short-run supply curve is the line labelled SS_0. It is clear from the diagram that if the price level is P_0, the economy is in

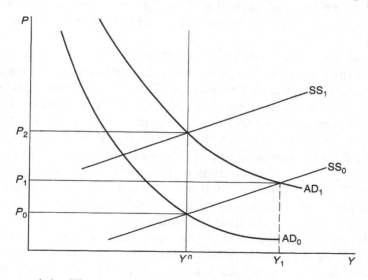

FIGURE 4.4 The interaction of aggregate supply and demand.

full equilibrium in the sense that the expected price level is equal to the actual price level and the level of output is therefore equal to its natural level. From this initial position of full equilibrium consider what happens if there is a shift in the aggregate demand curve from AD_0 to AD_1? If expectations of the price level remain at P_0 then the economy will move up the line SS_0 since this is the relevant short-run supply curve. Output will rise to Y_1 and prices will rise to P_1. It is this rise in the average level of prices above the level people are expecting, P_0, which stimulates the rise in output: on the *typical* island suppliers are tending to find a price higher than they guess the average price level to be and are responding by increasing their output and, since this is happening typically and not merely on one island, *aggregate* output is stimulated.

But this is not the only possible way in which the economy might respond to the upward shift of the aggregate demand curve. Another possibility is that as the aggregate demand curve rises from AD_0 to AD_1 the expected level of prices rises to P_2, and the relevant short-run supply curve is the line labelled SS_1. In this case there is no increase in output. Output remains at its natural level, while prices rise from P_0 to P_2. The reason why there is no increase in output is that the typical supplier has correctly realized that the price on his island is rising at the same rate as the average level of prices, and there has therefore been no change in his relative price and so no incentive to raise output above its natural level.

While these two possibilities are interesting special cases they by no means exhaust the ways in which the economy *could* respond to the shift in the aggregate demand curve that we have assumed. If expectations of the general level of prices rose to some level between P_0 and P_2 then there would be some stimulus to output and some rise in prices. If expectations of the general level of prices rose above P_2 then there would be a fall in output and a rise in prices above P_2. And if expectations of the general level of prices fell below P_0 there could be a fall in prices and a rise in output. All these cases can be simply illustrated using the apparatus depicted in figure 4.4; we leave it to the reader to do so.

The important point for our purposes is that until *some* assumption is made about the generally expected price level we cannot rule out *any* response of the economy to the upward shift in the aggregate demand curve. As we show in the next section, the assumption that expectations of the general price level are rational severely restricts the possible ways in which the economy can respond to the assumed change in aggregate demand. It thus turns a model which is untestable, since no conceivable data could prove it wrong, into a testable one.

4.4 RANDOM AND SYSTEMATIC MOVEMENTS IN AGGREGATE DEMAND

To see what these restrictions are we must first recall the emphasis placed in chapter 2 on variables being determined by *processes*. The variable we are interested in here is the variable which has caused the shift in the aggregate demand curve. It may be a change in government expenditure, it may be a change in the quantity of money, or it may be a change in some other variable. It does not really matter for our purposes what the variable is. What does matter is that if we view that variable and all other variables affecting the aggregate demand curve as being determined by processes, the aggregate demand curve itself can be seen as the result of a process and shifts in the aggregate demand curve occur in line with that process. Of course, they may be due to the stochastic component of the process and therefore be unpredictable, or they may be due to the systematic or predictable component. From this point of view the relevant question to ask about the shift of the aggregate demand curve in figure 4.4 from AD_0 to AD_1 is: Was it predictable on the basis of the available information relating to the process determining aggregate demand? To put that another way, would a person who was using all the available information concerning the process determining aggregate demand have predicted that the position of the aggregate demand curve was going to be AD_1?

If the answer to that question is 'yes', then the rational expectations hypothesis implies that the generally expected position of the aggregate demand curve will be AD_1. In that case the rational expectation of the average price level must be P_2. For if the generally expected price level is P_2 the relevant aggregate supply curve will be the one labelled SS_1 which cuts the expected aggregate demand curve AD_1 to give a price level equal to the one that is expected, P_2. So, if the rational person thinks that the aggregate demand curve will be at AD_1 he must also expect a price level of P_2. If he expected any other price level he would not be acting rationally since he would not be forming his expectation of the price level in line with the process determining it; that is, the aggregate supply and demand process depicted in figure 4.4. For example, if, despite expecting the aggregate demand curve to be at AD_1, people in general expected a price level of P_0, the actual price level will *not* be P_0: thus expectations and the model are in conflict. The only price level which it is rational to expect if the position of the aggregate demand curve is expected to be AD_1 is P_2, since only this expectation will generate an actual price level equal to it.

Therefore, if the shift in the aggregate demand curve from AD_0 to AD_1 is predictable on the available information relating to the process determining aggregate demand, the expected price level will be P_2, the relevant aggregate supply curve will be the one labelled SS_1 and the upward shift in the aggregate demand curve *will have no effect on the aggregate level of output*. This is an extremely important result, both because of its policy implications which we shall consider later in this chapter and because of the scope it offers for testing the rational expectations hypothesis. It implies that those movements in aggregate demand which are predictable will have no effect on real output and, by implication, employment or unemployment, but will only affect prices. Rational people will predict them and thereby annul any effect they might have on real variables.

Now consider the result of assuming that the shift in the aggregate demand curve from AD_0 to AD_1 was entirely unpredictable, the result of a positive value for the random error term in the process determining aggregate demand. Since the shift in demand was not predictable, even rational people would not have expected it, and so the typical supplier would be finding the price of the good on her island higher than she was initially expecting the average price to be. This might lead her to change her expectation of the average level of prices; after all, if she is rational she must know that unpredictable movements in aggregate demand can occur and that one symptom of them is that the price in her island is higher than she was expecting the average to be. So the very fact that she observes her price to be higher than the average price level she was originally expecting may make her adjust upwards her expected average price level. But she also knows that *relative* shifts in demand occur and that these too can lead to her price being higher than the average. So she may believe that her price is higher than she initially expected because of a relative demand shift in her favour, which she might just as well take advantage of by supplying more output.

She faces what is known as a *signal extraction* problem. The signal she wishes to extract, or the information she wants, is the precise size of the random *aggregate* influence on her good in that period and the precise size of the random *relative* demand influence. But the information she actually obtains from observing the price of her good tells her the *total* effect of these two influences and not their individual effects. Somehow she has to try to extract the information she wants from the information she gets. This is the signal extraction problem. Exactly how a rational person will solve it we shall show later on. For the moment notice that if the *typical* supplier infers that her price is higher than she was initially expecting solely because of a relative demand shift in her favour, then the *typical* expected average price level will remain at P_0 and the rise in the aggregate demand curve will lead to a rise in output equal to $Y_1 - Y^n$. If, on the other hand, she infers that there has been a random upward shift in the aggregate demand curve which, by its very nature, affects all markets alike she will infer that the average level of price has risen to P_2. The typical expectation of the average level of prices will rise to P_2 and the shift in aggregate demand will have no effect on real output. If she *partly* infers a higher average price level than she was originally expecting and *partly* infers a relative demand increase then the generally expected price level will be somewhere between P_0 and P_2, and hence there will be some increase in aggregate output above its natural level.

As we have said, later on in the chapter we shall consider what might determine the extent to which the observation that the price in your market is higher than you were originally expecting leads you to raise your expectation of what the average price level is. The result, which we obtain there, is that in general it will be rational for agents to infer from an own price higher than initially expected that there have been both positive aggregate and positive relative demand shocks. As a result a random increase in aggregate demand is likely to produce a positive deviation of aggregate output from its natural level. This occurs to the extent that the *typical* supplier mistakenly thinks that the higher price for the good on her island is due to a relative demand shift in her favour. By a similar argument a random decrease in aggregate demand will cause the typical agent to find the price in her market lower than she was initially expecting; she will partly (mistakenly) infer from this that her *relative* price is low and will supply less output.

We can now state the central result of applying the rational expectations hypothesis to the aggregate demand – aggregate supply model that we have been using in this chapter. Changes in desired nominal spending, that is shifts in the aggregate demand curve, can affect real output even when expectations are rational, but only if those changes in aggregate demand are *random* and unpredictable. Predictable, systematic changes in aggregate demand will affect prices but not output.

4.5   THE VOLATILITY OF AGGREGATE DEMAND

Under rational expectations, movements in aggregate demand can affect real output if those movements are random because, faced with an unexpectedly high price for the good on her island, the typical supplier will at least partly infer that there has been some positive, relative demand shock on her island. The reason why a rational person would draw this inference is that an unexpectedly high price can be due to a positive aggregate demand shock or a positive relative demand shock, and it can of course arise from a combination of the two. Since this is the nature of the economic environment within which the agent operates it is rational for the agent to use that information about her environment to draw inferences from the information that she has about the current state of the economy, that is to solve her signal extraction problem. And if these random shocks in aggregate and relative demand are normally distributed so that larger (absolute) values are less likely to occur than smaller ones, it is rational to infer from an unexpectedly high price in any market that this is due partly to a positive aggregate demand shock and partly to a positive relative demand shock. Similarly, an unexpectedly low price will be attributed partly to a negative aggregate demand shock and partly to a negative relative demand shock. (The assumption that large (absolute) shocks are less likely than small ones makes it irrational to infer from an unexpectedly *high* price that there has been a *negative* shock to, say, aggregate demand outweighed by a large positive shock to relative demand.)

The question now becomes that of deciding what precise proportion of any unexpectedly high price is due to the aggregate demand shock and what proportion is due to the relative demand shock. The precise answer to this question requires a mathematical statement of the model, which we leave until later in this chapter, but the general answer, which both has policy implications and can serve as the basis for a subtle test of the model, is this: under rational expectations the proportions of any unexpectedly high price which are attributed to the aggregate and relative demand shocks respectively should be based on the true process determining that unexpectedly high price; that is, on the true likelihood of any unexpectedly high price being due to a random aggregate demand increase or to a favourable relative demand shock. So, in an economy in which relative demand shocks are typically smaller than aggregate demand shocks, the rational agent would attribute most of an unexpectedly high price to a positive aggregate demand shock – that, from knowledge of the economy, is the more likely reason. But in an economy in which the reverse is true and relative demand shocks are large compared to aggregate demand shocks it would be rational to attribute most of an unexpectedly high price to a relative demand shock – that, again, is the more likely reason.

Therefore the signal extraction problem will yield different solutions depending upon the economic environment: economies with highly volatile aggregate demand movements will, *ceteris paribus*, be economies in which agents will attribute a high proportion of any unexpectedly high or low price to an aggregate demand shock; economies with highly stable aggregate demand will, *ceteris paribus*, be economies in which agents will attribute a low proportion of any unexpectedly high or low price to an aggregate demand shock. But, as we showed earlier, if a positive aggregate demand shock occurs, and if the unexpectedly high local price to which it leads is attributed by agents wholly to an aggregate demand shock, then that movement in aggregate demand, although it is random, will have *no* effect on real output; it will merely induce a change in the expected and actual level of prices. On the other hand, if the same shock to aggregate demand occurs and is attributed by agents wholly to a relative demand movement, then that aggregate demand shock will have its maximum impact on real output. In general, the higher the proportion of unexpected local price movements attributed to aggregate demand shocks the smaller the effect on real output of any aggregate demand shock. And from our analysis of the signal extraction problem we can deduce that economies with highly volatile aggregate demand will be economies in which a high proportion of unexpected local price movements are attributed to aggregate demand shocks, and will therefore be economies in which shocks to aggregate demand have little impact on real output.

We consider below the implications this result has for policy, and in chapter 6 we show how it can serve as the basis for an empirical test of the model. But first we briefly state the main result of this chapter so far. It is possible to extend Friedman's reconciliation of the broad principles of rationality and the perceived facts about the relationship between movements in nominal spending and real variables to allow for rationality of expectations. This reconciliation suggests that systematic movements in aggregate demand will have no effect on real variables such as output or employment. However, random aggregate demand movements can induce changes in these real variables: they do so by causing rational agents to become temporarily confused between relative and aggregate demand shocks. The extent to which such confusion occurs is related to the volatility of relative and aggregate demand shocks.

4.6   A FORMAL STATEMENT OF THE RATIONAL EXPECTATIONS MODEL

In this section we present a formal statement of the simplified rational expectations aggregate supply and demand model discussed above. We thereby demonstrate rigorously the results we have obtained more intuitively above, and also illustrate a mathematical technique which is often used in rational expectations models. The mathematics in this section may appear difficult, but in fact is only straightforward algebra.

As we have explained above, we are imagining that the economy consists of a large number of geographically separate markets or islands. We shall index these markets or islands by the subscript

z, where z can be any number between 1 and the number of islands in the economy, N. We begin the model by writing down the supply of output in the zth market as

$$y^s(z)_t = \beta_0 + \beta_1 [p(z)_t - E_t(z)p_t] \qquad (4.1)$$

where $y^s(z)_t$ is the quantity of output supplied in market z in period t; $p(z)_t$ is the price of output in market z in period t; $E_t(z)p_t$ is the expectation formed in market z of the economy-wide average price of output in period t, p_t, using all the information available in the zth market at the beginning of period t; and β_0 and β_1 are coefficients, where β_1 is positive. All variables are defined as natural logarithms.

This equation is merely a formal statement of the idea that the quantity of output supplied is primarily determined by the local price relative to suppliers' expectations of the economy-wide average price of output. If the local price and the expected price are the same, then output will equal its natural rate, β_0. Remember that the information available in the zth market at the beginning of period t includes knowledge of all past aggregate and local variables and of $p(z)_t$, but does not include knowledge of any other current price.

The next equation of the model formally states a simple hypothesis about demand in each market:

$$y^d(z)_t = \alpha_0 + m_t(z) - E_t(z)p_t \qquad (4.2)$$

where $y^d(z)_t$ is the quantity of output demanded in the zth market; $m_t(z)$ is the quantity of nominal money held by consumers in the zth market in period t; and α_0 is a coefficient. Once again, all variables are defined as natural logarithms.

This equation states that the major influence on demand in the zth market is the expected real quantity of money holdings of consumers in the zth market; that is, their actual nominal holdings deflated by their expectation of the aggregate price level. The actual nominal money holdings of consumers in the zth market can by definition be looked upon as the economy-wide average quantity of money plus the deviation of the actual from the average. We shall assume that this deviation is a random variable, $\epsilon_t(z)$, with mean of zero and constant variance, σ_ϵ^2. So we have:

$$m_t(z) = m_t + \epsilon_t(z) \qquad (4.3)$$

where m_t is the economy-wide average quantity of nominal money.

We can thus rewrite the demand function, equation (4.2), as

$$y^d(z)_t = \alpha_0 + m_t - E_t(z)p_t + \epsilon_t(z) \tag{4.4}$$

We can thus identify two influences on demand in any market. The first is common to all markets and is the average nominal quantity of money in the economy deflated by the expectation held in the particular market of the average price level. This is the term $m_t - E_t(z)p_t$. The second influence, $\epsilon(z)_t$, is a random variable, the value of which can be positive or negative in any period but has a mean value of zero. Its presence can perhaps most easily be seen as resulting from more (or fewer) demanders than average being located in the zth market. The first of these influences represents the influence of aggregate demand since the key term, m_t, is an economy-wide average: its influence is not specific to one particular market – it affects all markets and hence is not indexed on z. In terms of the aggregate demand curve developed in section 4.1 this specification is a simplification: it ignores the influence on aggregate demand of variables other than the quantity of money. The second influence represents relative demand shifts between markets. If $\epsilon(z)_t$ is positive then the zth market is experiencing a relative demand shift in its favour – demand is higher than average. If $\epsilon(z)_t$ is negative then the zth market is experiencing an unfavourable relative demand shift – demand is lower than average. Of course, if we were to add up the $\epsilon(z)_t$ term in every market/island in the economy we would have the answer zero – the markets with below-average demand cancel out those with above-average demand.

The fourth equation of the model describes the process by which the average quantity of nominal money holdings is determined. To keep things as simple as possible we shall assume that the quantity of money is determined by the government in accordance with the following process:

$$m_t = m_{t-1} + g + v_t \tag{4.5}$$

where g is a constant and v_t is a random, serially uncorrelated error with zero mean and constant variance σ_v^2.

This equation states that the average quantity of money in the economy equals its value last period, m_{t-1}, plus a constant, g, plus a random serially uncorrelated error term, v_t. Since the term m_t is a logarithm it follows that $m_t - m_{t-1}$ is a measure of the proportionate rate of growth of the quantity of money. We shall assume that g is known and we shall treat g as the predictable component of monetary growth; on the other hand, v_t is not known and is therefore the unpredictable component.

As we explained in section 4.2, the model we are considering assumes that prices in each market move each period to equate supply and demand in each market. Thus for each island we can write the following:

$$y^s(z)_t = y^d(z)_t \tag{4.6}$$

Combining equations (4.1) and (4.4)–(4.6) and solving for the equilibrium price in the zth market gives

$$p(z)_t = [1/\beta_1][(\alpha_0 - \beta_0) + m_{t-1} + g + (\beta_1 - 1)E_t(z)p_t \\ + v_t + \epsilon(z)_t] \tag{4.7}$$

This equation is not yet a true solution for $p(z)_t$ since it contains a term in $E_t(z)p_t$ and, as we have emphasized, a rational expectation is one formed in accordance with the true process or solution for the variable concerned. So until we know the solution we cannot write in an expression for $E_t(z)p_t$. A solution would be an expression for $p(z)_t$ in terms of all the variables in the model which are predetermined or exogenous. In this case the only predetermined variable is m_{t-1}, and the exogenous variables are g, v_t and $\epsilon(z)_t$. We might conjecture that the general form of the solution for $p(z)_t$ which we seek is as follows:

$$p(z)_t = \pi_0 + \pi_1 m_{t-1} + \pi_2 g + \pi_3 v_t + \pi_4 \epsilon(z)_t \tag{4.8}$$

That is, we *assume* that the solution for $p(z)_t$ links $p(z)_t$ to all the predetermined or exogenous variables in a simple, linear equation; that is, there are no expressions in, for example, v_t^2 or $v_t m_{t-1}$. The rationale for this is that all the equations of the model are linear and so we would expect the solution to be linear. Of course, we do not yet know the precise values of the coefficients of the solution, the π's, but we can now begin to work them out. This method of solving the model is therefore called the method of undetermined coefficients.

First note that *at the end of period $t - 1$*, but before period t each agent knows the value of m_{t-1} and g. Furthermore, under rational expectations each participant knows the values of the π's, the coefficients of the solution for $p(z)_t$ shown in equation (4.8). They can thus form an expectation of $p(z)_t$ *conditional on the information that they have at the end of period $t - 1$.* At the end of period $t - 1$ the best guess any agent can make of the values of ν_t and $\epsilon(z)_t$, the aggregate and relative demand shocks in the coming period, is that they will be zero. Therefore it must be the case that this rational but conditional expectation of the price the agent will find in his local market in period t will be:

$$E_{t-1}p(z)_t = \pi_0 + \pi_1 m_{t-1} + \pi_2 g \qquad (4.9)$$

where $E_{t-1}p(z)_t$ is the expectation formed on the basis of information available at the end of period $t - 1$ about $p(z)_t$.

When trading in period t begins and the agent becomes aware of the price in his market, $p(z)_t$, it is clear from equation (4.8) that this amounts to becoming aware of $\pi_0 + \pi_1 m_{t-1} + \pi_2 g + \pi_3 \nu_t + \pi_4 \epsilon(z)_t$. But since he knew the first three elements of this expression before he observed his local price, it follows that the observation of his local price amounts to an observation of $\pi_3 \nu_t + \pi_4 \epsilon(z)_t$. That is, he observes the *combined* impact on his local price of the current aggregate and relative demand shocks. What he does not observe, but would wish to, is their *separate* effects, the value of $\pi_3 \nu_t$ and the value of $\pi_4 \epsilon(z)_t$. This is, in a more mathematical form, the signal extraction problem discussed earlier: how to work out the values of $\pi_3 \nu_t$ and $\pi_4 \epsilon(z)_t$ separately from knowledge of $\pi_3 \nu_t + \pi_4 \epsilon(z)_t$.

It turns out that the best he can do is to form his expectation of $\pi_3 \nu_t$ *and* $\pi_4 \epsilon(z)_t$ in accordance with the following formulae:

$$E_t(z)\pi_3 \nu_t = \gamma[\pi_3 \nu_t + \pi_4 \epsilon(z)_t]$$

$$E_t(z)\pi_4 \epsilon(z)_t = [1 - \gamma][\pi_3 \nu_t + \pi_4 \epsilon(z)_t]$$

where $\gamma = \pi_3^2 \sigma_\nu^2 / [\pi_3^2 \sigma_\nu^2 + \pi_4^2 \sigma_\epsilon^2]$.

The intuitive explanation for this has already been discussed: the greater the proportion of the variance of the composite disturbance term which is due to the variance of $\pi_3 \nu$, the more sensible it is to attribute more of any period's composite disturbance to $\pi_3 \nu$. The variance of $\pi_3 \nu$ is $\pi_3^2 \sigma_\nu^2$ and the variance of the composite disturbance term is $\pi_3^2 \sigma_\nu^2 + \pi_4^2 \sigma_\epsilon^2$, provided that ν and ϵ are uncorrelated – hence the formula for γ given above.

More formally, if one were to use all the known past values of $\pi_3 \nu$ and $\pi_3 \nu + \pi_4 \epsilon(z)$ in a regression of $\pi_3 \nu$ on $[\pi_3 \nu + \pi_4 \epsilon(z)]$ one would, by the conventional ordinary least-squares formula, estimate the coefficient on $\pi_3 \nu$ to be γ, and one would estimate a constant of zero. This is the best equation one could use to *forecast* the current value of $\pi_3 \nu$, that is $\pi_3 \nu_t$, given knowledge of the current composite disturbance, $[\pi_3 \nu_t + \pi_4 \epsilon(z)_t]$, and is therefore the one which rational agents will use to forecast $\pi_3 \nu_t$ given their information.

Since $p(z)_t$ is the price of the good in the zth market, p_t, the economy-wide average price of the good, p_t, can be seen as the sum of all these individual prices divided by N, the number of markets. The solution for p_t can therefore be derived by summing the solution for $p(z)_t$ shown in equation (4.8) and dividing by N. The results will be:

$$p_t = \pi_0 + \pi_1 m_{t-1} + \pi_2 g + \pi_3 \nu_t \qquad (4.10)$$

Notice that in deriving this expression we have used the result that on summation the expressions in $\epsilon(z)_t$ cancel out because they represent relative demand shocks which sum to zero. The other terms, for example $\pi_3 \nu_t$, are all the same in each market, so on averaging they occur in the same form as they do in an individual market.

Since equation (4.10) is the solution of p_t if follows that the rational expectation in the zth market at period t of p_t will be formed in accordance with it, given the information available in the zth market at period t. This information includes the π's, m_{t-1} and g, but does not include ν_t. But we have just worked out what the rational expectation of $\pi_3 \nu_t$ is, and we can therefore write:

$$E_t(z)p_t = \pi_0 + \pi_1 m_{t-1} + \pi_2 g + \gamma [\pi_3 \nu_t + \pi_4 \epsilon(z)_t] \qquad (4.11)$$

We now have two equations which both describe the process determining $p(z)_t$; equation (4.8), and equation (4.7) with equation (4.11) substituted for the term in $E_t(z)p_t$. Since they both describe the process of the same variable, they must both give the same answer as each other for $p(z)_t$, whatever the values of m_{t-1}, g, ν_t and $\epsilon(z)_t$ in any period. Thus for all possible values of these variables the following must be true:

$$\pi_0 + \pi_1 m_{t-1} + \pi_2 g + \pi_3 \nu_t + \pi_4 \epsilon(z)_t =$$

$$[1/\beta_1]\{(\alpha_0 - \beta_0) + m_{t-1} + g + (\beta_1 - 1)(\pi_0 + \pi_1 m_{t-1} + \pi_2 g)\}$$

$$+ [1/\beta_1]\{(\beta_1 - 1)\gamma(\pi_3 \nu_t + \pi_4 \epsilon(z)_t) + \nu_t + \epsilon(z)_t\} \qquad (4.12)$$

This equality is guaranteed to hold for any values of m_{t-1}, g and so on if the constant terms on both sides of the equality are identically equal, and if the pair of coefficients attached to each variable are identically equal. And so the conditions for the equality always to hold can be written:

(i) $\pi_0 = [\alpha_0 - \beta_0]/\beta_1 + \pi_0[\beta_1 - 1]/\beta_1$

(ii) $\pi_1 = 1/\beta_1 + \pi_1[\beta_1 - 1]/\beta_1$

(iii) $\pi_2 = 1/\beta_1 + \pi_2[\beta_1 - 1]/\beta_1$

(iv) $\pi_3 = 1/\beta_1 + \pi_3\gamma[\beta_1 - 1]/\beta_1$

(v) $\pi_4 = 1/\beta_1 + \pi_4\gamma[\beta_1 - 1]/\beta_1$

These five conditions can be solved for the five π's, giving:

$$\pi_0 = \alpha_0 - \beta_0, \qquad \pi_1 = 1, \qquad \pi_2 = 1,$$

$$\pi_3 = \pi_4 = 1/[\gamma(1 - \beta_1) + \beta_1]$$

The fact that π_3 and π_4 are equal implies that the value for γ can be written more simply as $\gamma = \sigma_\nu^2/[\sigma_\nu^2 + \sigma_\epsilon^2]$.

Substituting these values for the π's in equations (4.8) and (4.1) and using equation (4.1) we can write the expression for output in the zth market, $y(z)_t$, as:

$$y(z)_t = \beta_0 + \{[\beta_1(1 - \gamma)]/[\gamma(1 - \beta_1) + \beta_1]\}\{\nu_t + \epsilon(z)_t\} \quad (4.13)$$

The equivalent expression for aggregate or average output, y_t, is

$$y_t = \beta_0 + \{[\beta_1(1 - \gamma)]/[\gamma(1 - \beta_1) + \beta_1]\}\{\nu_t\}$$

or, more conveniently,

$$y_t = \beta_0 + \{[\beta_1\sigma_\epsilon^2]/[\beta_1\sigma_\epsilon^2 + \sigma_\nu^2]\}\nu_t \qquad (4.14)$$

The two major results we derived more intuitively in the earlier sections of this chapter are apparent from equation (4.14). First, only the unpredictable component of monetary growth ν_t affects real output. The predictable component, g, does not appear in equation (4.14), which means that it does not influence real output.

Second, the greater the variance of v, that is the greater the unpredictability of monetary growth, the less is the influence of any given value of v on real output. This result is apparent from the presence of the term σ_v^2 in the denominator of the second term in equation (4.14).

The model's implications for inflation and the Phillips curve can be also be shown formally. The solutions for the π's suggest that the solution for the *aggregate* price level is:

$$p_t = \alpha_0 - \beta_0 + m_{t+1} + g + \pi_3 v_t \tag{4.15}$$

Using equation (4.5) we can rewrite this as:

$$p_t = \alpha_0 - \beta_0 + m_t + [\pi_3 - 1]v_t \tag{4.16}$$

Since p_t is the log of the price level, the first difference of p_t, Δp_t, is a measure of the inflation rate, $\dot{P}_t$. Similarly, the first difference of m_t is a measure of the rate of growth of the quantity of money, $\dot{M}_t$. So, by first differencing equation (4.16) we can derive the model's implication for inflation, as:

$$\dot{P}_t = \dot{M}_t + [\pi_3 - 1]v_t - [\pi_3 - 1]v_{t-1} \tag{4.17}$$

Notice that, in the absence of any shocks, inflation equals the rate of growth of the money supply.

Expected inflation, $\dot{P}_t^e$ can be defined as $E_t p_t - p_{t-1}$; once again, this follows from the fact that p is defined as a logarithm and hence the difference between the expected logarithm of the price level in period t and the logarithm of the actual price level in period $t - 1$ is a measure of the expected rate of change of actual prices between the two periods. The economy-wide expectation of the aggregate price level is given by summing equation (4.11) over z:

$$E_t p_t = \alpha_0 - \beta_0 + m_{t-1} + g + \gamma \pi_3 v_t \tag{4.18}$$

which we can rewrite as:

$$E_t p_t = \alpha_0 - \beta_0 + m_t + [\gamma \pi_3 - 1]v_t \tag{4.19}$$

By lagging equation (4.16) we obtain the expression for p_{t-1} as

$$p_{t-1} = \alpha_0 - \beta_0 + m_{t-1} + [\pi_3 - 1]v_{t-1} \tag{4.20}$$

Subtracting this from equation (4.19) gives the expected inflation rate as:

$$\dot{P}_t^e = \dot{M}_t + [\gamma \pi_3 - 1]\nu_t - [\pi_3 - 1]\nu_{t-1} \qquad (4.21)$$

The difference between actual and expected inflation can be found by subtracting equation (4.21) from equation (4.17), giving:

$$\dot{P}_t - \dot{P}_t^e = [1 - \gamma]\pi_3 \nu_t \qquad (4.22)$$

The expression for aggregate output, that is equation (4.13), can now be rewritten in terms of $\dot{P}_t - \dot{P}_t^e$ using the implication of equation (4.22) that $\nu_t = \{1/[(1 - \gamma)\pi_3]\} (\dot{P}_t - \dot{P}_t^e)$, and using the solution for π_3:

$$y_t = \beta_0 + \beta_1(\dot{P}_t - \dot{P}_t^e) \qquad (4.23)$$

Thus aggregate output is equal to its natural rate, β_0, and some positive function of the difference between actual and expected inflation. We now assume that there is a natural rate of unemployment, U^n, and that the relationship between unemployment and output is given by:

$$U_t - U_t^n = \beta_2[y_t - \beta_0] \qquad (4.24)$$

where β_2 is a negative constant.

This merely states that when output is at its natural rate, unemployment is at its natural level; and that when real output is above (below) its natural level, unemployment will be below (above) its natural level. Such an assumption is a plausible one: in booms unemployment is low and in slumps it is high. Combining equations (4.23) and (4.24) we can generate the natural rate Phillips curve in one of two forms:

$$U_t = U_t^n + \beta_2\beta_1(\dot{P}_t - \dot{P}_t^e) \qquad (4.25)$$

$$\dot{P}_t = \dot{P}_t^e + [1/\beta_2\beta_1][U_t - U_t^n] \qquad (4.26)$$

Both equations convey the essential message of the natural rate hypothesis: that a stable negative relationship between inflation and unemployment exists only when expectations of inflation are constant.

4.7 POLICY IMPLICATIONS

(a) Keynesian policy ineffectiveness

Imagine a government that follows the typically Keynesian approach to macroeconomic policy, relaxing fiscal or monetary policy whenever the economy moves into a recession and tightening fiscal or monetary policy when the economy is booming. In the standard Keynesian view of macroeconomics such a policy will soften the fluctuations in real output and other real variables to which any economy is prone and which are due to fluctuations in private-sector spending. Many governments have pursued this general approach to economic policy since the 1940s, and a vast amount of economic research has gone into forecasting recessions and booms, and estimating large-scale models of the economy with the aim of enabling governments to carry out such a policy successfully.

The model that we have explained above suggests that this approach to policy, and by implication the economic research undertaken to improve it, are flawed. The essence of the flaw is that as the process by which aggregate demand is determined becomes known and therefore predictable, rational people will predict the changes in aggregate demand that governments engineer. And as we have seen, predicted changes in aggregate demand will have no effect on real output, or real economic activity – they will only affect prices. Thus Keynesian economic policy is either impotent – or approaching impotence – as the process by which aggregate demand is determined becomes known. This impotence is *inherent* in the Keynesian approach to policy and not merely a feature of a specific version of that approach; for by its very nature it makes government influences on aggregate demand predictable in that it links government policy changes to the current or past state of the economy. Even if government policy is linked to the *future* state of the economy in the sense that it is influenced by the predictions of some government economic model, these predictions can be *currently* ascertained and used to make government policy predictable. And it is precisely its predictability which renders it impotent.

The only possible way in which a government might try to use its ability to affect aggregate demand, in order to influence the level of aggregate output, would be to introduce random movements in its policies and hence random movements in aggregate demand which, as we have shown above, would produce deviations of aggregate output away from its natural level. But to be effective these random changes in government expenditure or the money supply, or whatever, would have to be unpredictable; and that means unpredictable to the government too, for if the government could predict them, then so could others. Their effect would be not to stabilize output but to increase the fluctuations of output around its natural level – the precise opposite of what Keynesian policies aim to achieve.

Therefore a key implication of the rational expectations hypothesis when combined with the aggregate demand – aggregate supply model developed above is that the Keynesian approach to macroeconomic stabilization policy is badly flawed. Much of the controversy which originally surrounded the rational expectations hypothesis was because of this implication.

(b) The Lucas critique

Further doubt is cast on the Keynesian approach to macroeconomic policy by what is known as the Lucas critique (see Lucas, 1976). This critique has wide applicability but it is convenient to discuss it here.

Keynesian stabilization policy involves manipulation by the government of the instruments of macroeconomic policy, such as government expenditure, tax rates, interest rates and so on. In order for such a policy to be successful and efficient the government has to have some idea of the size of any changes in tax rates and so on required to stabilize the economy, and some idea of when precisely such changes are required. To give them this idea economists have put a considerable amount of research effort into estimating models of the economy. These models, some of which involve hundreds of equations, are then used to simulate the effects of different policies. Such policy simulation forms the basis of the advice that economists give to governments about what policies they should actually undertake. It is common practice in this sort of exercise to take the estimated coefficients of the model – its structure – as given and independent of whatever policies are being carried out or considered. If this assumption is incorrect, if the structure of the model is in fact dependent upon the policies being carried out, then a model of the economy estimated in a period when one set of policies, one policy regime, was in operation will give misleading advice about what to expect under a different policy regime. Lucas argues that rational expectations implies that just such a dependence of the structure of many macroeconomic models on the policy regime is likely to exist, and that existing estimated macroeconomic models are likely to be quite misleading.

We can show Lucas's argument using the model developed in section 4.6. Recall that we assumed that the nominal quantity of money in the economy, m_t, was determined in the following simple way:

$$m_t = m_{t-1} + g + v_t \qquad (4.27)$$

where g is a known constant; and v_t is a random, serially uncorrelated variable with mean zero, which represents the unpredictable component of the quantity of money, and which we might think of as arising because of, say, faults in the government's monetary control techniques. Equation (4.27) can be seen as representing a simple monetary policy regime: a different value for g, or the inclusion of other influences on the quantity of money, would indicate a different policy regime.

We also derived the result that aggregate output, y_t, would be disturbed from its natural level, β_0, only by the unpredictable component of the quantity of money, v_t. Thus we derived

$$y_t = \beta_0 + \varphi v_t \qquad (4.28)$$

where φ is a positive coefficient (see equation (4.14) above).

Now, since from equation (4.27) we can write $v_t = m_t - m_{t-1} - g$, we can rewrite equation (4.28) as:

$$y_t = \lambda_0 + \lambda_1[m_t - m_{t-1}] \qquad (4.29)$$

where $\lambda_0 = \beta_0 - \varphi g$, and $\lambda_1 = \varphi$.

Now although equation (4.29) is derived from a rational expectations model, it does not look like one on the surface. For if one ignores the relationship between the λ's and β_0, φ and g, equation (4.29) seems to say that the level of real output can be raised by an increase in the quantity of money, regardless of whether or not that increase is predictable. To put that another way: imagine an economist attempting to estimate a model of real output in this economy. And imagine that this economist is not working within the rational expectations framework and so makes no distinction between the predictable and unpredictable components of the money supply. Equation (4.29) shows that this economist will find that real output can be perfectly explained by the change in the money supply. Equation (4.29) will therefore be part of this economist's model, which he uses to advise the government. Of course, he does not realize that the constant, λ_0, is really $\lambda_0 = \beta_0 - \varphi g$, and that $\lambda_1 = \varphi$. To him, λ_0 and λ_1 are just numbers which are, from his perspective, the structure of his model and which, once estimated, he takes as given.

Taking equation (4.29) to represent the economist's model, it is easy to see that he would recommend to a government that if it wished to achieve a higher level of real output it should raise the rate of growth of the quantity of money. Assume that the government takes this advice so that the process describing the quantity of money becomes:

$$m_t = m_{t-1} + g + h + v_t \tag{4.30}$$

where h is a positive constant.

Will this succeed in raising the level of output? The model shown in equation (4.29) suggests, if we take the λ's as given, that it will. But the λ's should not be taken as given: in particular, λ_0 is dependent upon the money supply process. If this process changes to the one shown in equation (4.30) and if equation (4.28) is really the truth then the value of λ_0 will change to $\beta_0 - \varphi[g + h]$. In other words, the constant term in the economist's model – equation (4.29) – will fall, and by such an extent to ensure that the level of real output on average will equal the same as it did before, even though monetary growth is higher under the new policy regime. The economist's model has proved to be unstable in the face of a policy regime change and has provided unreliable advice.

We have used a simple model to illustrate the Lucas critique, but since the point is an important one with wide applications it is worth stating it more generally. The essence of it is that if expectations of a variable are rational they will be determined by the process governing that variable. Thus expectations about policy will be determined by the process governing that policy, the 'policy regime'; and changes in policy regime will alter the precise way in which people form their expectations about policy. Estimated models of the economy which do not allow for changes in expectations when policy regimes change are therefore likely to be seriously flawed, in that they will begin to predict the behaviour of the economy badly whenever a policy regime change occurs. By implication, these models should not be used, as they often are, to evaluate different policy regimes, since it is precisely when a different policy regime is adopted that they become unreliable.

To put that another way, there are reasons for thinking that what an econometric model builder might believe is a good estimate of the constant structure of the economy is in fact no such thing, but rather an estimate of a relationship or group of relationships which are dependent upon a particular policy regime. If the policy regime changes then so will what was thought to be the constant structure. Economists should therefore be cautious in making recommendations about policy changes. Such changes may well alter what appeared to be the constant structure of the economy itself, and these changes also have to be allowed for when evaluating different policies. More fundamentally, the Lucas point can be seen as suggesting that the constant structure of the economy, which it is a major aim of the macroeconomist to reveal, is much more deeply hidden than econometric model builders might previously have thought. As a result the Keynesian approach to policy-setting may be difficult to carry out successfully.

(c) Friedman's x per cent growth rule

A more positive policy implication of the model is the apparent support for the approach to macroeconomic policy, especially monetary policy, advocated by a number of economists, notably Friedman (1959). In sharp contrast to Keynes and his followers, these economists have suggested that monetary policy should not be changed in response to any booms or recessions which the economy experiences: it should not be more expansionary in a recession and more restrictive in a boom. Rather, the government should bind itself (or even be constitutionally bound) to expand the quantity of money each period at some specified percentage rate of growth, x per cent. The precise value of x in any year should be announced well in advance in, say, a five-year plan, and should be strictly adhered to. The actual state of the economy should not, except in quite exceptional circumstances, induce the government to depart from its announced strategy, its x per cent rule.

The proponents of this approach to policy claim that it will encourage a more stable background in which the private sector can make its own investment and spending plans with greater certainty about future government policy; that it will prevent abrupt and damaging shifts of policy; and that it will make government manipulation of monetary policy for electoral purposes more diffifult. For all these reasons some economists have for years advocated this approach to monetary policy and during the 1970s a number of governments began at least to pay lip service to it by announcing target rates of growth for the money supply over the coming year.

However, within the simple aggregate supply and demand framework that we have developed above it has always been possible to show that, if expectations of inflation are not rational, then Friedman's x per cent growth rule for the quantity of money will be inferior to some other policy which links monetary growth to the current or past state of the economy. Here, inferiority means that Friedman's x per cent growth rule would imply greater fluctuations of real output around its natural level than would a policy of appropriately varying monetary policy as the economy moved into boom or recession.

The intuitive reason for this inferiority is that *irrational* expectations always offer some scope for a government to 'fool' people systematically. We have already seen a number of examples of this. Take the case in which the price level expected next period is always equal to this period's actual price level. Then, if there is, for whatever reason, a large permanent fall in aggregate demand there will be an immediate fall in prices and a drop in output. Expectations of the price level will fall only gradually to their new equilibrium level, and while they do so output will remain below its natural level. If the government is locked into a policy of expanding the money supply at some pre-announced rate it cannot do anything about this possibly severe recession. But if it is not bound by such a policy it can induce a large increase in the money supply and prevent the recession, or at least bring it to an end quickly. Thus the more flexible monetary policy is superior to the Friedman x per cent growth rule.

But if expectations are rational then this superiority disappears, for if the fall in aggregate demand assumed above were predictable, it would have no effect on real output and would not need to be countered by a change of monetary policy. And if it were unpredictable, then while it would have an immediate effect on ouput, this could not be prevented by government policy since the government would not be able to foresee the fall in aggregate demand. The result that Friedman's approach to monetary policy is no longer inferior to a more 'flexible' approach, once one incorporates rational expectations into the basic aggregate supply and demand model, was demonstrated more formally and generally by Sargent and Wallace (1975) and is sometimes known as the Sargent–Wallace proposition.

Some additional support for a simple x per cent rule for the money supply is provided by the analysis explained earlier about the volatility of aggregate demand. For that analysis suggests that if aggregate demand shocks are kept to a minimum, ideally at zero, economic agents will be best able to recognize and respond to relative demand shocks even though they do not observe any other current prices than their own. This is, of course, because, in the absence of aggregate demand shocks, any unexpectedly high price must be due to a relative demand shock. The more predictable aggregate demand is, the less will rational agents be fooled into supplying quantities of output that they would not have supplied had they had perfect information. In this sense the more predictable aggregate demand is, the more efficient the economy is. If monetary policy is the key influence on aggregate demand then since the x per cent rule is extremely easy to understand aggregate demand will be highly predictable, provided of course that the authorities are successful in adhering to their rule. A more complex rule, linking monetary policy to last period's unemployment rate or balance of payments deficit or whatever, may be less easy to understand and more subject to error because of, for example, inaccuracies in the balance of payments figures. It may therefore produce greater uncertainty about aggregate demand. So this analysis too suggests some support for Friedman's x per cent rule.

In fact, the rational expectations hypothesis is sometimes seen as providing support for the 'strong' version of the Friedman approach to monetary policy in which the x per cent rule is made constitutionally binding. The reason for this is essentially that if expectations are rational, the government has an incentive to 'cheat' on its monetary rule which it does not have under other forms of expectations formation. For example, from the model derived above it is clear that output will be raised above its normal rate only if people in general are fooled into believing that the average price level is lower than it actually is. If expectations are formed, say, adaptively then it is always possible to specify a rule for government policy which will consistently fool people. For example, if the expected price level always equals last period's price level then, by linking the change in the money supply to last period's price level, it will always be possible to ensure that the actual price level exceeds the expected price level and hence that output is kept above its natural level. Such a policy would work even if it were fully announced, provided that expectations were formed in the way we have assumed. Thus there is no incentive for the government to cheat on this way of conducting monetary policy – that is, to follow a different policy from the one that is announced – for it can fool people without cheating. Consequently, there is little need to prevent cheating by making the government's announced monetary policy constitutionally binding.

But if expectations are rationally formed, the government cannot expect a policy of linking the change in the money supply to the previous price level to succeed, for people will not be fooled by it. On the contrary, they will change their method of forming expectations in line with the process announced for determining the money supply and hence aggregate demand. This will be true whatever the process determining monetary policy is. Thus the only way by which the government might achieve a higher level of output would be by cheating, by not following the rule it says it will follow. The fact that governments could cheat like this will clearly be known to rational agents and might introduce some uncertainty about government policy. This uncertainty could be partly removed by making government policy constitutionally binding (but only 'partly', since constitutions can be changed too).

(d) Time-inconsistency

The possibility of cheating and some of the issues which it raises have been more formally explored by Barro and Gordon (1983) and Barro (1985) within a Phillips curve framework. The Phillips curve (more formally derived above) shows a negative relationship between wage or price inflation and unemployment. Within the aggregate supply – aggregate demand framework of this chapter such a relationship can be seen to occur because if aggregate demand increases and firms can sell their goods for a higher price, they can afford to offer workers higher nominal wages. If workers in employment or those unemployed are not fully aware of the general nature of the price increases in the economy, it may look to them as if these nominal wage increases represent higher real wages. They may therefore take up the offer more speedily than they otherwise would, or be more reluctant to leave their existing job to search for another job. Either way, the rise in prices is likely to be associated with a lower level of unemployment.

However, this is only true if the aggregate demand change and associated price change are unanticipated. So, for a given level of inflationary expectations, say zero, a high rate of inflation will be associated with a low level of unemployment and a low level of inflation will be associated with a high level of unemployment; that is, there will exist a stable Phillips curve. But if the expected rate of inflation changes then the Phillips curve will shift. For example, if expected inflation rises to 5 per cent then actual inflation of 5 per cent no longer fools anyone: hence unemployment will be the same as it was when actual and expected inflation were both zero. Similarly, just as when expectations of inflation were zero actual inflation of 5 per cent might sufficiently fool workers to generate an unemployment rate of 3 per cent, now, if expectations of inflation are 5 per cent, actual inflation would need to be 10 per cent to fool them by the same amount as before and hence generate the same unemployment rate of 3 per cent. In other words, an increase in expected inflation of 5 percentage points shifts the Phillips curve upwards by 5 percentage points.

Another way of putting this is to say that there are many possible Phillips curves – one for each level of expected inflation. Since an increase in expected inflation of z percentage points shifts the Phillips curve vertically by z percentage points, it follows that the level of unemployment at which expected and actual inflation are equal is the same for all possible values of expected inflation. This level of unemployment is called the natural level of unemployment.

In figure 4.5 we draw a set of Phillips curves. Imagine for the moment that expectations of inflation are zero and so the relevant Phillips curve for the moment is the one labelled $PC_0[\dot{P}_0^e]$. Imagine also that we can define a set of 'iso-vote' lines: these are similar to indifference curves and each one shows combinations of inflation and unemployment which would yield the government equal popularity. Since inflation and unemployment are both unpopular these iso-vote lines are downward-sloping, and the

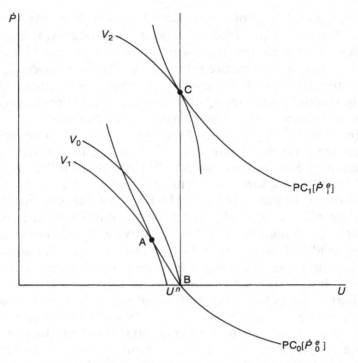

FIGURE 4.5   The Phillips curve and time-inconsistent policy.

further away from the origin they are the lower the popularity they imply. Their bowed shape can be justified on the assumption that both inflation and unemployment become increasingly unpopular the higher they are. Given that expectations of inflation are zero, and hence the relevant Phillips curve is $PC_0[\dot{P}_0^e]$, what is the maximum popularity the government can achieve through manipulation of monetary or aggregate demand policy? If expectations are fixed then the answer is that the government can achieve point A on the iso-vote line V_1 by expanding aggregate demand to generate inflation of $\dot{P}_1$ and unemployment of U_1. It cannot do any better than this since this is the iso-vote line which is tangential to the relevant Phillips curve. However, if agents are rational and aware of the economic environment in which they operate – here summarized by the shape of the Phillips curves and iso-vote lines, and by the government's objective of maximizing V – then V_1 is not a feasible equilibrium. It implies a level of inflation higher than people are expecting. Nor is point B on the iso-vote line labelled V_0 feasible, a point which involves inflation and expected inflation of zero and unemployment at its natural rate. If that position were to occur agents would be aware that the government would be tempted to create higher inflation to achieve iso-vote line V_1; they would come to expect that higher inflation and hence the relevant Phillips curve would not be the one labelled $PC_0[\dot{P}_0^e]$.

For a full equilibrium two conditions must be fulfilled: first the economy must be at the natural level of unemployment, where expectations of inflation are correct; and second the government must have no incentive to fool people by stimulating aggregate demand. Such a position occurs at point C in figure 4.5. Here the iso-vote line, V_2, is tangential to the relevant Phillips curve, $PC_1[\dot{P}_1^e]$, at the natural level of unemployment. So at this point expectations of inflation are correct, and given those expectations the government cannot achieve a higher iso-vote line.

But this full equilibrium position, at C, is inferior to the one at which inflation is zero and unemployment is equal to its natural rate, point B. This is clear from the fact that both have the same unemployment rate, but point C has a higher inflation rate; it is also indicated by the fact that at point C the popularity of the government is lower than it is at point B. We therefore have the odd result that the position which is optimal, point B, is not feasible, whereas the position that is feasible is sub-optimal. In terminology which is due to Kydland and Prescott (1977), the optimal position point B is said to be *time-inconsistent*. Loosely, a policy is said to be time-inconsistent if, once it has been adopted, there is an incentive at some later date to renege or cheat on it. Other examples in economics are the promise of an investment subsidy at some future date to encourage firms to invest: when the future date occurs and the investments has been carried out it is tempting for the government to renege on its promise.

In the present context the time-inconsistency problem suggests that the optimal combination of unemployment and inflation can only be achieved if there is some effective restraint to prevent the government from cheating on a commitment to zero inflation. An independent Central Bank might provide such a restraint, and so might the constitutional amendment, suggested in Friedman and Friedman (1980), which obliges the government to expand the money stock at some fixed rate and which would make cheating on this obligation illegal. Thus the rational expectation hypothesis can be seen as supporting Friedman's policy recommendation. At the same time it can be used to explain why in the absence of such effective restraints most governments have experienced positive inflation in the past 40 years. Barro and Gordon (1983) consider this analysis in more depth and use it to explain certain other macroeconomic phenomena such as the rising trend in unemployment and inflation, and the use of apparently ineffective counter-cyclical monetary policy by a number of governments.

4.8 SUMMARY

In chapters 6 and 7 we consider the empirical evidence relating to the model we have developed in this chapter. Before that we consider in the next chapter some of the criticisms of the model and of the major results we have derived from it. It is worthwhile restating here what those results are.

Shifts in aggregate demand will affect real output if they are random and unpredictable. Furthermore, such shifts will have less effect on output the more unpredictable aggregate demand is. Attempts to stabilize an economy's real output by systematic manipulation of aggregate demand will fail since, by making aggregate demand predictable, they also render it ineffective. Governments should aim to make their policy instruments as predictable as possible so as to minimize confusion and hence undesirable fluctuations in output. This all provides some support for an approach to policy quite different from that associated with Keynes, which has dominated policy-making since the 1940s. This new approach emphasizes the need for governments to operate macroeconomic policy in accordance with simple and predetermined rules which, on the whole, do not link policy to the current or past state of the economy. The emphasis on rules is further supported by consideration of the political influences on policy-setters.

SUGGESTIONS FOR FURTHER READING

Friedman (1968) and Phelps (1967) (see also Phelps, 1970) are the seminal statements of the natural rate hypothesis. Barro (1976),

Lucas (1972, 1975) are equally influential, formal statements of the rational expectations hypothesis within a natural rate framework. Kydland and Prescott (1977) analyse in some detail the problem of the time-inconsistency of policy. A useful introduction to the more technical aspects of the application of rational expectations can be found in Minford and Peel (1983). Open economy models with rational expectations are discussed in Dornbusch (1976), Calvo and Rodriguez (1977), Barro (1978b), Cox (1980) and Duck (1984).

5

Criticisms of the Flexible-price Rational Expectations Model

It is hardly surprising that such a powerful attack on conventional macroeconomic policy as that outlined in the previous chapter has provoked a number of counter-attacks. We shall consider these counter-attacks under two broad headings: those which maintain the assumption of price flexibility; and those which do not.

5.1 CRITICISMS WHICH MAINTAIN PRICE FLEXIBILITY

In this first category we consider three main criticisms: (a) that the model developed in chapter 4 cannot account for a major feature of all economies; (b) that the model relies for all its results on very simple specifications of the aggregate supply and demand curves; and (c) that even if one accepts the model as it stands governments might effectively stabilize the economy if they possess better information about the economy than the private sector, or indeed if different parts of the private sector possess different information.

(a) Serial correlation in aggregate real variables

The model developed so far suggests that only random movements in aggregate demand will cause real aggregate output to deviate from its natural or normal level. These random movements in aggregate demand are of course unpredictable and exhibit no clear pattern. The model therefore implies that the deviations of output from its natural rate should also be unpredictable and exhibit no pattern. But it is a common and easily observed fact that measures of aggregate output in any economy tend to be positively *serially correlated*; that is, a higher than average value for aggregate output in any period is more often than not followed by a higher than average value next period and, similarly, a low value in any period is more likely to be followed by another low one than by a high one. To put it more simply, all economies experience booms and slumps, many of which are quite drawn out or persistent. This persistence might be seen as an obvious contradiction of the prediction that deviations of output from its natural level should be random and hence a clear refutation of the rational expectations version of the aggregate supply and demand model developed above.

This is true, but of no great significance since it is easy to modify the model developed above and make it immune from this particular criticism, while ensuring that all its important features are retained. Such modification involves specifying some form of *propagation mechanism* which converts serially *uncorrelated* shifts in aggregate demand into serially *correlated* movements in aggregate output. One obvious propagation mechanism is provided by stocks of finished goods. Firms might hold such stocks so that when faced with an unexpectedly high level of demand they can meet it without recourse to a sharp and possibly very costly increase in production. So if an unexpected rise in demand occurs, they meet it partly by producing more and partly by running down their stocks of finished goods. But such a response implies that next period their stocks of goods will be lower than they feel is optimal, and they will therefore want to build them up again by producing more next period than they otherwise would. If they do this slowly then production will be higher than normal for a number of periods until stocks of goods are back at their optimal level. But this implies that a single random increase in aggregate demand in the current period can set up a serially correlated movement or boom in real output over a number of subsequent periods. Similarly, a single random decrease in aggregate demand could set up a multiperiod recession (see Blinder and Fischer, 1981; Demery and Duck, 1985; Duck, 1986).

All the results derived from the simpler model explained in the previous chapter could also be derived from one which allows stocks of finished goods to play this role. It will still be the case that only random aggregate demand will affect real output, and the more unpredictable aggregate demand is, the less effect it has on output. The policy conclusions drawn from the simpler model will also still follow. Other propagation mechanisms could be introduced with much the same result. For example, if it is costly for firms to hire more labour or adjust their capital stock it will be optimal for them to spread out over time their response to any relative price signals they receive. So, in this case too, a random increase in aggregate demand will typically produce a 'strung out' response in aggregate output. None of the major implications derived from the simple model would be affected by the introduction of these mechanisms.

This criticism of the model is thus more a criticism of the form in which it is put than of its substance; the form can be changed to take account of the criticism without changing any matter of substance.

(b) The simplicity of the model

A more telling criticism of the results we have derived from the rational expectations aggregate demand–supply model concerns their reliance on extremely simple specifications of the aggregate supply and demand curves. Minor changes in specification can alter the implications of the model significantly. For example, imagine a rise in the basic rate of income tax which is fully announced and anticipated. Standard economic theory suggests that this is likely to have an effect on the willingness of the population to work. The exact size or direction of the effect does not matter; what does is that there is a possibility of *some* effect. Thus a fully anticipated change in fiscal policy is quite likely to have some effect on real output in that it affects the willingness of the population to work to produce output.

Another, and more important, possible change of specification concerns the relative price term which enters the supply function. In the previous chapter we have defined this relative price term as the current price in the local market relative to the expected *current* average price across all markets. It has been argued that supply is more likely to show a positive response to relative price increases which are thought to be temporary than those that are thought to be permanent. Certainly the evidence from empirical studies of the supply of labour, for example, suggest little response of labour supply to long-term real wage increases. But this does not rule out a high response to real wage changes which are thought to be temporary: for example, suppliers of labour may well want to take advantage of a temporarily high real wage by supplying more labour, taking leisure (that is, supplying less labour) when the real wage has fallen back.

Within the present context, one way of taking account of this 'intertemporal' dimension to supply is to model suppliers as responding to the local price relative to their expectation of *next period's* average price. If this (expected) relative price is high then it will give suppliers an incentive to produce and sell more this period and hold the proceeds in monetary form, in anticipation that their real value will increase as the average price level falls next period. If the (expected) relative price is low then it will pay suppliers not to supply as much because they will be anticipating a drop in the real value of the proceeds. A similar relative price term may affect the demand for the good as well: if demanders feel that the price of the good is high relative to its likely future value, they may well delay purchases until the price is lower.

If supply is modelled as a function of this 'intertemporal' relative price term, one implication is that a permanent rise in the rate of growth of aggregate demand and hence in the rate of inflation may permanently reduce the quantity of output supplied, since it permanently reduces the real rate of return on holding the proceeds from sales in the form of money. Thus fully anticipated changes in the rate of growth of aggregate demand may affect the level of real output even where expectations are rational. This point, together with a proof that stabilizing monetary policy *can* have a role within rational expectations models which emphasize 'intertemporal substitution', can be made after modifying the island parable model developed earlier. The first modification is to respecify the relative price term in the supply function as $p(z)_t - E_t(z)p_{t+1}$ and allow a similar term to influence demand; the second is to respecify the major influence on aggregate demand as $m_t + E_t(z)\Delta m_{t+1} - E_t(z)p_{t+1}$, where $E_t(z)\Delta m_{t+1}$ is the expectation of the change in the money stock between periods t and $t + 1$. This second modification makes the model more in line with that developed by Barro (1976), and is justified on the grounds that what motivates agents' spending this period is their desire to have a sum of real money available next period. Such a specification allows us to make the point about stabilization policy mentioned above, and to point out an error in Barro's influential paper that was originally uncovered by Marini (1985). A third modification is to introduce an explicit private-sector aggregate demand shock and to eliminate the random component of monetary growth. The fully modified system consists of the following equations:

$$y_t^s(z) = \beta_0 + \beta_1[p_t(z) - E_t(z)p_{t+1}], \tag{5.1}$$

$$y_t^d(z) = \alpha_0 + m_t + E_t(z)\Delta m_{t+1} - E_t(z)p_{t+1} + \eta_t + \epsilon_t(z)$$
$$- \alpha_1[p_t(z) - E_t(z)p_{t+1}], \tag{5.2}$$

$$\eta_t = \eta_{t-1} + \xi_t, \tag{5.3}$$

$$m_t = m_{t-1} + g + \gamma_1\xi_{t-1} + \gamma_2\xi_{t-2} \tag{5.4}$$

Equations (5.1) and (5.2) have already been explained: η_t is the aggregate demand shock which is assumed to follow the 'random walk' process shown in equation (5.3), that is it equals its value in the previous period plus ξ_t, a serially uncorrelated random error with zero mean and constant variance σ_ξ^2. Equation (5.4) is a respecification of the process driving the quantity of money: it assumes that the quantity of money in period t equals its value in period $t - 1$ plus a constant, g, plus a function of the shocks to aggregate demand in periods $t - 1$ and $t - 2$. The γ's are constant coefficients and are policy parameters: the government can choose their value in order to stabilize output. One aim of this respecified model is to show that the choice of the γ's is *not* irrelevant to the behaviour of output, and hence that there is a stabilizing role for monetary policy even in a flexible-price rational expectations model.

The technique we use to solve this model (that of undetermined coefficients) is as described in the previous chapter. Briefly, we can write an expression for $p_t(z)$ as

$$p_t(z) = [1/(\alpha_1 + \beta_1)][\alpha_0 - \beta_0 + m_{t-1} + g + \gamma_1\xi_{t-1} + \gamma_2\xi_{t-2}$$
$$+ \epsilon_t(z) + [1/(\alpha_1 + \beta_1)][\eta_{t-1} + \xi_t$$
$$+ E_t(z)\Delta m_{t+1} + (\alpha_1 + \beta_1 - 1)E_t(z)p_{t+1}] \tag{5.5}$$

We can also assume a solution for $p_t(z)$ of the following form:

$$p_t(z) = \pi_0 + \pi_1 m_{t-1} + \pi_2 g + \pi_3\xi_t + \pi_4\xi_{t-1} + \pi_5\xi_{t-2}$$
$$+ \pi_6\eta_{t-1} + \pi_7\epsilon_t(z) \tag{5.6}$$

Since all the terms in equation (5.6) except $\pi_3\xi_t$ and $\pi_7\epsilon_t(z)$ are known at the end of period $t - 1$, it follows that observation of the local price, $p_t(z)$, amounts to an observation of $\pi_3\xi_t + \pi_7\epsilon_t(z)$. And from this we can deduce that

$$E_t(z)\pi_3\xi_t = \theta[\pi_3\xi_t + \pi_7\epsilon_t(z)] \tag{5.7}$$

where $\theta = \pi_3^2\sigma_\xi^2/[\pi_3^2\sigma_\xi^2 + \pi_7^2\sigma_\epsilon^2]$.

Equation (5.6) implies that the process driving the average price level, p_t, can be written as

$$p_t = \pi_0 + \pi_1 m_{t-1} + \pi_2 g + \pi_3\xi_t + \pi_4\xi_{t-1} + \pi_5\xi_{t-2} + \pi_6\eta_{t-1} \tag{5.8}$$

By updating this one period we can derive the process for next period's price, p_{t+1}, as

$$p_{t+1} = \pi_0 + \pi_1 m_t + \pi_2 g + \pi_3\xi_{t+1} + \pi_4\xi_t + \pi_5\xi_{t-1} + \pi_6\eta_t \tag{5.9}$$

which, after substituting for m_t and η_t from equations (5.3) and (5.4) respectively, we can write as

$$
\begin{aligned}
p_{t+1} = {}& \pi_0 + \pi_1 m_{t-1} + [\pi_1 + \pi_2]g + [\pi_6 + \pi_4]\xi_t \\
& + [\pi_5 + \pi_1\gamma_1]\xi_{t-1} + \pi_1\gamma_2\xi_{t-2} + \pi_3\xi_{t+1} + \pi_6\eta_{t-1}
\end{aligned} \tag{5.10}
$$

From this equation and equation (5.7) we can derive:

$$
\begin{aligned}
E_t(z)p_{t+1} = {}& \pi_0 + \pi_1 m_{t-1} + [\pi_1 + \pi_2]g + [\pi_6 + \pi_4][\theta/\pi_3] \\
& \times [\pi_3\xi_t + \pi_7\epsilon_t(z)] + [\pi_5 + \pi_1\gamma_1]\xi_{t-1} + \pi_1\gamma_2\xi_{t-2} \\
& + \pi_6\eta_{t-1}
\end{aligned} \tag{5.11}
$$

And by updating equation (5.4) and using equation (5.7) we can also derive:

$$E_t(z)\Delta m_{t+1} = g + [\gamma_1\theta/\pi_3][\pi_3\xi_t + \pi_7\epsilon_t(z)] + \gamma_2\xi_{t-1} \tag{5.12}$$

Substituting equations (5.11) and (5.12) into equation (5.5), and setting the result identically equal to equation (5.6), allows us to solve for the π's and obtain the following solution for output in the zth market, $y_t(z)$:

$$y_t(z) = \beta_0 - \beta_1 g + [\beta_1/(\alpha_1 + \beta_1)][1 - (1 + \gamma_2)\theta][\xi_t + \epsilon_t(z)] \tag{5.13}$$

The aggregate equivalent of equation (5.13) is simply

$$y_t = \beta_0 - \beta_1 g + [\beta_1/(\alpha_1 + \beta_1)][1 - (1 + \gamma_2)\theta]\xi_t \qquad (5.14)$$

Two features of equations (5.13) and (5.14) are important. The first is that the constant component of monetary growth, g, does now exert an influence on real output. However, the method by which a change in predictable monetary growth leads to a change in aggregate real output is not the familiar one – a higher rate of growth does *not* fool people into supplying more output. Indeed, it does not lead to a rise in output at all, but to a fall. An increase in the anticipated growth of the money supply raises the anticipated inflation rate and thereby lowers the attractiveness of holding the proceeds of output sales. Therefore output will be lowered. One way of thinking of this result is that variations in g cause simultaneous variations in the actual and the natural level of output: a higher value for g implies a lower natural and actual level of output. Variations in g then do not lead to deviations of output from its natural level, which is the result derived in chapter 4.

However, even this argument cannot overcome the second feature of equations (5.13) and (5.14): that while the policy parameter γ_1 does not appear in either equation, the policy parameter γ_2 does. In other words the choice of the parameter γ_2 affects the behaviour of real output, while the choice of γ_1 does not. This suggests that governments can use monetary policy to stabilize output by appropriate selection of γ_2; that is, by appropriately selecting the link between the money stock and the aggregate demand shock two periods before. Barro (1976) appears to have overlooked this point. He considered the link between the money stock and aggregate demand shock only one period before, that is the policy parameter γ_1, and found, as we have, that the size of that policy parameter was unimportant. He thus concluded that stabilization policy was unimportant. But this is true only of stabilization which links the money stock to last period's aggregate demand shock; it is not true in the more general case in which the money stock is linked to earlier aggregate demand shocks. To see clearly that the selection of the parameter γ_2 affects the distribution of output around its natural level, we follow Barro's procedure and first derive what real output in a typical market would be if there were full current information; that is, if everyone knew the current value of all the shocks affecting the economy. We might think of this full information value of output, $y_t^*(z)$, as the value of output which government policy is trying to achieve even though there is not full information; or, more loosely, one might think of it or its aggregate equivalent as the natural level of output.

If everyone knows the value of the current shocks then we can replace equation (5.7) with the following:

$$E_t(z)\pi_3\xi_t = \pi_3\xi_t \qquad (5.7a)$$

Then, following the procedure outlined above, and using equation (5.7a) rather than equation (5.7) to obtain expressions for $E_t(z)p_{t+1}$ and $E_t(z)\Delta m_{t+1}$, we can derive the following:

$$y_t^*(z) = \beta_0 - \beta_1 g + [\beta_1/(\alpha_1 + \beta_1)][\epsilon_t(z) - \gamma_2\xi_t] \qquad (5.15)$$

The difference between the full information value of output in the zth market and the actual value with imperfect information is, from equations (5.13) and (5.15),

$$y_t(z) - y_t^*(z) = [\beta_1/(\alpha_1 + \beta_1)][1 - \theta][1 + \gamma_2]\xi_t$$
$$- [\beta_1/(\alpha_1 + \beta_1)\theta][1 + \gamma_2]\epsilon_t(z) \qquad (5.16)$$

It is clear from this expression that the difference between full information output and actual output can be made zero each period; that is, perfect stabilization policy can be achieved, if the government sets the policy parameter γ_2 equal to -1. Any other setting for γ_2 would be less efficient. Thus even in the type of rational expectations model used by Barro to show that stabilization policy was ineffective, such policy can be shown to be at least potentially effective.

The intuition behind this result is as follows. By setting γ_2 equal to -1 the government can ensure that next period's price level is immune to current shocks. This immunity arises because any aggregate demand disturbance will induce the government to change the money supply in such a way as to nullify the effect of the aggregate demand disturbance on the future price level. So an aggregate demand disturbance in period t will raise prices in period t but leave prices in period $t + 1$ unchanged. In such circumstances agents do not have to concern themselves with whether an unexpectedly high price in period t is due to a relative or aggregate demand shock. The two shocks have identical effects: they both leave prices in period $t + 1$ unaffected and they both induce a difference between prices in period t and $t + 1$ which can be responded to by increasing output in accordance with equation (5.1). So by selecting the appropriate value for γ_2 the government can render the distinction between aggregate and relative demand shocks irrelevant and create for agents a situation similar to one of full current information.

Selecting a value for γ_1 cannot achieve the same result because such a policy leaves the distinction between an aggregate and a relative demand shock no less important than before: a positive relative demand shock will raise current prices above expected future ones; a positive aggregate demand shock will not. For example, if γ_1 is -1 then a positive aggregate demand shock in period t, ξ_t, will imply expected values for Δm_{t+1} and for m_{t+2} lower, *ceteris paribus*, by an amount $-\xi_t$. But from equation (5.5) the former affects prices this period by an amount $-\xi_t$ and the latter affects prices next period by an amount $-\xi_t$. So the selection of this value for γ_1 causes no change in the price term which influences supply, $p_t(z) - E_t(z)p_{t+1}$. This will be true whatever the value of γ_1; therefore whatever value of γ_1 is selected it cannot make the distinction between aggregate and relative demand shocks any less important. This is essentially the point made by Barro (1976). The point he overlooked, which was pointed out by Marini (1985), is that this argument only applies to γ_1. By linking monetary policy to further lags in aggregate demand shocks one can establish a potential role for monetary policy even within Barro's rational expectations framework.

Of course, this analysis only provides a *potential* role for monetary policy. In more realistic models the optimum value for γ_2 would depend upon the structural parameters of the economy. For example, if we had assumed in the above model that $\eta_t = \rho\eta_{t-1} + \xi_t$, where ρ is a fraction, then the optimum value for γ_2 would be a complex function of ρ, β_1 and α_1. For monetary policy to be successful the values of these parameters would need to be known. If they are not, then governments may well select a value for γ_2 which makes the performance of the economy worse rather than better.

However, this analysis is important in showing that it is not rational expectations itself which produces the result that monetary policy cannot be used to stabilize real variables in the economy; rather, it is the combination of rational expectations and a particular class of model.

(c) Asymmetric information

The same point can be made by considering models which assume that different agents in the economy have access to a different quality of information. So far we have considered models in which all agents face the same information problem, although obviously agents in the island model have different information depending upon which island they are located on. In this section we consider two situations in which different agents have access to different types of information. The first, and simplest, is where the government has access to better information than the private sector; the second is where consumers have better access than producers to information about current shocks.

The first case can be dealt with quite simply. Imagine a random decrease in aggregate demand which, for the private sector, is unpredictable. In the absence of any change in government policy this unpredictable downward shift in the aggregate demand curve would induce a fall in real output. If the downward shift in aggregate demand was also unpredictable to the government, then clearly the government could take no steps to offset it. But if it had better information about what was likely to happen in the economy than the private sector, the government could take such measures. In the case we are considering this would involve some increase in government spending or some increase in the quantity of money, or some combination of both. Provided that the government acted efficiently, the result would be that the aggregate demand curve would not shift down: the tendency for it to do so would be offset by government action. Hence there would be no fall in real output – the government would have successfully stabilized it.

There is no inconsistency between this result and rational expectations: as far as the private sector is concerned there has been a negative unpredictable random movement in private-sector aggregate demand offset by a positive, unpredictable random movement in the money supply or government spending. The fact that the two random movements are linked is no help to the private sector in predicting them. Thus, in rational expectations models in which the government has an informational advantage, there is scope for the government to use policy to stabilize output.

The question is: How important are such differences or asymmetries in information likely to be? On the whole it seems difficult to believe they are very important. Most macroeconomic data are published fairly quickly, and any delay is often due more to the time it takes to collect them than a strict publication lag. Government models of the economy have their counterpart in private-sector models of the economy which, although not exactly the same, nevertheless exhibit much the same features. Besides, it is often the case that the government model is known to those outside government. Furthermore, of course, if the government did possess an important informational advantage there would be a strong incentive for the private sector to obtain the same information, so one might expect the advantage to be gradually eroded.

The same objections might also be applied to models which suggest a role for government policy arising out of asymmetries of information between groups in the private sector. To illustrate these models we consider a simplified version of the intertemporal substitution model developed above: we shall assume that consumers or demanders have full current information, but suppliers do not. Because of this asymmetry of information, expectations differ between suppliers and demanders, a fact we recognize by indexing the expectations terms by s and d for suppliers and demanders respectively. Supply in each market is determined by the difference between the price in each market and suppliers' expectations of next period's price level. Demand is determined by the difference between the price in each market and demander's expectations of next period's price level, and also by the expected real value of next period's money balances. Further influences on demand are a relative demand shock, $\epsilon_t(z)$, and a private-sector aggregate demand shock, η_t, which is assumed to follow the process shown in equation (5.3). The equations of the model are:

$$y_t^s(z) = \beta_0 + \beta_1[p_t(z) - E_t^s(z)p_{t+1}], \tag{5.17}$$

$$y_t^d(z) = \alpha_0 + m_t + E_t^d(z)\Delta m_{t+1} - E_t^d(z)p_{t+1} + \eta_t + \epsilon_t(z)$$
$$- \alpha_1[p_t(z) - E_t^d(z)p_{t+1}] \tag{5.18}$$

$$\eta_t = \eta_{t-1} + \xi_t \tag{5.19}$$

In the money supply equation we adopt a policy rule which Barro (1976) showed would lead to policy ineffectiveness; that is, we assume that the quantity of money is linked only to the once-lagged value of ξ:

$$m_t = m_{t-1} + g + \gamma_1 \xi_{t-1} \tag{5.20}$$

Using the technique of undetermined coefficients we can write the process for $p_t(z)$ as

$$p_t(z) = \pi_0 + \pi_1 m_{t-1} + \pi_2 g + \pi_3 \xi_t + \pi_4 \xi_{t-1} + \pi_6 \eta_{t-1} + \pi_7 \epsilon_t(z) \tag{5.21}$$

We assume that demanders know the value of all current shocks, but suppliers do not, so we can write:

$$E_t^d(z)p_{t+1} = \pi_0 + \pi_1 m_{t-1} + [\pi_1 + \pi_2]g + \pi_1 \gamma_1 \xi_{t-1} + [\pi_4 + \pi_6]\xi_t + \pi_6 \eta_{t-1}, \tag{5.22}$$

$$E_t^s(z)p_{t+1} = \pi_0 + \pi_1 m_{t-1} + [\pi_1 + \pi_2]g + \pi_1 \gamma_1 \xi_{t-1} + [\pi_4 + \pi_6][\theta/\pi_3][\pi_3 \xi_t + \pi_7 \epsilon_t(z)] + \pi_6 \eta_{t-1}, \tag{5.23}$$

$$E_t^d(z)\Delta m_{t+1} = g + \gamma_1 \xi_t \tag{5.24}$$

Substituting these expressions for the respective expectations terms and using the technique of undetermined coefficients, we obtain:

$$\pi_0 = \alpha_0 - \beta_0, \qquad \pi_1 = 1, \qquad \pi_2 = 1 + \alpha_1 + \beta_1,$$

$$\pi_3 = [1 + \gamma_1][\alpha_1 + \beta_1 \theta]/[\alpha_1 + \beta_1], \qquad \pi_4 = \gamma_1, \qquad \pi_6 = 1,$$

$$\pi_7 = [\alpha_1 + \beta_1 \theta]/[\alpha_1(\alpha_1 + \beta_1)]$$

and hence,

$$y_t(z) = \beta_0 - \beta_1 g + [\beta_1(1 + \gamma_1)\alpha_1(1 - \theta)/(\alpha_1 + \beta_1)]\xi_t + [\beta_1(1 - \theta)/(\alpha_1 + \beta_1)]\epsilon_t(z) \tag{5.25}$$

With γ_2 assumed equal to zero, the full information value of $y_t(z)$ can be written, as from equation (5.15),

$$y_t^*(z) = \beta_0 - \beta_1 g + [\beta_1/(\alpha_1 + \beta_1)]\epsilon_t(z) \tag{5.26}$$

and so the difference between $y_t(z)$ and $y_t^*(z)$ can be written as

$$y_t(z) - y_t^*(z) = [\beta(1 + \gamma_1)\alpha_1(1 - \theta)/(\alpha_1 + \beta_1)]\xi_t - [\beta_1 \theta/(\alpha_1 + \beta_1)]\epsilon_t(z) \tag{5.27}$$

It is clear from this equation that the selection of the policy parameter γ_1 is now important for the distribution of output around its full information value. In fact, in the simple case above, the optimum setting for this parameter is -1, for then aggregate demand shocks cause no change in either actual or full information output.

The reason for this is that with γ_1 set to -1 a shock increase to aggregate demand, that is a positive value for ξ_t, will induce the authorities to reduce next period's money supply by an amount equal to $-\xi_t$. Since the expected value of next period's money supply enters the current demand function, and since demanders are assumed to know the value of ξ_t, it follows that, in general, demand will be immunized from the influence of ξ_t. Because of this, the only shock that can disturb current prices from the value they are expected to take next period is a relative demand shock. With only this single shock affecting prices the signal extraction problem facing suppliers disappears: they can infer with confidence from their local price what the relative demand shock is.

If suppliers had the same, full information that demanders have, or if demanders had the same, imperfect information that suppliers have, the setting of γ_1 would be irrelevant. In the former case this is because there would be full information, and in the latter case the reason for the irrelevance of γ_1 was explained when we discussed the intertemporal substitution model.

This illustrates one particular case in which differences in information amongst economic agents allows policy to be effective even within a full price flexible rational expectations model. Other cases are discussed in Turnovsky (1980), Weiss (1980) and King (1982).

5.2   THE IMPLICATIONS OF ASSUMING PRICE STICKINESS

In the previous chapter the theory of rational expectations was combined with a macroeconomic model which assumed full price flexibility: on each island, each period the price of the good moved to equate supply and demand. A major result of that model was that *systematic* aggregate demand policies would be ineffective in stabilizing real output, employment and other real variables. It is commonly agreed that while in some markets prices move in the way the model assumes – very quickly to equate changes in supply and demand – in other markets they do not. For example, in the foreign exchange market or the stock markets the prices of currencies or stocks and shares change by the hour to equate supply and demand. The prices of certain goods (such as agricultural produce) also seem to respond very promptly to changes in supply and demand. Even in certain labour markets, for example casual day labour, the price of labour can move apparently very freely. But there are other markets in which prices appear to move sluggishly and to be, at least in the short run, unresponsive to changes in supply and demand. Many labour markets appear to fall into this category, with wage rates being determined through complex institutional arrangements and bargaining processes which seem to imply that they will be less than fully flexible. The prices of certain goods too – notably manufactured goods – appear to be 'administered', or set for some time so that they do not respond immediately to changes in supply and demand.

Of course, prices may appear to be more sticky than they actually are, for there are many ways of changing the 'price' of a good without changing the amount of £'s printed on the good's label. For example, a firm could offer better after-sales service for a microcomputer or a longer guarantee for a television; it could waive delivery charges for a new table or throw in a set of free wine glasses with the purchase of petrol. All such measures can be seen as changing the terms on which a good is bought, a broad inter-pretation of its price, without necessarily changing the quoted price for the good. Thus the fact that quoted prices appear to be inflexi-ble may not necessarily imply that prices broadly interpreted are.

Furthermore, pointing to inflexibility in some prices does not by itself show that the assumption of general price flexibility is unreasonable. It may be that the cited deviations from price flexibility are empirically unimportant; that is, they do not signi-ficantly affect the 'average' behaviour of prices.

However, following a study of prices in the US, Carlton (1986) has recently concluded that the degree of price rigidity in many industries is significant. He found that it is not unusual in some industries for prices to individual buyers to remain unchanged for several years. And in one case study Cecchetti (1986) has shown that the news-stand price of magazines has been very rigid (*Reader's Digest* changed its price six times between 1950 and 1980). Of course, the fact that a price may be constant over a given interval of time may not itself mean that it is inflexible; the price could be equal to its equilibrium value and the latter could in fact be constant as well. To demonstrate, then, that prices are inflexible in the sense that we mean in the remainder of this chapter, it has to be established that the price may deviate from its equilibrium value over a given interval. Since the equilibrium price is not observed, tests for sticky prices thus require a model of the equilibrium price. For this reason prices may appear flexible or otherwise, depending on the theory of the equilibrium price used in the test. Despite these considerations many economists believe that the tendency of prices to remain unchanged over several periods suggests strongly that they are not in equilibrium, as one would expect the equilibrium price to have changed over that interval.

Most economists would agree then that there is, at the very least, *prima-facie* evidence that a significant number of prices are not fully flexible, and that one ought therefore to consider the implications of sticky prices in macroeconomic models. In the rest of this chapter we shall drop the assumption that prices are fully flexible and examine the implications of assuming that they are either fixed or at least move only slowly to their equilibrium values. We shall maintain the assumption that expectations are rational, and show that it is not this assumption *per se* which leads to the ineffectiveness of systematic stabilization policy but its combination with (*inter alia*) the assumption of price flexibility. Thus even if expectations are fully rational there may be a role for systematic stabilization policy provided that prices are sufficiently inflexible.

(a) The McCallum Model

We begin the analysis of sticky prices by recalling the policy implications of the flexible-price model developed in the previous chapter. In figure 5.1, AD_0 represents the level of aggregate demand (rationally) expected to prevail at time t. The typical expectation of the general price level is therefore P_0. If the actual level of aggregate demand is greater than that expected (say, AD_1 in figure 5.1), the actual level of prices will move above P_0 to equate supply and demand, and output will rise above Y^n. The reason for the rise in output is the familiar one: the unexpectedly high level of aggregate demand has led to the typical supplier observing an unexpectedly high price. Partly misinterpreting this as due to a favourable relative demand shift the typical supplier increases output to take advantage of what (wrongly) appears to be a high relative price. Any rise in aggregate demand which was rationally anticipated would have had no such effect – it would merely have led to a rise in prices. Systematic changes in the instruments of monetary and fiscal policy would produce only predictable changes in aggregate demand and therefore cannot be used to stabilize real output – policy is ineffective.

How would the implications of this model be changed if prices were temporarily fixed or 'sticky'? The answer depends upon the precise nature of price rigidity. The definition of price stickiness which we shall employ in this section does not in fact alter very much the policy implications of the model developed in the previous chapter, although it may have implications for the test of that model. This definition was suggested by McCallum (1977, 1978). In his model firms set prices at the end of period $t - 1$ to cover period t. Once set, prices cannot be changed within period t. At the end of period t prices are then set for period $t + 1$, and so on. In this sense prices in period t are sticky: they are set one period in advance and are then unresponsive to the level of demand which actually occurs in period t. McCallum assumes that firms set their prices for period t in the following way. Given all the information available to them at the end of period $t - 1$, firms expect that the position of the aggregate demand curve in period t will be AD_0 in figure 5.1. Firms aim to set prices so that their

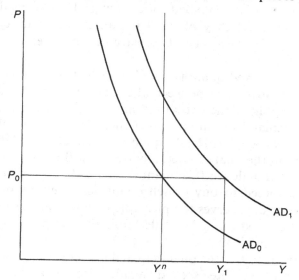

FIGURE 5.1   Sticky prices and excess demand.

expected level of production is in each period (in total) Y^n. Given that the typical firm expects the aggregate demand curve to be AD_0, it follows that the general level of prices set at period $t - 1$ for period t will be P_0.

If the actual aggregate demand curve is AD_0, the general level of prices will be P_0 and the level of output will be Y^n, but what happens if the aggregate demand curve is higher than expected, say at AD_1? Of course, such a shift in the level of aggregate demand can only occur, given rational expectations, if it is the result of a random, unpredictable movement in, for example, monetary or fiscal policy. It cannot occur through any systematic movement or it would have been predicted. But if such a random movement occurs, how will firms react to it? In particular, given that prices have already been set and cannot be changed, what will happen to real output? The answer requires some specification of a 'quantity rule'; that is, a description of agents' behaviour when, because of price stickiness, disequilibrium prevails.

To understand the need for some quantity rule, consider figure 5.1 again. It is clear from that figure that at the price level P_0 the level of actual aggregate demand is Y_1, whereas firms initially wanted to produce Y^n. In other words, there is excess demand for goods. Output could be as high as Y_1 if firms adopt the rule of producing whatever is demanded, or as low as Y^n if firms decide to produce only what they planned initially. The quantity rule determines where between these two extremes the level of output will actually be.

A frequently invoked quantity rule is that if there is disequilibrium, that is a difference between the quantity demanded and the quantity supplied, the actual quantity traded will equal the minimum of demand or supply. So if there is excess supply the quantity actually traded will be the quantity demanded, and if there is excess demand the quantity actually traded will be the quantity supplied. The rationale for this quantity rule is that it implies that no agents are forced to buy or sell quantities in excess of their wishes, so the rule preserves the principle of voluntary exchange. In the present context this rule would imply that output will equal Y^n in figure 5.1 with the gap $Y_1 - Y^n$ being unsatisfied excess demand. So the result of the unanticipated movement in aggregate demand is merely to create excess demand: prices are already fixed at P_0 and the quantity rule implies that output remains at Y^n.

An alternative quantity rule sets output equal to the level of demand. The rationale here is that firms may wish to preserve customer goodwill by preventing shortages. They may therefore agree to sell at price level P_0 whatever is demanded. In figure 5.1 this implies that output would rise to Y_1 if aggregate·demand unexpectedly rose to AD_1.

Clearly, then, different quantity rules imply different solutions for output. With the 'minimum' quantity rule, unexpectedly high levels of aggregate demand do not raise output above Y^n, but unexpectedly low levels of aggregate demand will depress output below Y^n (the reader may wish to verify this by imagining an actual aggregate demand curve to the left of AD_0). Setting output equal to aggregate demand means that output will exceed Y^n when aggregate demand is unexpectedly high and output will fall below Y^n when aggregate demand is unexpectedly low. Whatever the rule, the mechanism by which random movements in aggregate demand lead to fluctuations in output is not the same as the one explained in chapter 4. There the random movement in aggregate demand leads to an unexpectedly high price and it is this which induces a rise in output. But here such a change in price cannot occur since prices are fixed at the end of period $t-1$ and their values are therefore known. Thus in McCallum's model unexpected fluctuations in aggregate demand can cause changes in real output even though they do not cause unexpected movements in prices. In this model, as with others discussed in the remainder of this chapter, changes in aggregate demand can be said to have real output effects because of *imperfect competition* (that is, price stickiness), whereas real effects of such changes discussed in the previous chapter arose because of *imperfect information*. This difference may account for the fact that although there is now a great deal of empirical evidence linking monetary or aggregate demand shocks to real output fluctuations – evidence which we shall discuss in later chapters – the evidence that unexpected *price* changes affect output is much weaker (see, for example, Fair, 1979).

What happens to the 'policy ineffectiveness proposition' in this model? McCallum assumes that the government decides its monetary and fiscal policies for period t at the end of period $t-1$ and cannot or does not change them in period t. In this sense he assumes that government policy is subject to the same degree of stickiness as prices. Since aggregate demand policies are decided on the basis of the information available at the end of period $t - 1$, it follows that the systematic component of aggregate demand will, as before, have no effect on real output. For, by definition, the systematic element in aggregate demand can be predicted at the end of period $t - 1$ and will be reflected purely in the prices firms set at the end of that period for the next period. The stickiness in prices assumed in the model is not sufficiently severe to change the key result of chapter 4: only the random component of aggregate demand can affect real output. Thus the policy ineffectiveness proposition can survive in a model in which prices exhibit some degree of stickiness, provided that the policy instruments exhibit the same degree of stickiness.

More generally, prices could be sticky and yet the major implication of the flexible-price model developed in chapter 4 could still be true. The shorter the period over which *prices* are sticky in relation to the period over which *government policy instruments* are sticky, the more likely it is that the policy implications of chapter 4 will remain.

To complete this section we present a simplified formal version of the McCallum model. In this version we shall in fact assume that it is *wages* that are set by trade unions one period in advance and that prices are flexible; that is, we shall examine a *sticky wage* rather than a *sticky price* model. In the quantity trading rule for the labour market we shall assume that employment is determined by the demand for labour. We further assume that the demand for labour is a function of the real wage so that we can write

$$n_t = \alpha[p_t - w_t] \tag{5.28}$$

where n_t is the logarithm of the demand for labour or the level of employment at time t, w_t is the logarithm of the nominal wage rate at time t, p_t is the logarithm of the price level at time t, and α is a positive constant.

Now assume that the wage set at the end of period $t - 1$ for period t is determined by

$$w_t = E_{t-1}p_t \tag{5.29}$$

This assumes, for simplicity, that workers are anxious to keep their wage in period t in line with the (rationally) expected level of prices for that period. Given the existence of an aggregate production function of the form $y_t = \beta n_t$, an expression for the logarithm of output can be obtained by substituting equation (5.29) into equation (5.28) and then substituting the resulting equation into the production function. This gives:

$$y_t = \alpha\beta[p_t - E_{t-1}p_t] = [p_t - E_{t-1}p_t] \tag{5.30}$$

where for simplicity we have assumed that $\alpha\beta = 1$. Equation (5.30) is the aggregate supply curve: firms will produce more output if the price level is higher than that expected by workers or their trade union. Now assume a simple aggregate demand function of the following form:

$$y_t = m_t - p_t + v_t \tag{5.31}$$

where m_t is the logarithm of the money supply in period t; and v_t is an aggregate demand shock.

Setting aggregate demand (equation (5.31)) equal to aggregate supply (equation (5.30)) and solving for the price level we obtain

$$p_t = \tfrac{1}{2}[m_t + v_t + E_{t-1}p_t] \tag{5.32}$$

Taking expectations of equation (5.32) and collecting terms, we can derive

$$E_{t-1}p_t = [E_{t-1}m_t + E_{t-1}v_t] \tag{5.33}$$

Substituting equation (5.33) into equation (5.32) gives

$$p_t = \tfrac{1}{2}[m_t + E_{t-1}m_t + v_t + E_{t-1}v_t] \tag{5.34}$$

Equations (5.34) and (5.33) may be substituted back into equation (5.30) to give the following solution for output:

$$y_t = \tfrac{1}{2}[m_t - E_{t-1}m_t] + \tfrac{1}{2}[v_t - E_{t-1}v_t] \tag{5.35}$$

The policy implications of equation (5.35) are identical to those of chapter 4 and discussed less formally above: only the random and unpredictable component of monetary policy has real effects.

(b) The Fischer–Phelps–Taylor model

In a contrasting approach, a number of writers have introduced the possibility that private agents, such as firms or workers, may bind themselves to fixed prices over periods long enough to permit within-period reaction by policy-makers. In such models the policy ineffectiveness proposition no longer holds, even though expectations are assumed to be rational. The original application of rational expectations to this type of sticky price model was by Fischer (1977), Phelps and Taylor (1977) and later by Taylor (1979). For simplicity we shall refer to this model in what follows as the Fischer model. As with the McCallum model we shall begin by illustrating the models with the use of the aggregate supply and demand model of chapter 4, and follow this with a more formal presentation of the model.

Imagine an economy in which firms, for whatever reason, agree to fix prices at the end of period t to cover period $t + 1$ and $t + 2$ and not to alter these prices in either period $t + 1$ or $t + 2$ if circumstances differ from those expected at the close of period t. Similarly, at the end of period $t + 2$ firms set prices to cover periods $t + 3$ and $t + 4$ and these prices may not be altered in periods $t + 3$ and $t + 4$. In other words, prices are set at the end of every even period (0, 2, 4, and so on) to cover the next two periods. In deciding what prices to set, firms form expectations (which, of course, we shall assume are rational) of what the price level is likely to be in the next two periods.

Using figure 5.1 again we might imagine that firms, at the end of period 0, expect that the position of the aggregate demand curve will be AD_0 in period 1. For simplicity we shall also assume that firms expect that the position of the aggregate demand curve in period 2 will also be AD_0. Given their (rational) expectations, firms agree to set prices at P_0 in periods 1 and 2 and therefore expect to produce a level of output in both periods equal to Y^n. But imagine that the aggregate demand curve is at AD_0 in period 1 but shifts out to AD_1 in period 2: What will happen then? The answer, of course, depends upon the quantity rule that firms employ, in particular how they react to a higher level of demand than they were expecting. If firms are anxious to maintain customer goodwill and therefore agree to produce whatever is demanded at the set price, then the effective supply curve for periods 1 and 2 is the horizontal line from P_0. Thus, in period 2, if the aggregate demand curve is in fact AD_1, output will rise to Y_1, price remaining at P_0. Of course, if aggregate demand were to fall below the level indicated by AD_0, then the level of output would fall below Y^n.

It is now straightforward to show how government policies,

even anticipated ones, can stabilize real output in this model of 'sticky' prices. Imagine that firms have set their prices at the end of period 0 to give a price level of P_0 in periods 1 and 2. They have done this because they rationally expect the aggregate demand curve to be AD_0 in periods 1 and 2. Imagine that private-sector investment, a component of aggregate demand, turns out to be unexpectedly high in period 2, so that in period 2 the aggregate demand curve is in fact AD_1. In the absence of any change in government policy, and if firms are following the quantity rule of setting output equal to demand, output will rise to Y_1 in period 2. It is important to realize that firms may have enough information at the end of period 1 to predict the rise in aggregate demand in period 2, so that the rise in aggregate demand from period 1 to period 2 is anticipated at the end of period 1. But the rise in aggregate demand was not anticipated at the end of period 0 when the price was set.

Despite their ability to predict the coming rise in aggregate demand, firms are obliged to keep prices at P_0 and to produce Y_1. Thus, in this model, even anticipated movements in aggregate demand may affect the level of output. Whether or not they do depends upon their timing. If they can be anticipated at the end of one of the even periods they will have no effect on real output: prices will merely adjust to keep output at its natural rate Y^n. But if they can only be anticipated at the end of one of the odd periods, they will have an effect on real output because prices are fixed.

Furthermore, government policy can now be used to stabilize real output. For if at the end of period 1 a rise in aggregate demand is predictable, the government could reduce its own spending and thereby maintain the position of the aggregate demand curve at AD_0 and hence maintain aggregate real output at Y^n. Such a policy would work even if, at the end of period 1, it was perfectly predictable. It does not rely for its efficacy on the government having access to better information for, as we have said, firms may well be able to anticipate the rise in aggregate demand between period 1 and 2. What it does rely on is the government's ability to change its policy instruments more quickly than firms can change prices. The government can therefore act to avoid unwanted macroeconomic effects of 'market failure', or the failure of prices to move to clear markets.

As with the McCallum model, we now present a more formal

statement of the Fischer model. We shall also assume that *wages* rather than prices are set in advance, so that our formal model is one of 'wage stickiness' rather than 'price stickiness'. Imagine an economy in which the wage rate for half its workers is set at the end of every *even* period to cover the following two periods, while the wage rate for the other half is set at the end of every odd period, again to cover the following two periods. The 'overlapping' nature of the contracts in this economy is set out diagrammatically in figure 5.2. Note the wage rate at any point in time (t) is made up of an average of wages which were set one period earlier and those set two periods before.

As with the formal McCallum model above, the level of employment for both groups of workers is determined by the demand for labour, so the aggregate level of employment is given by

$$n_t = \alpha[p_t - w_t] \qquad \text{or} \qquad n_t = \alpha[p_t - \tfrac{1}{2}(w_{1t} + w_{2t})] \qquad (5.36)$$

since w_t (the aggregate wage) is defined as $\tfrac{1}{2}(w_{1t} + w_{2t})$. This definition follows from the assumption that half the labour force establish contracts in even periods and half in odd periods. Note that we are assuming that both sets of firms sell their output at the

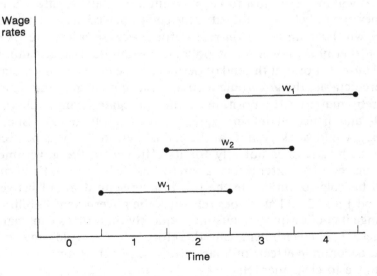

FIGURE 5.2　Overlapping contracts.

price p_t and that they have identical real wage elasticities of demand $(-\alpha)$: that is, the firms are identical in every respect other than the timing of their wage contracts.

If t is an even number, then w_{1t} was in fact *set* two periods earlier and w_{2t} was *set* at the close of the previous period. If t is odd, then w_{1t} was set at the end of the previous period and w_{2t} was set two periods earlier. This feature is illustrated in figure 5.2, in which it can be seen that in period 3 (odd) w_1 was set the end of the period 2 (even) but w_2 was actually set two periods earlier in period 1 (odd).

Both groups of workers set their wage rates given their (rational) expectations of the level of prices in the two periods covered by the wage contract. Again, for simplicity we shall assume that the price level is believed to remain unchanged over the period of the contract, so we can write:

$$\left.\begin{aligned} w_{1t} &= E_{t-1}p_t & = E_{t-1}p_{t+1} \\ w_{2t} &= E_{t-2}p_{t-1} & = E_{t-2}p_t \end{aligned}\right\} \text{ when } t \text{ is odd,}$$

$$(5.37)$$

$$\left.\begin{aligned} w_{1t} &= E_{t-2}p_{t-1} & = E_{t-2}p_t \\ w_{2t} &= E_{t-1}p_t & = E_{t-1}p_{t-1} \end{aligned}\right\} \text{when } t \text{ is even}$$

Notice that workers who set their wages at the end of even periods believed, in the even period $t - 1$, that the price level in odd period t would remain unchanged in period $t + 1$. Similarly, we assume that workers who set their wages at the end of odd periods believed, in the odd period $t - 2$, that the price level would be the same in periods $t - 1$ and t.

Consider the case in which t is odd. Given an aggregate production function of the form $y_t = \beta n_t = \beta[n_{1t} + n_{2t}]$, we can substitute the relevant rows of equation (5.37) into equation (5.36), and substitute the resulting expressions into the production function to give:

$$\begin{aligned} y_t &= \alpha\beta\tfrac{1}{2}[p_t - E_{t-1}p_t + p_t - E_{t-2}p_t] \\ &= \tfrac{1}{2}[p_t - E_{t-1}p_t + p_t - E_{t-2}p_t] \end{aligned}$$

$$(5.38)$$

where we again have assumed for simplicity that $\alpha\beta = 1$. Output is thus affected by the deviation of the price level from both that expected by workers in period $t - 1$ and in period $t - 2$. The former reflects the effects of contracts formed last period currently in their first period, and the latter reflects the effects of contracts formed two periods ago now in their second period.

Assume again a simple aggregate demand curve of the form given in equation (5.31), which we repeat here for convenience:

$$y_t = m_t - p_t + v_t \tag{5.31}$$

Setting aggregate supply (equation (5.38)) equal to aggregate demand (equation (5.31)) we obtain an expression for the price level:

$$p_t = \tfrac{1}{2}[m_t + v_t] + \tfrac{1}{4}[E_{t-1}p_t + E_{t-2}p_t] \tag{5.39}$$

Of course, this is not a solution as there are expectation terms to be solved on the right-hand side. To solve these terms, by taking expectations of equation (5.39) conditional on information dated $t - 2$ we obtain:

$$E_{t-2}p_t = [E_{t-2}m_t + E_{t-2}v_t] \tag{5.40}$$

and by taking expectations conditional on information dated $t - 1$ we obtain:

$$E_{t-1}p_t = \tfrac{2}{3}[E_{t-1}m_t + E_{t-1}v_t] + \tfrac{1}{3}E_{t-2}p_t$$

or

$$E_{t-1}p_t = \tfrac{2}{3}[E_{t-1}m_t + E_{t-1}v_t] + \tfrac{1}{3}[E_{t-2}m_t + E_{t-2}v_t] \tag{5.41}$$

Substituting these expressions for expectations back into the price equation we can write:

$$p_t = (\tfrac{1}{2})(m_t + v_t) + (\tfrac{1}{4})(\tfrac{2}{3})(E_{t-1}m_t + E_{t-1}v_t)$$
$$+ (\tfrac{1}{4})(\tfrac{1}{3})(E_{t-2}m_t + E_{t-2}v_t) + (\tfrac{1}{4})(E_{t-2}m_t + E_{t-2}v_t) \tag{5.42}$$

By substituting equations (5.42), (5.41) and (5.40) into the expression for aggregate supply, equation (5.38), we obtain the solution:

$$y_t = \tfrac{1}{2}[\tfrac{1}{3}(m_t - E_{t-1}m_t) + \tfrac{2}{3}(m_t - E_{t-2}m_t)]$$
$$+ \tfrac{1}{2}[\tfrac{1}{3}(v_t - E_{t-1}v_t) + \tfrac{2}{3}(v_t - E_{t-2}v_t)] \tag{5.43}$$

Now imagine that v_t is in fact a random walk given by

$$v_t = v_{t-1} + \xi_t$$

where ξ_t is a serially independent random variable. This states that other non-monetary effects on aggregate demand (such as private investment expenditure) are determined by their values in the previous period plus a random or surprise term. To show how policy can be effective in this model we first consider the case in which the authorities simply set the money supply to be constant, so that $m_t - E_{t-1}m_t$ and $m_t - E_{t-2}m_t$ are zero (that is, expectations are always correct). In this case the solution for y_t, which we denote by y_t^1, is

$$y_t^1 = \tfrac{1}{2}(\xi_t + \tfrac{2}{3}\xi_{t-1}) \tag{5.44}$$

Now imagine that the authorities followed a simple rule linking the money supply in period t to the aggregate demand shock in period $t - 1$ (ξ_{t-1}). The rule we shall consider is

$$m_t = -\xi_{t-1} \tag{5.45}$$

It follows from this rule that $E_{t-1}m_t = -\xi_{t-1}$ and $E_{t-2}m_t = 0$. Thus $m_t - E_{t-1}m_t = 0$ and $m_t - E_{t-2}m_t = -\xi_{t-1}$. Given this, our solution for output, which we denote by y_t^2, is now

$$y_t^2 = \tfrac{1}{2}\xi_t \tag{5.46}$$

It is now clear that the variation in y_t^1 is greater than that of y_t^2 because the former has the additional term in ξ_{t-1} which does not appear in equation (5.46). Thus the monetary authorities could reduce the variation in output by adopting a simple rule that links the level of money supply to the lagged shock to aggregate demand, and this dominates the more simple rule that just set money supply equal to a constant that was independent of the state of aggregate demand.

(c) Sticky prices and general equilibrium

The sticky price models we have considered so far tend merely to 'tack on' the assumption of sticky prices to the sort of model developed in chapter 4. In recent years a number of economists have developed models which make price stickiness and the ensuing failure of markets to clear central to their analysis. In these models much attention has been focused on the *interaction* between markets which fail to clear, and the mechanisms by which agents' actions are coordinated when prices are sticky. Early macroeconomic models with quantity rationing were developed by Solow and Stiglitz (1968), Barro and Grossman (1971) and Malinvaud (1977). In what follows the main ideas of these models are discussed in general terms and the implications of allowing expectations to be rational within them are very briefly mentioned. We do not have the space in this book to discuss the models in any depth; the interested reader is referred to Muellbauer and Portes (1978).

The central contribution of these models has been to focus on the 'spill-over' effects that result from the failure of markets to clear. If one market fails to clear, this will have repercussions in other markets and these in turn may further affect the disequilibrium in the initial market. These spill-over effects require a 'general equilibrium' analysis; that is, one in which the interaction between all markets is considered,

As an illustration of such spill-over effects, imagine an economy with only two markets – a labour market and a goods market. Households supply labour and demand goods; firms supply goods and demand labour. Because wages and prices are rigid, both markets may fail to clear. Initially we assume that there is excess supply in both markets. Once again we note that the failure of each market to clear requires a quantity trading rule for each. We shall assume that output is determined by the minimum of supply and demand, so that with excess supply in both markets, the quantities traded in each will be determined by *demand*. In the labour market, employment is determined by the demand for labour by firms; in the goods market actual output traded is determined by the demand for goods by households.

Excess supply of labour means that households are *rationed* in the labour market: they cannot sell the quantity of labour services they wish to at current wages and prices. This may mean that some workers are unemployed or that all workers are underemployed, or a combination of both. Because households do not realize their desired labour supply, they will not be able to achieve their desired demand for goods. This arises from the fact that unemployment or underemployment will reduce the household's income and *constrain* the demand for goods. The *effective* demand for goods (to use a familiar Keynesian term) is below what households would optimally choose *given current wages and prices* (referred to as the *notional* demand). The rationing of the household in the labour market *spills over* into the goods market by constraining the household's demand for goods.

Similarly, consider the effects of rationing in the goods market. Here excess supply of goods means that output is determined by demand and firms cannot sell the desired volume of output. Firms are rationed in the goods market. Because of this (and assuming for simplicity that firms do not carry inventories) they will demand only enough labour to produce the output they *can* sell, for any additional inputs of labour will either be idle or else will produce output which will remain unsold. It is therefore only profitable for the firm to demand just enough labour to meet the demand for output. The demand for labour is therefore *constrained* by the fact that the firm is rationed in the goods market. In this way a ration in the goods market *spills over* into the labour market by constraining the demand for labour.

Since the constrained demand for goods (by households rationed in the labour market) will exacerbate the ration of firms in the goods market, and since the constrained demand for labour will further ration the household in the labour market, it is natural to ask whether the behaviour of both sets of agents can be mutually consistent. To be mutually consistent the constrained demand for goods must ration firms in a manner that restricts their demand for labour to give rise to the initial constrained demand for goods. The nature of such a 'quantity-constrained equilibrium' is discussed in the references cited above. The coexistence of excess supplies of labour and goods is referred to as a 'Keynesian' quantity-constrained equilibrium. Depending on the precise values assumed for the (fixed) levels of wages and prices, other non-market clearing regimes are:

- Classical: excess supply of labour; excess demand for goods.
- Repressed inflation: excess demand for both goods and labour.
- Underconsumption: excess demand for labour; excess supply of goods.

The significance of these regimes for economic policy has been explored in a number of papers, notably in Muellbauer and Portes (1978) and Malinvaud (1977). In these and other models, households save for future consumption (by accumulating money balances) and in some cases firms can accumulate inventories for future sales. Because of this, expectations of the future have important effects on the present. For example, if the household expects to be rationed in the goods market in the future, there is less reason to save out of current income and, consequently, the current demand for goods will rise. If a firm expects to be rationed in the future in the goods market, it is more likely to increase its current sales rather than produce for inventories. There is, of course, no reason why expectations of future rations should not be rational (that is, based on current information, including the economic model of how these rations arise). Indeed, Neary and Stiglitz (1983) have introduced the idea of 'rational constraint expectations' into a model characterized by rationing and constrained equilibrium.

The analysis of such models under rational expectations is too complicated to discuss here, but the main implications of the Neary and Stiglitz model are worth sketching. When Keynesian quantity-constrained equilibrium exists in the current period (that is, excess supply of both labour and goods) the multiplier effect of government spending (whether that spending is anticipated or otherwise) is greater under rational expectations than under 'static' (non-rational) expectations. Similarly, an increase in the supply of money will have real output effects whether it is anticipated or otherwise. The allowance for spill-over effects between markets does not alter the policy implications discussed in simpler models earlier in this chapter, in other words that anticipated policies (both monetary and fiscal) can be used to stabilize output. Moreover, the increase in the expenditure multiplier led Neary and Stiglitz to argue that the introduction of rational expectations into 'quantity-constrained' models 'actually enhances the effectiveness of government policy' (p. 224).

5.3 MICRO-FOUNDATIONS FOR STICKY PRICES

The previous section has shown that the precise nature of price stickiness is of major importance to the results usually derived from rational expectations macroeconomic models. For if prices are rigid in the McCallum sense, the main results of the flexible-price models carry through: in particular, systematic attempts to stabilize real output, employment and other real variables will fail; whereas if prices are sticky over long enough to permit policy adjustments by the government, the case for the type of stabilization policy advocated by Keynesian economists is restored even if expectations are rational.

Proponents of the view that Keynesian stabilization policies are futile have been quick to point out the key role that wage and price rigidity play in justifying such policies, and the need for advocates of such policies to provide some theory of why prices should be rigid in the way they claim they are. Imposing exogenously a particular form of price rigidity which happens to produce the result that Keynesian stabilization policies can work is hardly enough by itself to justify such policies. After all, it seems likely that the form of wage and price rigidity in an economy will reflect the economic environment, one component of which is likely to be the behaviour of aggregate demand. For example, in the two-period model described in the previous section it would seem likely that if aggregate demand became more volatile firms would become much more reluctant to agree to set prices two periods in advance, and so perhaps they would set prices only one period in advance: the nature of price rigidity would change in response to a change in the economic environment.

It is for this reason that Keynesian stabilization policies have been criticized for relying on the 'unexplained postulate' of wage rigidity and for assuming that the form of wage and price rigidity, the form of wage and price *contracts*, is exogenously given rather than determined by, amongst other things, the type of monetary and fiscal policies being carried out. This is a good example of the 'Lucas critique' discussed in chapter 4.

This point has been forcefully expressed by two of the leading proponents of rational expectations, Lucas and Sargent:

> So the key issue here is really the fundamental one involved in the dispute between Keynes and the classical economists: is it adequate to regard certain surperficial characteristics of existing wage contracts as given when analysing the consequences of alternative monetary and fiscal regimes? Classical economic theory denies that those characteristics can be taken as given. To understand the implications of long-term contracts for monetary policy, one needs a model of the way those contracts are likely to respond to alternative monetary policy regimes. An extension of existing equilibrium models in this direction might well lead to interesting variations, but it seems to us unlikely that major modifications of the implications of these models for monetary and fiscal policy will follow from this.
>
> (Lucas and Sargent, 1978, p. 65)

The need to find a sound theoretical basis for wage and price stickiness has inspired a large and growing literature on what has become known as 'contract theory'. It is not possible to review comprehensively the research into the micro-foundations here, and the reader is directed to Rotemberg (1987) for an interesting survey. However one recent series of contributions are worthy of mention. A number of authors (Akerlof and Yellen, 1985; Mankiw, 1985a; Parkin, 1986) have argued that if firms have set optimum prices, a small change in the optimum may not persuade firms to change their price as the gain in profit is marginal. This is because the profit function before the change must have been horizontal at the optimum, so a small change in the optimum price will make only a marginal difference to the firms' profits. If there are small administrative costs of changing prices (so-called 'menu costs'), it may not be worth the firm changing its price as the adjustment costs may dominate the small gain in profitability. Yet the cited studies have shown that the macroeconomic effects of such rigidities can be quite substantial. Thus it is argued that the gain in profits of changing prices may only be of *second order*, whereas the welfare losses from the resulting rigidities may be of *first order*.

Of course, there may be other costs of changing prices (other than purely administrative ones). Okun (1981) and Rotemberg (1982) consider the cost of customer dissatisfaction with firms whose pricing appears erratic. Whatever the nature of price adjustment costs, one important development in establishing the micro-foundations of Keynesian wage or price rigidity has emphasized that these costs need not be substantial to lead to rigidities which can have important macroeconomic consequences.

However, one problem that applies to a number of theories seeking to explain nominal wage rigidities has been highlighted by Barro (1977b) and can be illustrated here by reference to figure 5.1. Suppose that a contract to sell at a given price for a specified period is, for whatever reason, advantageous to both buyers and sellers. A contract is therefore concluded to sell at a price P_0 for a set period (the exact length of this period is of no immediate concern). If unpredictable changes in aggregate demand occur, disequilibrium results: for example, an unexpectedly high level of aggregate demand would cause excess demand to arise. In such a circumstance a quantity rule has to be adopted in order to determine what actual output will be, and the one which we adopted was that actual output would equal the level of demand, thus obliging firms to produce and sell more than they initially considered optimal at the

price set. If they are rational, firms will realize that such disturbances can occur, even though they cannot forecast their precise
timing. Furthermore, they will know that such disturbances will
force them to produce a level of output which is not the optimal
one in the sense that it is not what they would in advance choose
to produce at a price of P_0. Barro's question is as follows: Why
should firms agree to a course of action which they know in certain
circumstances will force them to do something which in advance
or *ex ante* appears sub-optimal? To put this a slightly different
way: a contract which fixes prices but specifies that output will
equal whatever is demanded must *ex ante* be sub-optimal for firms.

A similar question can be asked about consumers when the quantity rule is that output equals the minimum of demand and supply.
For this implies that if there is an unexpected rise in demand in
period t consumers will not be able to buy the quantity of the good
they at time period $t - 1$, or *ex ante*, considered optimal at the set
price. Knowing that such disturbances can occur, why should consumers agree to a form of contract which, in such circumstances,
forces them to acquire a quantity of goods at the agreed price which
they consider sub-optimal? Such a contract must *ex ante* be
sub-optimal.

As Barro points out, the only quantity rule which does not carry
with it the implication that at times buyers and sellers will, *at the
price set*, trade a quantity of the good they consider *in advance* to
be sub-optimal is a rule which sets output equal to the value it
would take in the absence of any unanticipated disturbances; that
is, Y^n. For then if the price is set at P_0 the quantity traded will
equal the quantity that buyers and sellers at the end of period $t - 1$
thought optimal at that price. Of course, if disturbances occur to
aggregate demand, buyers or sellers who have agreed on a price
P_0 and a quantity to be traded Y^n will find themselves buying or
selling more or less than they now think is optimal, but that is not
the point. At the time they agreed the contract, period $t - 1$, it
appeared optimal to trade Y^n if the price level was P_0. And since
that is what the contract binds both sides to do, it is at period $t - 1$
an optimal contract.

The force of Barro's point should now be clear: in order to
explain quantity movements when prices are sticky, Keynesian
economists must provide some theoretical justification for the
quantity rule they use. A quantity trading rule which fixes price but

not output (or employment) appears to be sub-optimal. If economic agents are assumed to be rational optimizers when forming expectations, why should they not also be rational optimizers when drawing up contracts? As we have said, these questions are the subject of a large amount of current research which it is beyond the scope of this book to consider.

5.4 SUMMARY

In this chapter we have dealt with the major criticisms of the model developed in chapter 4. In particular, we have shown the implications of applying rational expectations to a variety of alternative models, some of which maintain the idea of wage and price flexibility and some which do not. We have established that rational expectations *per se* do not imply policy ineffectiveness, for when rational expectations are combined with alternative models of the macroeconomy systematic policy *can* influence the behaviour of output and allow the authorities to undertake stabilization policies. The case for stabilization policy is further strengthened when one assumes that either wages or prices are sticky over time, although the microeconomic foundations for long-term contracts are very much in their development stage. The counter-examples to the policy ineffectiveness proposition that we have considered in this chapter have led one notable proponent of rational expectations to write 'the potential usefulness of activist policy rules in dampening fluctuations . . . may survive the rational expectations revolution' (McCallum, 1980, p. 738).

SUGGESTIONS FOR FURTHER READING

Buiter (1980) summarizes and develops a number of criticisms of the rational expectations equilibrium macroeconomic model. Marini (1985) demonstrates that stabilization through monetary policy is possible in Barro's (1976) model. Rotemberg (1987) and Blanchard (1987) provide useful surveys of recent developments in the foundations for Keynesian macroeconomics and Gray (1976) analyses certain conditions under which 'sticky' wages might be optimal.

6

Rational Expectations and Macroeconomics: Two Influential Empirical Studies

In this chapter we shall examine two influential tests of rational expectations models in macroeconomics. The contributions of Lucas (1973) and Barro (1977a) initiated a major applied research programme, the main aim of which was the empirical evaluation of the model presented and discussed in chapter 4. Because of the historical importance of these papers we devote most of this chapter to them, and to the subsequent empirical research which has either corroborated or extended their results. We leave the more recent research which has challenged their findings to the following chapter.

The Lucas paper, which we cover in section 6.1, concentrates on testing the prediction of the model developed in chapter 4 that the more unpredictable aggregate demand is, the less is the effect on real output of any given unpredictable movement in aggregate demand. Barro focused on the other major prediction of that model: that only the unpredictable movement in aggregate demand affects real variables such as output and unemployment – his contribution is discussed in section 6.2. Finally, in section 6.3 we consider some of the modifications and extentions to these key contributions.

6.1 THE LUCAS TEST

The model developed in chapter 4 suggested that only the unpredictable component of aggregate demand would cause output to deviate from its natural level, and the more unpredictable it was the less effect it would have on the deviation of real output from its natural rate. Formally, we could write a simple version of that model (see, for example, equation (4.14) as

$$y_t = y_t^n + \beta_t(\sigma_\nu^2, \sigma_\epsilon^2) \nu_t \tag{6.1}$$

where y_t is the aggregate real output, y_t^n is the natural level of output, ν_t is the unpredictable component of aggregate demand, σ_ν^2 is the variance of ν, σ_ϵ^2 is the variance of the relative demand shocks, and $\beta_1(\sigma_\nu^2, \sigma_\epsilon^2)$ is a function explained below, the value of which is positive. All variables are in logarithms.

This equation states that in the absence of any aggregate demand shock (that is, if ν_t is zero), output will equal its natural level, y_t^n. If the aggregate demand shock is positive, then real output will rise above its natural level; if it is negative it will fall below it. The actual size of the rise or fall for any given value for ν_t will depend upon the variances of the aggregate and relative demand shocks. The higher the variance of the aggregate demand shock, the more unpredictable the aggregate demand shock is, and therefore, as explained in chapter 4, the lower will be the effect of any given ν_t. In other words, the greater the value of σ_ν^2 the lower, *ceteris paribus*, the value of $\beta_1(\sigma_\nu^2, \sigma_\epsilon^2)$. The model also predicts that the higher the value of σ_ϵ^2 the greater, *ceteris paribus*, the value of $\beta_1(\sigma_\nu^2, \sigma_\epsilon^2)$. The focus of the Lucas (1973) paper is on the first of these predicted relationships; that is, between the volatility of aggregate demand and its impact on real output. He tests it using data from a number of different countries over the same time period, reasoning that if equation (6.1) were true, then those countries in which aggregate demand has been highly unpredictable should be those countries in which unpredictable aggregate demand has little effect on real output.

In fact, Lucas uses a slightly more complicated version of equation (6.1) in his study. First he rewrites equation (6.1) as:

$$y_{cit} = \beta_{1i}(\sigma_{\nu i}^2, \sigma_{\epsilon i}^2) \nu_{it} \tag{6.2}$$

where y_{cit} is by definition the deviation of aggregate output in the ith country from its natural rate (that is, $y_{it} - y_{it}^n$). The other variables with i subscripts are as before but now refer to the ith country.

Then he allows for the effects of a 'propagation mechanism' (see section 5.1(a)) by adding the lagged value of y_{cit} to equation (6.2) and attaching a positive coefficient β_{2i} to it, giving:

$$y_{cit} = \beta_{1i}(\sigma_{vi}^2, \sigma_{\epsilon i}^2)\, v_{it} + \beta_{2i} y_{cit-1} \tag{6.3}$$

The addition of y_{cit-1} implies that any aggregate demand shock will have a drawn-out effect on real output: a positive value of v_{it} will, *ceteris paribus*, lead to a positive value for y_{cit} (that is, output will be above its natural level); next period, even in the absence of a positive value for v_{it+1}, y_{cit+1} will be positive because of the influence of the positive value of $\beta_{2i} y_{cit}$. Provided that the value of β_{2i} is less than one, the effect of the positive value of v_{it} will gradually become negligible. If β_{2i} were greater than one, the effect of a non-zero v_{it} would increase over time, so a value of β_{2i} of less than one is a requirement for the model's stability.

Three final assumptions permit Lucas to carry out his test. First, he assumes that $\sigma_{\epsilon i}^2$ is a constant which is roughly the same for all countries. Second, he assumes that the natural level of output grows at a rate which for any individual country is a constant over time but which may differ between countries. This assumption allows Lucas to measure y_{cit} as the deviation of actual real output, y_{it}, from the value predicted from a regression of y_{it} on a constant and time (where time might take the value of 1 in the first year of the data period, 2 in the second and so on). Using this as his measure of y_{cit}, Lucas can carry out a separate regression of y_{cit} on y_{cit-1} and v_{it} for each of the countries for which he has data, once he has solved the problem of how to measure v_{it} for each country. The method employed by Lucas to measure v_{it} appears now to be rather simplistic, as we shall see when we discuss later empirical studies. He measures each country's aggregate demand at any time by its total nominal spending. He then assumes that for each country the rate of growth of aggregate demand or nominal spending has followed a very simple process; that is,

$$DX_{it} = \chi_{0i} + v_{it} \tag{6.4}$$

where DX_{it} is the rate of growth of the ith country's nominal spending, χ_{0i} is the mean value of DX_i over the whole period, and v_{it} is the deviation of DX_{it} from its mean.

Rationality of expectations implies that if equation (6.4) adequately describes the process determining DX_{it}, then for each country the anticipated rate of growth of aggregate demand will be χ_{0i} and the unanticipated rate of growth will be ν_{it} in any period t. Thus Lucas measures the unanticipated rate of growth of aggregate demand in the ith country in any period t by ν_{it}, the deviation of the actual rate of growth of nominal spending from its mean value over the whole period. And he measures the unpredictability of aggregate demand in the ith country by the variance of ν_{it}, $\sigma_{\nu i}^2$. Of course, this procedure is only valid if equation (6.4) does adequately describe the process determining DX_{it} in each country. The extreme simplicity of the process suggests that this is unlikely, although Lucas (1973, p. 328 fn. 5) recognizes the problem and argues that the process he has assumed (that is, equation (6.4)) appears 'roughly accurate for most countries' in his study. The simplicity of the process assumed for aggregate demand is something we shall return to later, since it has some bearing on the interpretation of Lucas's results.

If, for each country, $\sigma_{\nu i}^2$ is constant over time it follows that $\beta_{1i}(\sigma_{\nu i}^2, \sigma_{\epsilon i}^2)$ will be a constant, although of course for different countries it will be a different constant. Thus for each country one could use Lucas's measure of unanticipated aggregate demand to estimate the following OLS regression based on equation (6.3):

$$y_{cit} = \beta_{1i}\nu_{it} + \beta_{2i}y_{cit-1} + \xi_{it} \qquad (6.5)$$

where β_{1t} is a coefficient, and ξ_{it} is a random error which is assumed to be serially uncorrelated with zero mean.

In fact, Lucas actually substitutes for ν_{it} from equation (6.4) and estimates the following regression for each country:

$$y_{cit} = -\beta_{1i}\chi_{0i} + \beta_{1i}DX_{it} + \beta_{2i}y_{cit-1} + \xi_{it} \qquad (6.6)$$

Strictly, equations (6.5) and (6.6) are equivalent only if in estimating equation (6.6) the restriction is imposed that the coefficient estimated on DX_{it} is equal to the negative of the constant term divided by the mean of DX_{it}, χ_{0i}. It appears that Lucas did not in fact impose this restriction, but estimated equation (6.6) freely. However, in what follows we shall assume that Lucas estimated the equivalent of equation (6.5). Thus Lucas can be seen to be estimating a regression for each country in which that country's deviation of real output from its natural level is regressed on its own lagged value and Lucas's measure of the unpredictable and therefore unanticipated component of aggregate demand.

Lucas's study used data from 18 countries, and the regression equation (6.5) was estimated for each of them using annual data over the period 1952-67. If the rational expectations macroeconomic model summarized in equation (6.3) has any validity, one would expect, first of all, that the estimate of β_1 for each of the 18 countries would be positive and that the estimated value of β_2 would be between zero and one. In general, these predictions of the theory are confirmed by Lucas's results. However, in a number of cases the variables on the right-hand side of equation (6.5) account for rather a small proportion of the variance of the left-hand side variable, y_{cit}, suggesting that some important influences on y_{cit} have been omitted from the estimating equation.

The second and crucial prediction of equation (6.3) is that those countries in which aggregate demand is volatile should be those countries in which β_1 is estimated to be low. Countries with volatile aggregate demand are identified by Lucas as those countries for which the variance of unanticipated aggregate demand, ν, is high. To test this prediction rigorously Lucas should estimate equation (6.6) for his 18 countries jointly, imposing the restriction implied by his model that the β_1 coefficients are negatively related to the estimated variances of ν. The Lucas model could then be tested along the lines suggested in chapter 3, by testing for the validity of this restriction. In fact, Lucas adopts a much less rigorous approach. He tabulates for each country the estimated variance of the unanticipated aggregate demand term, ν, and that country's estimated value for β_1. If the prediction is correct then a negative relationship should be observed. Lucas claims that such a relationship can be discerned in his data. As an illustration of this negative relationship Lucas notes that for the US his estimate of the variance of aggregate demand is 0.00064, while for Argentina it is more than 20 times higher at 0.01555; the estimate of β_1 for the US is 0.910, whereas for Argentina it is much lower at 0.011.

One problem with the Lucas study, recognized by Lucas (1973, p. 331), is that his 18 countries fall into two distinct groups. The first group consists of 16 countries in which aggregate demand has been reasonably stable; the second consists of two countries – Argentina and Paraguay – in which aggregate demand has been highly expansive and volatile. The apparent negative relationship between Lucas's estimate of the aggregate demand volatility for any country and his estimate of β_1 for the country is heavily dependent upon these two highly volatile countries. To base conclusions on such a small sample is unsatisfactory. However, a number of other authors (for example, Alberro, 1981; Kormendi and Meguire, 1984) have employed something like the Lucas approach using data from more countries, and have generally found much the same result as that reported in Lucas.

Despite the slightly unsatisfactory nature of the data set used by Lucas, and although the tests he applied were hardly rigorous, his paper was influential in that it was one of the first to show that certain of the predictions made by the rational expectations hypothesis were not entirely inconsistent with the data. We shall consider in chapter 7 a more fundamental econometric problem with the Lucas study which casts doubt on the interpretation which Lucas puts on his results.

6.2   THE BARRO TEST

A second series of influential studies that gave support to the model presented in chapter 4 – this time to its prediction that only unanticipated changes in aggregate demand have real output effects – were those of Barro (1977a, 1978a; see also Barro and Rush, 1980). The starting point of Barro's model is the assumption that the rate of growth of the quantity of money in an economy is the prime determinant of the rate of growth of aggregate demand in that economy. The distinction drawn in chapter 4 between the predictable and unpredictable components of aggregate demand can be easily translated into a distinction between the predictable and unpredictable components of monetary growth. In particular, if the quantity of money is the prime determinant of aggregate demand, it follows from the analysis in chapter 4 that the predictable component of the rate of growth of the quantity of money will have no effect on any real variable such as the level of output or the level of unemployment; only the unpredictable or random component of monetary growth will affect real variables.

In accordance with the theory of rational expectations, Barro identifies the predictable component of monetary growth as that part of the process determining monetary growth which could have been predicted on the basis of the information available at the time. His initial task then is to identify this process. In his original paper

Barro (1977a) used annual data for the US covering the period from 1941 to 1973 and, in contrast to Lucas (1973), who after all was considering a much larger number of countries, Barro investigated the process determining monetary growth in some detail. In accordance with certain theoretical considerations and after some empirical experimentation, Barro obtained the following fairly complex equation as his best estimate of the process determining the annual rate of growth of the quantity of money over the period 1941–73:

$$\hat{DM}_t = 0.087 + 0.24\,DM_{t-1} + 0.35\,DM_{t-2} + 0.082\,FEDV_t$$
$$+ 0.027\,UN_{t-1} \qquad (6.7)$$

where $\hat{DM}_t$ is the rate of growth of the quantity of money predicted by the process shown in equation (6.7) to occur in period t, and DM_{t-i} is the actual rate of growth of the quantity of money in period $t - i$. The rate of growth is defined logarithmically, that is $DM_t = \log M_t - \log M_{t-1}$, where M_t is the annual average of the M1 definition of the US money stock; $FEDV_t$ is a measure of federal government expenditure relative to 'normal', and UN_t is a measure of unemployment, defined as $\log[U/(1 - U)]$, where U is the annual average unemployment rate.

So, according to Barro's estimate, the predictable component of money growth, $\hat{DM}_t$, depends upon the following:

1 $FEDV_t$, a measure of the deviation of government expenditure from its normal level. Barro's argument for the inclusion of this variable is that if government expenditure is equal to its normal level, it will tend to be financed by orthodox taxation, but if it is, say, abnormally high it is more likely to be financed by measures which increase the rate of monetary growth. The exact method by which Barro measures normal government expenditure is not vital for our purposes: essentially, it is through a regression of actual expenditure on its own lagged values.
2 UN_{t-1}, a lagged measure of unemployment. Barro argues that the presence of this variable reflects the counter-cyclical response of money to the level of economic activity. When unemployment is high the US authorities have tended to respond by allowing monetary policy to accelerate.
3 Two lagged money growth terms to pick up any elements of serial dependence or lagged adjustment not captured by the other explanatory variables.

It should be emphasized that equation (6.7) is the result obtained from an ordinary least-squares (OLS) regression of actual monetary growth, DM_t, on the variables on the right hand-side. It amounts to the 'best' statistical description of the process determining DM_t which Barro could find for the period covered by his data. Because of this Barro treats $\hat{DM}_t$ as the best prediction that could be made by rational agents of the value of DM_t. Thus $\hat{DM}_t$ is identified by Barro as his estimate of the rationally anticipated component of DM_t, or $E_{t-1} DM_t$. In other words, Barro assumes that rational agents over the period were aware that the rate of growth of the quantity of money was being determined by the process described in equation (6.7), and were using their knowledge of that process and the coefficients involved in it to predict future monetary growth.

For this assumption to be consistent with rational expectations, equation (6.7) must exhibit three key characteristics: first, the variables on the right-hand side of equation (6.7) should include all those which exert an important impact on monetary growth. In fact, the right-hand side variables in equation (6.7) account for about 90 per cent of the movements in DM, so this criterion seems likely to be satisfied. Second, the component of DM which this equation does not account for should not exhibit any pattern for, if it did, then rational agents would exploit that pattern to improve their forecasts. Barro presents some evidence that no such pattern exists: this evidence is from the Durbin–Watson statistic (see Johnston, 1984, pp. 314–17) which tests the null hypothesis that the error in predicting DM in any period t made by equation (6.7) is unrelated to the error made in the previous period. From the Durbin–Watson statistic which Barro reports one cannot reject the null hypothesis (although, strictly speaking, the Durbin–Watson test is not applicable because of the presence of the lagged dependent variable). The third key characteristic is that the actual value of all the variables which according to equation (6.7) determine $\hat{DM}_t$ should be known at the end of period $t - 1$; otherwise they cannot be used to predict DM_t. In all cases except $FEDV$ this criterion is satisfied since all other variables are dated $t - 1$ or earlier, and we assume that such variables are in agents' information sets. But $FEDV$ is a currently dated variable and so, strictly, should not be included in equation (6.7). Barro (1977a, fn. 9) acknowledges this criticism but argues that the principal movements in *FEDV*, which are dominated by changes in wartime activity, would be known to agents in advance. The role of *FEDV* is explored critically by Pesaran (1982), whose study is considered in more detail in chapter 7.

Having obtained a measure of anticipated monetary growth, Barro computes the unanticipated component of monetary growth in each period as the difference between actual monetary growth in the period and the anticipated component of monetary growth in that period; that is, $D\hat{M}R_t = DM_t - D\hat{M}_t$. To put this another way, $D\hat{M}R$ is the estimated residual from the OLS regression, the coefficients of which are shown in equation (6.7) and the dependent variable of which is actual monetary growth DM_t.

To test the prediction that the unpredictable component of monetary growth affects real variables, Barro first regresses the level of unemployment on the current and lagged values of his $D\hat{M}R$ variable and on two other variables which are seen as influencing the natural rate of unemployment. (The presence of the lagged $D\hat{M}R$'s is taken to reflect the presence of some 'propagation mechanism' such as those described in chapter 5.) Thus Barro carries out an OLS regression of the following form:

$$UN_t = \beta_0 + \beta_1 D\hat{M}R_t + \beta_2 D\hat{M}R_{t-1} + \beta_3 D\hat{M}R_{t-2} + \beta_4 MIL_t$$

$$+ \beta_5 MINW_t + \xi_t \tag{6.8}$$

where ξ_t is the equation error term; MIL = (military personnel)/ (male population aged 15–44), for years in which selective military draft law was in effect, and $MIL = 0$ for the non-selective draft-law years; and $MINW$ is the minimum wage level.

The rationale for including *MIL* is that conscription works towards reducing the unemployment rate if individuals are more likely to be drafted into the services if they are unemployed. The variable *MINW* measures the impact of minimum wage legislation on the unemployment rate. The number of lagged $D\hat{M}R$ terms that enter into equation (6.8) are determined empirically by Barro; that is, he only retains lagged $D\hat{M}R$ terms the coefficients of which are significantly different from zero. One would expect that if the unpredictable growth in the money stock were positive, then output would rise and unemployment fall. Thus one would expect to observe negative coefficients on the current and lagged $D\hat{M}R$'s.

Notice that Barro assumes that $FEDV_t$ and UN_{t-1} do not exert an independent influence on UN_t. This is an example of the 'exclusion restrictions' discussed in chapter 3.

The results of carrying out an OLS regression of equation (6.8) using annual US data from 1946 to 1973 were:

$$\hat{UN}_t = -3.07 - 5.8\,\hat{DMR}_t - 12.1\,\hat{DMR}_{t-1} - 4.2\,\hat{DMR}_{t-2}$$
$$\quad\;\;(0.15)\;\;(2.1)\qquad\quad(1.9)\qquad\qquad(1.9)$$

$$-4.7\,MIL_t + 0.95\,MINW_t \qquad R^2 = 0.78 \quad DW = 1.96$$
$$(0.08)\qquad(0.46)$$

$$(6.9)$$

Estimated standard errors are in parentheses.

Notice that, as the theory suggest, the unpredictable monetary growth variables have significant negative effects on the level of unemployment. The values of the student's 't' test statistics, for a test of the null hypothesis that the coefficients on the $\hat{DMR}$ variables are zero, are 2.8 for $\hat{DMR}_t$, 6.4 for $\hat{DMR}_{t-1}$ and 2.2 for $\hat{DMR}_{t-2}$. These values are to be compared with 2.07, the critical value at the 5 per cent significance level under the 't' distribution with 22 degrees of freedom. So we can reject the hypothesis that each of the coefficients on the DMR variables are zero, and conclude that current $\hat{DMR}$ and up to two lags in $\hat{DMR}$ had a significant impact on the unemployment rate. Thus the first part of the prediction which Barro set out to test appears to be confirmed by these results – unpredictable monetary growth does affect a real variable in the way suggested. Notice also that the coefficients on the $\hat{DMR}$ variables imply that the lag pattern has a triangular shape with the strongest effect, -12.1, occurring after a one-year lag and then dying away.

Next, Barro tests the proposition that it is *only* the unpredictable part of money growth that influences the rate of unemployment. He does this by including total money growth, DM, in the unemployment equation as well as the unanticipated component, $\hat{DMR}$; that is, equation (6.8) becomes:

$$UN_t = \beta_0 + \beta_1\,\hat{DMR}_t + \beta_2\,\hat{DMR}_{t-1} + \beta_3\,\hat{DMR}_{t-2} + \beta_4\,MIL_t$$
$$+\,\beta_5\,MINW_t + \gamma_1\,DM_t + \gamma_2\,DM_{t-1} + \gamma_3\,DM_{t-2} + \omega_t$$

$$(6.10)$$

where ω_t is the equation error term.

The null hypothesis that $\gamma_1 = \gamma_2 = \gamma_3 = 0$ can then be tested by using the F distribution as explained in chapter 3. Barro obtains a value of 1.4 for his test statistic, which is less than the critical value under the F distribution with 3 and 19 degrees of freedom at the 5 per cent significance level. So the null hypothesis that the γ coefficients are all zero cannot be rejected, and therefore neither the current nor the lagged DM's appear to have any influence on the rate of unemployment. Notice that this test is equivalent to testing whether the *anticipated* component of monetary growth has an additional effect on unemployment over and above the effect of the $D\hat{M}R$'s. To see this substitute $DM_t = D\hat{M}_t + D\hat{M}R_t$ into equation (6.10) to give:

$$UN_t = \beta_0 + [\beta_1 + \gamma_1]D\hat{M}R_t + [\beta_2 + \gamma_2]D\hat{M}R_{t-1}$$
$$+ [\beta_3 + \gamma_3]D\hat{M}R_{t-2} + \beta_4 MIL_t + \beta_5 MINW_t$$
$$+ \gamma_1 D\hat{M}_t + \gamma_2 D\hat{M}_{t-1} + \gamma_3 D\hat{M}_{t-2} + \omega_t \qquad (6.11)$$

So including current and lagged total money growth in the output equation and testing the null hypothesis that the coefficients on these variables are all zero is exactly equivalent to including current and lagged predictable components of money growth in the output equation and testing for zero coefficients on these variables. That is, constraining the γ coefficients to zero in equation (6.11) will produce exactly the same sum of square residuals as in equation (6.10) when the γ coefficients are constrained to zero.

Barro's statistical tests all seemed to support one of the main predictions made by the simple rational expectations model developed in chapter 4: that unpredictable monetary growth is important in the determination of the level of unemployment while predictable monetary growth is irrelevant.

In subsequent papers Barro (Barro, 1978a; Barro and Rush, 1980) extended the analysis in two directions. First, he examined the influence of predictable and unpredictable monetary growth on real output rather than unemployment: he found evidence here too that only the unpredictable component of monetary growth affected real output, a positive monetary surprise leading to a rise in output above its natural level. Second, he introduced a further equation – a price equation – and found that, as the rational expectations theory predicts, an anticipated rise in monetary growth, of say χ per cent, leads to an immediate χ per cent rise in the price level, whereas a similar unpredictable rise in monetary growth leads initially to a less than χ per cent rise in the price level.

In general then, Barro's results appear to represent a small but significant body of evidence in support of the sort of rational expectations macro-economic model developed in chapter 4.

One criticism of Barro's approach to the estimation and testing of the rational expectations model is that he employs a two-stage estimation procedure and this is not statistically efficient. That is, he first carries out an OLS regression of monetary growth on a number of other variables – the *DM* equation – and obtains the residuals from this equation; then, in a second stage, uses these residuals, the $D\hat{M}R$'s, in an OLS regression in which unemployment or output is the dependent variable. Such a procedure is not fully efficient in that it does not use all the information contained in the model. In particular, it fails to take account of its cross-equation restrictions. It therefore bypasses one of the main methods of testing the rational expectations hypothesis which we explained in chapter 3, namely testing the restrictions it imposes. An asymptotically efficient and more fruitful estimation procedure would involve the estimation of all coefficients *jointly*, imposing the cross-equation restrictions ('asymptotically' means 'as the sample size tends to infinity'). To explain this point (which Barro (1977a) recognizes in a footnote, p. 107 fn. 15) and also to demonstrate that Barro's results appear to hold true for countries other than the US, we shall outline a model similar to Barro's which Attfield, Demery and Duck (1981a) (henceforth ADD) applied to UK annual data for the period 1946–77. Their model consists of the following equations:

$$DM_t = \alpha_0 + \alpha_1 DM_{t-1} + \alpha_3 DM_{t-2} + \alpha_3 B_t + \alpha_4 S_{t-1} + DMR_t$$

$$y_t = \beta_0 + \beta_1 DMR_t + \beta_2 DMR_{t-1} + \beta_3 DMR_{t-2} + \beta_4 DMR_{t-3}$$

$$+ \beta_5 t + \beta_6 VP_t + \xi_t \qquad (6.12)$$

where *DM* is the rate of growth of the money stock, *B* is the real value of the government borrowing requirement and *S* is the real current account balance of payments surplus. In the output equation *y* is the log of real GDP, *t* is a time trend and *VP* is a measure of the variability of the inflation rate; DMR_t and ξ_t are equation errors.

The first equation in this model is an estimate of the process that monetary growth followed over the period considered. The second is an output equation in which the variables t and VP determine the natural rate of output. The rationale for the inclusion of B in the money equation is that governments may finance expenditures which they are reluctant to pay for through taxes by methods which expand the money stock. Since a given nominal value for the borrowing requirement implies a progressively lower value for DM, the appropriate 'fiscal' influence on monetary growth is the real value of the borrowing requirement (B). ADD argue that their method of dealing with the relationship between fiscal and monetary policy is simpler than that used by Barro (1977a), in which the equivalent fiscal variable is government expenditure relative to its normal level. The use of B avoids the problem of estimating the normal level of government expenditure which, ADD argue, Barro handles inconsistently since he assumes that agents form their expectations about normal government expenditure using an adaptive expectations mechanism, while assuming that agents form their expectations rationally elsewhere in the system. The justification for the inclusion of the lagged real current account balance of payments surplus, S_{t-1}, is that it reflects the concern of successive UK governments with the external balance; a large surplus encourages (or at least allows) a more expansionary monetary policy, while a large deficit tends to bring about a contractionary one.

The structure of the output equation reflects the assumptions that the natural level of output is a function of two variables: time, t, and a measure of the variability of the inflation rate, VP. The time trend accounts for the effects of a constant natural rate of growth of output while VP allows for the possibility that the efficiency of the economy, and hence the natural level of output, is reduced by a variable inflation rate. ADD suggest that the reasons efficiency might be impaired in periods of variable inflation are that the price system fails to transmit as efficiently the information on relative prices needed to coordinate economic plans, that the optimum wage and price contract length shortens, making existing arrangements inappropriate, and that government interference in markets is likely to be increased.

From the money growth equation in (6.12) we have:

$$DMR_{t-i} = DM_{t-i} - \alpha_0 - \alpha_1 DM_{t-1-i} - \alpha_2 DM_{t-2-i} - \alpha_3 B_{t-i}$$
$$- \alpha_4 S_{t-1-i} \tag{6.13}$$

Substituting the expressions for DMR_{t-1}, DMR_{t-2} and DMR_{t-3} into the output equation in (6.12) gives the two-equation model:

$$DM_t = \alpha_0 + \alpha_1 DM_{t-1} + \alpha_2 DM_{t-2} + \alpha_3 B_t + \alpha_4 S_{t-1} + DMR_t,$$

$$y_t = \beta_0 + \beta_2 [DM_{t-1} - \alpha_0 - \alpha_1 DM_{t-2} - \alpha_2 DM_{t-3} - \alpha_3 B_{t-1}$$
$$- \alpha_4 S_{t-2}] + \beta_3 [DM_{t-2} - \alpha_0 - \alpha_1 DM_{t-3} - \alpha_2 DM_{t-4}$$
$$- \alpha_3 B_{t-2} - \alpha_4 S_{t-3}] + \beta_4 [DM_{t-3} - \alpha_0 - \alpha_1 DM_{t-4}$$
$$- \alpha_2 DM_{t-5} - \alpha_3 B_{t-3} - \alpha_4 S_{t-4}] + \beta_5 t + \beta_6 VP_t$$
$$+ \beta_1 DMR_t + \xi_t \tag{6.14}$$

From the model in equation (6.14) it is possible to explain the cross-equation restrictions. Take, for example, the coefficient estimated on B_t in the DM_t equations: this is an estimate of α_3. But the coefficients estimated on B_{t-1}, B_{t-2} and B_{t-3} in the output equation are estimates, respectively, of $-\beta_2 \alpha_3$, $-\beta_3 \alpha_3$ and $-\beta_4 \alpha_3$ and so we can deduce from these four estimated coefficients estimates of β_2, β_3 and β_4. Similarly, by taking the coefficient estimated on S_{t-1} in the DM_t equation, α_4, and the coefficients estimated on S_{t-2}, S_{t-3} and S_{t-4} in the output equation, which are estimates of $-\beta_2 \alpha_4$, $-\beta_3 \alpha_4$ and $-\beta_4 \alpha_4$, we can deduce other estimates of β_2, β_3 and β_4. The two sets of estimates of β_2, β_3 and β_4 should, in large samples, be approximately the same, if the restrictions are correct. This restriction – that the two ways of obtaining estimates of β_2, β_3 and β_4 should give the same results – is an example of the cross-equation restrictions implied by the model in equation (6.14). Barro's procedure ignores such restrictions entirely because he estimates the monetary growth and real output equations separately and does not impose the restrictions. There is therefore no guarantee that the restrictions which are implied by his model will be satisfied. As we have said, an asymptotically efficient procedure would estimate the coefficients in both equations jointly, imposing all the cross-equation restrictions.

ADD (1981a) employ such a procedure – full information maximum likelihood – to estimate the model in equation (6.14) where the current monetary shock DMR_t times its coefficient β_1 is relegated to the error term in the output equation. That is, if we let the whole error term in the output equation be η_t, then $\eta_t = \xi_t + \beta_1 DMR_t$. The variance–covariance matrix of equation errors is then:

$$E\begin{bmatrix} DMR_t \\ \eta_t \end{bmatrix} [DMR_t, \eta_t] \equiv \sum \equiv \begin{bmatrix} \sigma^2_{DMR} & \beta_1 \sigma^2_{DMR} \\ \beta_1 \sigma^2_{DMR} & \beta_1 \sigma^2_{DMR} + \sigma^2_\xi \end{bmatrix}$$

where σ^2_{DMR} is the variance of DMR_t and σ^2_ξ is the variance of ξ_t and, to ensure that the structural parameters in the model are identified, it is assumed that the covariance between DMR_t and ξ_t is zero. ADD obtain maximum likelihood estimates by maximizing the criterion

$$-|n/2| \log \left[\det \left(\hat{\sum} \right) \right] = -|n/2| (\log \hat\sigma^2_{DMR} + \log \sigma^2_\xi) \qquad (6.15)$$

with respect to the α_i's and β_i's in the structure in equation (6.14), where n is the sample size. Notice that an estimate of β_1 can be obtained by dividing the top right-hand element of the estimated Σ matrix, that is the estimate of the $\text{cov}(DMR_t, \eta_t)$, by the top left-hand element of the covariance matrix.

ADD obtain the following estimates for their model:

$$\hat{DM}_t = 0.56 + 0.46\, DM_{t-1} + 0.33\, DM_{t-2} - 0.001\, B_t$$
$$\quad (1.0) \quad (0.17) \qquad (0.22) \qquad\qquad (0.0004)$$
$$+ 0.0027\, S_{t-1},$$
$$(0.008) \qquad\qquad\qquad\qquad\qquad\qquad (6.16)$$

$$\hat{y}_t = 10.68 + 0.002\, DMR_{t-1} + 0.002\, DMR_{t-2} + 0.003\, DMR_{t-3}$$
$$(0.016)\,(0.001) \qquad\qquad (0.001) \qquad\qquad (0.0009)$$
$$+ 0.025\, t - 0.025\, VP_t,$$
$$(0.0007) \quad (0.009)$$

$$R^2 = 0.994, \qquad DW = 2.21, \qquad \hat\beta_1 = 0.0017$$
$$\qquad\qquad\qquad\qquad\qquad\qquad\qquad (0.0008)$$

where asymptotic standard errors are given in parentheses and a '^' denotes an estimate of a variable or a coefficient.

In the money equation ADD did try a number of other variables such as the lagged inflation rate, nominal and real rates of interest and real income (as a deviation from trend) to obtain the most satisfactory explanation of the monetary growth process. The variables in equation (6.16) proved to be the most suitable determinants of monetary growth.

In the output equation the unpredictable monetary growth variables do have a significant, positive effect on real output, although the impacts of DMR_{t-1} and DMR_{t-2} are less significant than Barro found for the US. Notice also that the estimates for the UK do not display the strong triangular pattern found by Barro in the US.

ADD then tested the hypothesis that it is *only* unpredictable money growth that has an impact on real output by inserting actual money growth into the output equation in (6.14) for the periods t, $t - 1$, $t - 2$ and $t - 3$, and comparing the likelihood from this model with the model in equation (6.16). The resulting test statistic is 5.49, which has to be compared with 9.49, the critical value under the chi-square distribution at the 5 per cent significance level with 4 degrees of freedom. So the null hypothesis that it is only unpredictable monetary growth which influences real output cannot be rejected.

The above tests are carried out by estimating the system as a whole and not, as in Barro (1977a), by estimating separately the money growth equation and the unemployment (or output) equation. Since all the coefficients are estimated simultaneously, the estimated model (6.16), which has all the cross-equation restrictions imposed, can be compared with another model which has the same variables on the right-hand side of each equation but in which the cross-equation restrictions are relaxed; that is, the coefficients on each variable are freely estimated as

$$DM_t = \pi_0 + \pi_1 DM_{t-1} + \pi_2 DM_{t-2} + \pi_3 B_t + \pi_4 S_{t-1} + \nu_{1t},$$

$$y_t = \pi_5 + \pi_6 DM_{t-1} + \pi_7 DM_{t-2} + \pi_8 DM_{t-3} + \pi_9 B_{t-2}$$
$$\quad + \pi_{10} S_{t-2} + \pi_{11} DM_{t-4} + \pi_{12} B_{t-2} + \pi_{13} S_{t-3} +$$
$$\quad + \pi_{14} DM_{t-5} + \pi_{15} B_{t-3} + \pi_{16} S_{t-4} + \pi_{17} t + \pi_{18} VP_t$$
$$\quad + \nu_{2t} \tag{6.17}$$

where ν_{it} are equation errors.

Since in equation (6.16) we have relaxed the cross-equation restrictions implied by the rational expectations model (6.14), we can carry out a likelihood ratio test of the restrictions in equation (6.14) by comparing its likelihood with that of equation (6.17). As explained in chapter 3, if the likelihood ratio test suggests that the cross-equation restrictions are not valid, it implies that the model which imposes them is invalid. For their UK data ADD carried out such a test and obtained a test statistic of 17.93 which has to be compared with a critical chi-square value of 15.5 at the 5 per cent level and 20.1 at the 1 per cent level, with 8 degrees of freedom. Given that they are working with a small sample and that the likelihood ratio test is a large sample test, ADD do not consider the evidence to be strong enough to reject the null hypothesis.

ADD (1981b) further extend this research by estimating a three-equation quarterly model of unanticipated monetary growth, output and the price level for the UK over the period 1963–78. Apart from the use of quarterly data, the main difference in this study is that the current monetary shock is included in the output equation rather than being incorporated in the error term, in what – ADD demonstrate – is an asymptotically efficient estimation procedure. That is, they show that the coefficients of the model are still identified in this case provided that it is assumed that the equation errors in the money growth equation and in the output equation are contemporaneously uncorrelated. They reach broadly the same conclusion as in the paper using annual data: monetary growth affects real output only if it is unpredictable, and the cross-equation restrictions imposed by the model cannot be rejected. Thus the ADD (1981a, b) results lend support to the findings of Barro for the US.

6.3　THE LEIDERMAN TEST

Soon after the publication of Barro's studies it was pointed out by Leiderman (1980) that Barro's model embodied two important but separate hypotheses – rational expectations and what is called structural neutrality – and that it was possible to test for rational expectations separately, and then, given rational expectations, test for structural neutrality. The structural neutrality hypothesis in the Barro model is simply the assumption that any growth in the quantity of money which is anticipated, whether or not those anticipations are formed rationally, will not affect the level of real output or unemployment. To understand Leiderman's argument clearly, consider the following simplified version of the Barro model:

$$DM_t = E_{t-1} DM_t + DMR_t,$$

$$E_{t-1} DM_t = \alpha_1 DM_{t-1} + \alpha_1 DM_{t-2} + \alpha_3 FEDV_t,$$

$$UN_t = \beta_1 [DM_t - E_{t-1} DM_t] + \xi_t \tag{6.18}$$

The structural neutrality hypothesis is embodied in this model because the coefficient on $E_{t-1} DM_t$ in the unemployment equation has a coefficient which is equal but opposite in sign to the coefficient on DM_t. Thus a rise in monetary growth which is anticipated will have no effect on the level of unemployment.

If it is now assumed that the coefficients on DM_t and $E_{t-1} DM_t$ in the unemployment equation are different, so that we are *not* assuming structural neutrality, we can rewrite the unemployment equation as:

$$UN_t = \beta_{11} DM_t - \beta_{12} E_{t-1} DM_t + \xi_t \tag{6.19}$$

A test for structural neutrality therefore reduces to the simple test of the null hypothesis $\beta_{11} = \beta_{12} = \beta_1$. If this equality restriction is not supported by the data, we can *reject* the neutrality postulate.

We can therefore test for rational expectations by substituting for $E_{t-1} DM_t$ and DM_t into equation (6.19) to give the system:

$$DM_t = \alpha_1 DM_{t-1} + \alpha_1 DM_{t-2} + \alpha_3 FEDV_t + DMR_t,$$

$$UN_t = [\beta_{11} - \beta_{12}][\alpha_1 DM_{t-1} + \alpha_1 DM_{t-2} + \alpha_3 FEDV_t] + \xi_t$$

$$+ \beta_{11} DMR_t \tag{6.20}$$

where we have allowed the term $\beta_{11} DMR_t$ to accumulate in the equation error in the unemployment equation in (6.20). (Notice that this means that the covariance between the equation errors in (6.20) is $\beta_{11} \sigma_{DMR}^2$, which is unlikely to be zero.) The equations in (6.20) embody the hypothesis of rational expectations but *not* the assumption of structural neutrality. Assume that we estimated the unrestricted version of equation (6.20); that is,

$$DM_t = \pi_1 DM_{t-1} + \pi_1 DM_{t-2} + \pi_3 FEDV_t + \xi_{1t}$$

$$UN_t = \pi_4 DM_{t-1} + \pi_5 DM_{t-2} + \pi_6 FEDV_t + \xi_{2t} \qquad (6.21)$$

where the π_i's are coefficients and ξ_{it} are equation errors.

In equation (6.21) there are six unrestricted coefficients. In the system in equation (6.20), however, there are only five coefficients to be estimated, namely α_1, α_2, α_3, β_{11} and β_{12}. The rational expectations hypothesis thus places one restriction on the reduced form. A test of the rational expectations hypothesis can therefore be constructed by computing the likelihood from the equations in (6.20) and the likelihood from (6.21), and comparing the likelihood ratio test statistic with the chi-square distribution with, for this example, one degree of freedom.

If the rational expectations hypothesis is not rejected by this test we can test the structural neutrality hypothesis by comparing the likelihood from the system in equation (6.20) with the likelihood from the same system with the restriction imposed that β_{11} equals β_{12}. Leiderman carried out this test using Barro's (1977a) data set (in which the real variable is unemployment). He uses a full information maximum likelihood technique and concludes that 'the restrictions implied by the constituent hypothesis of rational expectations and "structural neutrality", as well as by the joint neutrality hypothesis, are not rejected by the sample information at the usual significance levels of five and one per cent' (Leiderman, 1980, p. 80).

6.4   THE LUCAS AND BARRO APPROACHES COMBINED

The Lucas (1973) paper tests one of the major predictions of the rational expectations model developed in chapter 4 and summarized in equation (6.1) by using cross-country data; the Barro studies test the other major prediction of that model using data from a single country. A natural extension of the two approaches is to combine them and test both predictions at the same time. This has been done in a number of papers and in this sections we outline the results of a study by Attfield and Duck (1983) (henceforth AD).

In simplified form, their model consists of the following three equations:

$$DM_t = \alpha_i Z_{it} + DMR_{it}, \qquad y_{cit} = \beta_i[DM_{it} - \alpha_i Z_{it}] + \xi_{it},$$
$$(6.22,\ 6.23)$$

$$\beta_i = \phi/[\phi + \sigma^2_{DMRi}] \tag{6.24}$$

where DM_{it} is the rate of growth of the money stock in country i; Z_{it} is a variable, the value of which is known at the end of the previous period and which influences monetary growth; α_i and β_i are coefficients for country i; DMR_{it} and ξ_{it} are normally and independently distributed random errors, with zero means and variances σ^2_{DMRi} and $\sigma^2_{\xi i}$ respectively; and ϕ is a constant.

The first of these equations merely states that for any country the quantity of money grows in accordance with an identifiable but stochastic process. This process may differ from country to country; that is why the coefficient α_i is indexed on i. The second equation embodies the structural neutrality and rational expectations hypothesis: for each country only the unpredictable component of monetary growth causes output to deviate from its natural rate. These two equations then are essentially the Barro model applied to a number of different countries.

Equation (6.24) is a particular form of the relationship derived in chapter 4 and tested in Lucas (1973). The derivation of the specific form need not concern us. Its essential implication is that the coefficient linking the deviation of output from its natural rate to the unpredictable component of monetary growth depends *negatively* on the variance of unpredictable monetary growth.

The three equations taken together embody *both* of the major predictions outlined in the rational expectations macroeconomic model developed in chapter 4. To test the two predictions, AD test the restrictions implied in equations (6.22)–(6.24). To see what these are, first rewrite equations (6.22)–(6.24) as a two-equation model:

$$DM_{it} = \alpha_i Z_{it} + DMR_{it},$$

$$y_{cit} = [\phi/(\phi + \sigma^2_{DMRi})][DM_{it} - \alpha_i Z_{it}] + \xi_{it} \tag{6.25}$$

For any single country there are no restrictions imposed on equation (6.25) by equation (6.24). To see this, imagine estimating the DM equation in equation (6.25) by OLS to obtain an estimate of α_i ($\hat{\alpha}_i$), and using the sum of squared residuals from this equation to construct an estimate of σ^2_{DMRi}. The estimate of α_i could then be substituted into the output equation in (6.25) and, from the regression of y_{cit} on $(DM_{it} - \alpha_i Z_{it})$, a unique estimate of ϕ obtained by using the estimate of σ^2_{DMRi}. But if there are two countries used in the sample then, since ϕ is assumed to be a constant across countries, that is it is not indexed on i, there will be a restriction on the model. To see this, imagine repeating for a second country the process just described for the first. Since ϕ is a constant across countries you should obtain the same estimate of it in this second case. Thus when estimating the model (6.25) using data from two countries, the restriction must be imposed that in each case the estimate of ϕ must be the same. As the number of countries in the sample increases, so does the complexity of the restrictions imposed by equation (6.25). In fact, within the full AD model there are restrictions across equations within countries, between variances and coefficients within countries and between coefficients across all countries.

To test the restrictions on the model, AD use annual data for the period 1951–78 from 11 different countries (the US, the Netherlands, Canada, Denmark, Australia, the UK, the Philippines, Columbia, El Salvador, Guatemala and Argentina). The particular countries were selected because an adequate explanation of monetary growth was possible on the basis of a simple and common process. The process consisted of lagged government real expenditure and, for some countries, the lagged rate of monetary growth. For the output equation AD assume that real output is a function of time, its own lagged value and current or one-period lagged unanticipated monetary growth (AD, 1983, p. 448). They estimate the model using maximum likelihood techniques and find that unanticipated monetary growth does generally have a positive effect on real output. Of the 11 countries, 8 have estimates of β that are significantly positive. In addition, a likelihood ratio test of the cross-equation restrictions does not reject the restrictions at the 1 per cent significance level for any of these countries. These results support the prediction that the unpredictable component of monetary growth exerts a significant influence on real output.

AD then test the prediction that it is *only* the unpredictable component of DM that has an impact on real output in the way described in section 6.2. They find that the null hypothesis that the

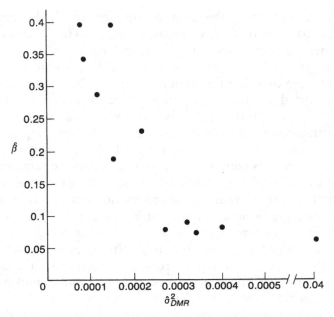

FIGURE 6.1   The influence of monetary shocks and their volatility.

anticipated component of monetary growth exerts no influence on real output cannot be rejected for any country at the 1 per cent level.

As a preliminary test of the prediction that the larger the variance of *DMR*, the smaller the coefficient β, AD present a figure which we reproduce in figure 6.1, which is a plot of the 11 estimates of the coefficient on unanticipated monetary growth in the output equations, the β_i's, against the corresponding estimates of σ^2_{DMRi}, the unpredictability of monetary growth as measured by the sum of squared residuals in the money growth equations.

From the points plotted in figure 6.1, the relationship between β and the variability of the unanticipated component of monetary growth is a downward-sloping one. Such a figure gives the same sort of support to the prediction that the volatility of aggregate demand and its impact on real output are negatively related, as was found by Lucas (1973). AD develop a much more formal likelihood ratio test of this relationship by estimating the model across all countries with the β_i's unrestricted and then with the β_i's restricted, according to the formula given in equation (6.24). For details of the derivation of the test statistic, interested readers are referred to AD (1983, p. 446). The result of the test was that the restrictions imposed by the rational expectations hypothesis on the β_i coefficients could not be rejected.

The overall conclusion of the AD paper is that there is some support for the proposition that monetary growth affects real output only if it is unpredictable, and that the impact on output of unpredictable monetary growth declines the more unpredictable monetary growth becomes. Kormendi and Meguire (1984) reach broadly the same conclusion using a similar model, but with a much larger sample of 47 countries.

6.5 SUMMARY

This chapter has explained and reported the results of two of the most influential empirical studies of the rational expectations hypothesis within a simple macroeconomic model. It has also discussed further applications and some extensions of these models. In general, the results that we have reported in this chapter have been favourable to the rational expectations hypothesis, suggesting at the very least that the usefulness of that hypothesis in one area of macroeconomics cannot be dimissed lightly. But these studies have had their critics, and it is to some of the key criticisms of them that we now turn in chapter 7.

SUGGESTIONS FOR FURTHER READING

Hanson (1980), Koskela and Viren (1980) and Lawrence (1983) are all attempts to apply something like the Lucas (1973) test to different data sets. Wogin (1980) and Demery, Duck and Musgrave (1984) are applications of the Barro model to two other countries, Canada and West Germany respectively. McCallum (1976) and Sargent (1976b) are other attempts to test for rational expectations within a simple macro-model of the economy. Alogoskoufis and Pissarides (1983) and Demery, Duck and Musgrave (1983) concentrate on the price equation in Barro's model, in particular whether there is evidence in the UK that prices are 'sticky'. Tests of policy neutrality exploiting regime-switching for identification are a feature of Bean (1984) and Attfield and Duck (1986).

7

Criticism and Reappraisal of the Lucas and Barro Models

In this chapter we shall examine a number of criticisms and extensions of the Lucas and Barro models. The chapter is in two parts. In the first we examine an important problem with the Barro and Lucas tests, one which, in the case of the Lucas model especially, may considerably weaken the force of the results. Secondly, we shall examine some extensions to the Lucas and Barro tests which are generally unfavourable to the rational expectations hypothesis. We show how, in more recent research, predictable changes in both nominal income growth and monetary growth have been shown to have significant output and unemployment effects, contrary to the central propositions of both the Barro and Lucas models. We show that some of this research has raised doubts over the importance of monetary factors in explanations of the business cycle.

7.1 THE EFFECT OF MEASUREMENT ERROR AND MODEL MISSPECIFICATION

In this section we shall examine two related objections to the Lucas and Barro results. The first concerns the possibility that the aggregate demand variable is measured with error. We shall show that the results obtained by Lucas in particular may be due to the fact that nominal income growth is measured with error – an error which varies from country to country. Secondly – and more importantly – we shall investigate the implications of choosing the wrong process determining the behaviour of the aggregate demand variable.

One of the most serious defects in the Lucas (1973) paper is that a simple 'errors in variables' model can produce the same apparent results. If nominal income growth, DX, contains a measurement error, the Lucas results may have little or nothing to do with the prediction of the economic model he was seeking to test. To see the point clearly, consider Lucas's output equation (6.6). For simplicity we will drop the term y_{cit-1} and, for convenience we will drop the country subscripts, so the equation to be estimated becomes

$$y_{ct} = -\beta_1\chi_0 + \beta_1 DX_t + \xi_t \qquad (7.1)$$

where ξ_t is a random error term. Suppose, however, that the 'true' change in nominal income is DX_t^*, and the relationship between the truth and the variable actually measured is

$$DX_t = DX_t^* + \epsilon_t \qquad (7.2)$$

with $DX_t^* = \chi_0 + \nu_t^*$; where ϵ_t is a measurement error with zero mean and which is uncorrelated with DX_t, and ν_t^* is the 'true' unanticipated nominal income growth. Note that the expected mean of both DX and DX^* is χ_0.

Let the true relationship be

$$y_{ct} = -\beta_1\chi_0 + \beta_1 DX_t^* + \omega_t \qquad (7.3)$$

with ω_t assumed to be uncorrelated with DX_t^* and with ϵ_t. Equivalently, we can write

$$y_{ct} = \beta_1\nu_t^* + \omega_t$$

If we substitute $DX_t^* = DX_t - \epsilon_t$ from equation (7.2) into equation (7.3) we obtain

$$y_{ct} = -\beta_1\chi_0 + \beta_1 DX_t - \beta_1\epsilon_t + \omega_t \qquad (7.4)$$

So we can interpret the equation to be estimated in (7.1) as equation (7.4) with $\xi_t = \omega_t - \beta_1\epsilon_t$. The problem is then that the ordinary least-squares estimator of β_1 is (now assuming, to simplify notation, that all variables are measured as deviations from sample means):

$$\hat{\beta}_1 = \sum_1^n DX_t y_{ct} \bigg/ \sum_1^n (DX_t)^2 \qquad (7.5)$$

where n is the sample size.

Since the numerator is $\sum_1^n DX_t y_{ct}$, which equals $\sum_1^n (DX_t^* + \epsilon_t)(\beta_1 DX_t^* + \omega_t)$, taking expectations we obtain:

$$E\left(\sum_1^n DX_t y_{ct}\right) = n\beta_1 \sigma_*^2$$

where σ_*^2 is the variance of DX_t^*. We obtain this expression because the components ϵ_t, DX_t^* and ω_t all have zero covariances. The expectation of the denominator in equation (7.5) is, of course, $n\sigma_{DX}^2$ (where σ_{DX}^2 is the variance of DX_t), so in large samples the ordinary least-squares estimator of β_1 in (7.5) tends to the ratio

$$\beta_1 \sigma_*^2 / \sigma_{DX}^2 \qquad (7.6)$$

That is, because DX_t in equation (7.4) is correlated with the measurement error term ϵ_t, the estimator of β_1 is *biased towards zero* because $\sigma_*^2 / \sigma_{DX}^2$ is greater than zero but less than one. The reason that $0 < \sigma_*^2 / \sigma_{DX}^2 < 1$ is that $\sigma_*^2 / \sigma_{DX}^2$ is the ratio of two positive numbers (variances) and because $\sigma_{DX}^2 = \sigma_*^2 + \sigma_\epsilon^2$, where σ_ϵ^2 is the variance of ϵ_t.

The conclusion from expression (7.6) is that if DX_t is measured with error then we would observe that countries with a value of σ_{DX}^2 which is large relative to σ_*^2 could have a relatively small estimated β_1, not because of Lucas's argument but because the estimator of β_1 is biased towards zero. On the other hand, those countries in which σ_{DX}^2 and σ_*^2 are approximately the same will have little or no downward bias in the estimator of β_1: that is, Lucas's results could have been obtained because 'unstable price countries' such as Argentina have a larger measurement error component in the data on nominal output than in stable price countries such as the US.

This interpretation of Lucas's results is important, because it suggests that even where there is no relationship between the true variance of aggregate demand and β_1, an observed relationship may be found between the measured variance in aggregate demand and the estimated coefficient β_1. However, there is a related and even more important problem with Lucas's test. Some may argue that measurement errors are likely to be relatively small compared with the total variance of the true change in aggregate demand. But even if measurement error did not arise, Lucas's test may still be misleading. This is because he specifies a very simple process determining nominal income growth (see equation (6.4)): one in which aggregate demand change is a constant plus a random, and therefore unpredictable, error term. Reverting now to levels (rather than deviations from means), the rational forecast for DX_t, given information dated $t - 1$, is simply the constant χ_0. The unanticipated component can therefore be written as

$$\nu_t = DX_t - \chi_0 \qquad (7.7)$$

Note that the variance of the unanticipated component is the same as the variance of DX_t, since the variance of the mean must be zero. Suppose that for each country examined, Lucas omitted a variable which influenced DX_t, and which was known to agents at the time they formed an expectation of DX_t. This would imply that the true process determining DX_t is given by

$$DX_t = \chi_0 + \chi_1 Z_{t-1} + \nu_t^* \qquad (7.8)$$

where Z_{t-1} is the variable omitted by Lucas, and where ν_t^* is the true unanticipated change in aggregate demand. Again for simplicity we will assume that Z_{t-1} is a random variable with zero mean, so that χ_0 in equation (7.8) is the same as that given in equation (6.4). The important point to note is that Z_{t-1} is known to agents when they are forecasting DX_t. Solving equation (7.8) for ν_t^* we obtain

$$\nu_t^* = DX_t - \chi_0 - \chi_1 Z_{t-1} \qquad \text{or} \qquad \nu_t^* = \nu_t - \chi_1 Z_{t-1} \qquad (7.9)$$

The 'true' equation is

$$y_{ct} = -\beta_1 \chi_0 + \beta_1 DX_t - \beta_1 \chi_1 Z_{t-1} + \omega_t \qquad (7.10)$$

whereas Lucas estimated

$$y_{ct} = -\beta_1 \chi_0 + \beta_1 DX_t + \xi_t \qquad (7.11)$$

Note that equation (7.10) is equivalent to equation (7.4) with $\chi_1 Z_{t-1}$ equal to ϵ_t. Since higher values of Z_{t-1} will be associated with higher values of DX_t (by equation (7.8)), the results we derived from the 'errors in variable' case will carry over to the case of a wrongly specified nominal income growth process. Countries with a high variance in Z_{t-1}, and hence in DX_t, will tend to have estimated values for β_1 which are lower simply because Lucas failed to account for the influence of Z_{t-1} on DX_t. In this case an omitted variable from equation (7.11) is negatively correlated with the included one, DX_t, leading to incorrect estimates of β_1. By adopting such a simple process for nominal income growth, Lucas's test may be very open to this weakness and his results must be interpreted with caution.

The 'errors in variable' problem also affects the models of Barro and Attfield and Duck. In these models we can treat the problem from the point of view of a misspecification of the monetary growth equation; that is, biases may arise when a variable is omitted from the money growth equations. We write a simplified version of the Barro model as

$$DM = \alpha X + \delta Z + DMR, \qquad y = \beta DMR + \epsilon \qquad (7.12)$$

where we have dropped the t subscript. We will assume in what follows that the value of the parameter α is known. This simplifies the algebra considerably without much loss in generality.

The relationships in equation (7.12) are assumed to be the 'truth'; that is, the true processes which generate monetary growth and output. Now, suppose that when equations (7.12) are estimated, the term δZ is omitted, so that the output equation actually estimated is

$$y = \beta[DM - \alpha X] + \omega \qquad (7.13)$$

where ω is an error term. Since the true output equation from equation (7.12) is

$$y = \beta(DM - \alpha X - \delta Z) + \epsilon$$

we must have, in equation (7.13), that $\omega = \epsilon - \beta\delta Z$. So we can see why a misspecification of the money growth equation – in the sense that a variable is omitted – is the equivalent of an errors in variables problem. It is because the true equation error, DMR, in equation (7.12) is measured incorrectly in equation (7.13), and the measurement error, δZ, enters into a term in the output equation error in equation (7.13). It follows that since the explanatory variable in equation (7.13) is $DM - \alpha X$, which is equal to $\delta Z + DMR$ from equation (7.12), then the explanatory variable and the equation error in equation (7.13) are correlated as they both contain δZ. So, if we use ordinary least squares to estimate the relationships in equation (7.13) we obtain, with variables now measured as deviations from means,

$$\hat{\beta} = \frac{\Sigma(\delta Z + DMR)y}{\Sigma(\delta Z + DMR)^2} = \frac{\Sigma(\delta Z + DMR)(\beta DMR + \epsilon)}{\Sigma(\delta Z + DMR)^2} \qquad (7.14)$$

In large samples, therefore, the estimator of β will tend to

$$\frac{\beta \sigma_{DMR}^2}{\delta^2 \sigma_z^2 + \sigma_{DMR}^2} \tag{7.15}$$

where σ_z^2 and σ_{DMR}^2 are the variances of Z and DMR respectively.

So we have same result as that given in expression (7.6); that the estimator of β is 'biased' towards zero by the ratio $\sigma_{DMR}^2/(\delta^2 \sigma_z^2 + \sigma_{DMR}^2)$, the term $\delta^2 \sigma_z^2$ being, of course, the variance of the measurement error in DMR. Attfield and Duck (1983, p. 447) derive a similar result under the much more general conditions: that α is a vector which has to be estimated; that there are other exogenous variables in both the money and output equations; and that the coefficients in both equations are estimated jointly using the maximum likelihood procedure.

In the context of the Attfield and Duck model, the importance of the expression in (7.15) is that the larger $\delta^2 \sigma_z^2$ is relative to σ_{DMR}^2, the closer the expression in equation (7.15) is to zero. Therefore, even though there is no relationship between β and σ_{DMR}^2 in the true model in equation (7.12), if variables are omitted from the money growth equation we might observe an *apparent* relationship between the estimated β and the estimated error variance obtained from the money growth equation, $\delta^2 \sigma_z^2 + \sigma_{DMR}^2$, in a cross-country sample.

Attfield and Duck argue, however, that the 'bias' could work in the *opposite* direction. First, suppose that in equation (7.15) the variance due to the omitted variable $\delta^2 \sigma_z^2$ is a constant across countries. Then, with β constant, any differences in estimates of β are due solely to variations in σ_{DMR}^2. But an increase in σ_{DMR}^2 in equation (7.15) leads to an *increase* in the estimator of β. If then β really does decline as σ_{DMR}^2 rises according to the formula we developed, that is $\beta = \phi/(\sigma_{DMR}^2 + \phi)$, then in equation (7.15) the estimator of β will tend to

$$\phi \sigma_{DMR}^2/(\sigma_{DMR}^2 + \phi)(\delta^2 \sigma_z^2 + \sigma_{DMR}^2) \tag{7.16}$$

and so, as σ_{DMR}^2 rises, if $\delta^2 \sigma_z^2$ is constant, the apparent relationship between σ_{DMR}^2 and the estimator of β will *understate* the true relationship.

Secondly, suppose that the proportion of the variance of the true unanticipated money growth component, σ_{DMR}^2, to the total variance in the denominator of equation (7.15) is approximately the same from country to country, that is $\sigma^2_{DMR}/(\delta^2\sigma^2_z + \sigma^2_{DMR}) = g$, where g is a constant across countries. In this case, observed differences in the estimator of β, that is $\hat{\beta}$, for different countries must be due to differences in β because $\hat{\beta}$ tends to βg and, since $0 < g < 1$, the relationship between the estimator of β and the estimated error variance from the money growth equation may underestimate the relationship between the true parameter β and σ^2_{DMR}.

In the context of the Barro model that we discussed in chapter 6, it can be seen from equation (7.14) that the estimator of the coefficient on the current monetary shock in the output equation will be biased towards zero by any misspecification of the money growth equation. Attfield (1983) extends the above result to the case in which a current money shock and a number of lagged shocks are included in the output equation, and shows that all the coefficients on the monetary shock variables are biased towards zero by the same factor. Attfield also shows in this paper that tests can still be carried out on the significance of anticipated money growth even where the money growth equation is misspecified in the sense described in this chapter.

7.2   EXTENSIONS TO THE LUCAS MODEL

(a) Structural neutrality

The Lucas model can be criticized along two related lines. First, Lucas did not test for 'structural neutrality'; that is, he did not test whether anticipated changes in aggregate demand had real output effects. Examination of equation (6.6) will suggest how such a test could have been carried out (we repeat the equation here for convenience but drop the country subscript):

$$y_{ct} = -\beta_1\chi_0 + \beta_1 DX_t + \beta_2 y_{ct-1} + \xi_t \tag{6.6}$$

where, to repeat, χ_0 is the mean of DX_t. Since χ_0 can be estimated from the sample of observations on DX_t, the constant term in a regression of output on nominal income growth and lagged output should be the negative of the mean of DX_t times the coefficient on DX_t itself. This restriction could have been imposed and tested (for example, by subtracting χ_0 from DX_t and estimating the equation without an intercept term), but Lucas failed to do so.

Imagine that such a test were performed and the restriction rejected. This would imply that an additional constant term would be significant in equation (6.6) and this could be the effect on output of the anticipated component of nominal income growth (that is, χ_0). An alternative interpretation of the rejection is possible, however: y_{c_t} (which, you recall, is a deviation from the natural level of output) could be measured with a constant error, so that one might expect a constant term which differs from $-\beta_1 \chi_0$ to appear in equation (6.6). In this case it would not be possible to test for structural neutrality. Since anticipated nominal income growth is a constant and since there is a legitimate constant in the output equation, it is impossible to disentangle their separate effects. In formal terms, the coefficient on anticipated nominal income growth is not identified.

The second weakness of the Lucas test concerns his failure to allow for other influences on changes in aggregate demand, influences that rational agents could incorporate into their forecasts of DX_t. An obvious extension of the Lucas test would involve an investigation of such other influences on DX_t in much the same way as Barro and others have done for the money supply. Tests of structural neutrality can be performed once variables influencing DX_t are identified, provided of course that those variables do not also have an independent influence on y_{c_t} (another example of the 'exclusion restrictions' discussed in chapter 3). This extension to the Lucas test was the main feature of an empirical paper by Gordon (1982), to which we now turn.

(b) Gordon's test

Gordon (1982) examined the behaviour of nominal income growth net of the natural growth of output (which we shall call DX_t^T) using quarterly data over the period 1890–1980 in the US. He fitted a 'first-stage' regression of DX_t^T on its main determinants. These were mainly lagged DX_t^T, lagged monetary growth, lagged inflation and $y_{c_{t-1}}$. We write this first-stage regression as

$$DX_t^T = \alpha' Z_{t-1} + \nu_t \qquad (7.17)$$

where Z_{t-1} is a vector of variables known to agents at time $t-1$ which influence DX_t^T; α is a vector of coefficients and ν_t is the equation error term which is considered to be unanticipated nominal income growth (net of the natural growth of output). According to the Lucas model, only the unanticipated component of DX_t^T will affect real output: its anticipated component will have no measurable output effect. To test this implication, Gordon set up the following estimating equation:

$$y_{ct} = \beta_0 \hat{\alpha}' Z_{t-1} + \beta_1 \nu_t + \beta_2 y_{ct-1} - \sum_i^n \beta_{2+i} \dot{P}_{t-i} + \omega_t \qquad (7.18)$$

where $\hat{\alpha}' Z_{t-1}$ is an estimate (from equation (7.17)) of anticipated nominal income growth, $\dot{P}_{t-i}$ is a measure of lagged inflation for period $t - i$, and ω_t is the equation error. The inflation terms are included because Gordon wanted to test for possible effects of lagged inflation on currrent output – a feature of an alternative model he wished to compare with that of Lucas.

The Lucas model would imply that $\beta_0 = \beta_{2+i} = 0$ (for all i), but β_1 and β_2 would be positive constants. The results obtained by Gordon for the sub-period 1954(1) to 1980(4) are typical of his findings: β_0 was estimated to be 0.91 and was statistically greater than zero; $\sum_1^n \beta_{2+i}$ was estimated to be -1.06, which was again statistically less than zero; β_1 and β_2 were estimated to be 0.75 and 0.94 (respectively) and were also statistically significant. Gordon's results represent a clear rejection of the Lucas model, because both adjusted anticipated nominal income growth and lagged inflation influence real output.

These findings directly contradict the evidence put forward by Barro and Attfield, Demery and Duck, discussed in the previous chapter, for in these studies anticipated monetary growth (presumably a major determinant of nominal income growth) was found to have no real output effect in either the US or the UK. Gordon suggested an explanation for these contradictory findings. Since anticipated aggregate demand (as measured by anticipated adjusted nominal income growth) does influence output but anticipated money does not, Gordon argues that anticipated money growth does not influence the growth in nominal spending (or income). This interpretation is very reminiscent of traditional Keynesian views on the impotence of monetary policy. Gordon summarizes this interpretation as follows: policy ineffectiveness 'is more related to factors set forth in early Keynesian models than those advanced by Lucas' (Gordon, 1982, p. 1197).

The test performed by Lucas was not a particularly powerful one in the sense that it was not possible to test for the effects of anti-cipated changes in nominal income. Gordon provides a more powerful test and rejects the main feature of the Lucas model; that only unanticipated changes in aggregate demand affect real output. Similar results were obtained for the UK by Demery (1984).

7.3 EXTENSIONS TO THE BARRO MODEL

Although the initial empirical research gave considerable support to the hypothesis that only unanticipated money growth affects real output, a great deal of subsequent research has not only challenged this hypothesis, but has raised doubts about whether the business cycle is a monetary phenomenon at all. We shall survey this research in this section.

(a) Mishkin's test

The first challenge came in two papers by Mishkin (1982a,b). The distinguishing feature of Mishkin's tests was the length of the lag allowed in the transmission of money supply to output changes. In Barro and Rush's (1980) quarterly model of the US, for example, lag lengths of seven or eight quarters were most common and, similarly, Attfield, Demery and Duck found a lag length of six quarters using UK data. In Mishkin's test, lagged terms in anti-cipated and unanticipated money growth up to 20 quarters were included in the output equation.

Following Leiderman, Mishkin estimated aggregate demand and output equations simultaneously, imposing the relevant cross-equation restrictions in a similar manner to that described in chapter 6. This permitted him to test separately for rational expec-tations and structural neutrality (see section 6.3). He adopted three alternative measures of aggregate demand: inflation, $\dot{P}$, nominal income growth, DX, and money growth, DM. According to struc-tural neutrality, only unanticipated values of each of these should influence output. The likelihood ratio tests of the rational expecta-tions and structural neutrality restrictions are set out in table 7.1.

Mishkin's model was estimated using quarterly US data over the period 1954–76. When adopting money growth as the aggregate demand variable, his results constitute an emphatic reversal of the

TABLE 7.1 Mishkin's extension to the Barro test: likelihood ratio statistics in the output equation

Test for	Aggregate demand variable		
	DM	DX	$\dot{P}$
Rationality	29.17*	12.86	10.23
Neutrality	15.45*	30.22*	18.52*
Joint test	43.83*	43.19*	28.45**

* Indicates a rejection of the null at the 1 per cent level.
**Indicates a rejection of the null at the 5 per cent level.

Barro–Leiderman result. The tests of rationality and neutrality both imply rejection of the null hypothesis at the 1 per cent level of significance. Interestingly, when Mishkin performed the same test on a model restricted to only seven lags in unanticipated money, his results were similar to those of Leiderman. The likelihood ratio test statistics were 19.44, 3.36 and 22.69 respectively for the rationality restrictions, the neutrality restrictions and the two combined, none of which constitute a rejection of the null hypothesis at the 5 per cent level. For this reason, Mishkin emphasizes that the rejection of rationality and neutrality arise only because he allows for a longer lag in the monetary transmission mechanisms. Similar results were obtained by Mishkin when unemployment rather than output was used as the dependent variable.

The rejection of the neutrality restrictions implies that anticipated money growth (which, of course, is measured conditional on the rational expectations restrictions) has real output effects, contrary to the Barro hypothesis. The pattern of the lagged effects of anticipated money growth on output is also of some interest. The coefficients attached to the first ten-quarter lagged terms in anticipated money growth were found to be significantly positive; the remaining ten terms were found to have a negative and significant effect on output. It is clear from these results that the relationship between monetary growth and output is both drawn-out and complex. Similar patterns were observed when nominal income growth was the aggregate demand variable (the first seven lagged terms in anticipated nominal income growth carried positive coefficients and the last 13 carried negative coefficients).

There is another feature of Mishkin's results that is worthy of comment. The rationality restrictions are rejected when money growth is adopted as the aggregate demand variable. Of course, this invalidates the neutrality test as the latter requires the rationality restrictions to be true in order to identify and measure the anticipated component of money growth. It follows that, strictly speaking, nothing can be said about the effects of anticipated money, as Mishkin's test has failed to model satisfactorily the manner in which expectations of money growth are formed. This failure could arise either because Mishkin has misspecified the money growth equation itself (that is, he has not identified the explanatory variables for monetary growth that rational agents are in fact using) or because the assumption of rationality itself is invalid.

However, when Mishkin adopts nominal income growth and inflation as the aggregate demand variables, the rationality restrictions are not rejected (at the 5 per cent level) so the neutrality tests in these cases are valid. As can be seen from table 7.1, neutrality is rejected for models in which nominal income growth, DX, and inflation, P, are the aggregate demand variables. Again, similar results were obtained from estimates of the unemployment (rather than output) equations (although rationality was rejected at the 5 per cent level when inflation was the aggregate demand variable). Mishkin concludes:

> Rejection of the joint hypotheses of rationality and neutrality are thus seen to occur primarily because of neutrality rather than rationality. This result might give some encouragement to those who are willing to assume rationality of expectations in constructing their macro models, yet are unwilling to assume the short-run neutrality of policy.
>
> (Mishkin, 1982b, p. 799)

Mishkin and Gordon adopt very different ways of modelling 'persistence' of the deviation of output from its natural or normal level. Gordon includes the lagged dependent variable, as Lucas had done in the original paper. Mishkin formally allows for persistence by extending the lagged influence of money for a period of five years. Yet despite these different approaches both papers come to the same conclusion: anticipated changes in aggregate demand have significant output effects. Their results offer encouragement to those who wish to maintain a role for government stabilization policy, although it is clear from Mishkin's results that policy design will have to take into account the drawn-out effects of changes in aggregate demand on output and economic activity.

(b) Pesaran's test

In another challenge to the Barro model, Pesaran (1982) makes an important methodological point. He argues that the tests conducted by Barro are inadequate in one important respect: it is quite possible for Barro's model to be 'conformable' to the data and yet be rejected when compared with an alternative model which is also conformable to the data. 'A proper test of a hypothesis', argues Pesaran, 'invariably requires consideration of at least one *genuine* alternative' (p. 535). Pesaran attempted to do this by comparing the Barro model with a 'Keynesian' alternative, using Barro's (1977a) data set.

He first modified the Barro model to remove what he considered to be an unsatisfactory feature of Barro's original formulation. You will recall from chapter 6 that Barro included a variable $FEDV_t$ as a determinant of money growth: this is the deviation of federal government expenditures from their normal levels. Pesaran's concern with this variable is simply that its value may not be known to agents at time $t - 1$ when they are attempting to forecast money growth. To avoid this problem, Pesaran developed a forecasting model for government expenditure and hence $FEDV_t$. Pesaran then re-estimated Barro's money growth equation, replacing $FEDV_t$ with $E_{t-1}FEDV_t$, and recomputed Barro's anticipated money growth variable. Because the forecasted $FEDV$ will differ from the actual value, Pesaran's computed values for DMR_t will differ from those used by Barro. In particular, because $FEDV_t$ will have greater variance than $E_{t-1}FEDV_t$, Pesaran's measure for DMR (say, $D\tilde{M}R$) will have greater variability than Barro's (which we shall now refer to as $D\hat{M}R$). In fact, the two are related by the following formula:

$$D\tilde{M}R_t = D\hat{M}R_t + 0.0656\,DGR \tag{7.19}$$

where DGR is Pesaran's measure of the unanticipated growth of government expenditure, and 0.0656 converts unanticipated government expenditure growth into unanticipated money growth via unanticipated $FEDV_t$. Pesaran's series for unanticipated money is thus 'noisier' than Barro's. Indeed, because Pesaran's forecasting model for government expenditure growth explains only half its variance, the *DGR* term in equation (7.19) makes an important contribution to Pesaran's measure of *DMR*. Put simply, in Pesaran's model economic agents will make less accurate forecasts of money growth because they are assumed to be poorly informed about one of its important influences – *FEDV*. Barro argues that *FEDV* is in fact dominated by military expenditures associated with wars, and that rational agents will be well informed beforehand about these expenditures. If Barro is correct in his assumption, Pesaran's model can be viewed as introducing an error into the 'true' measure of unanticipated money. If Pesaran is correct, then Barro is invalidly imputing an unanticipated component of money growth to its anticipated component.

Pesaran's 'genuine alternative' hypothesis is a 'Keynesian' model, in which unemployment is a linear function of, *inter alia*, current and lagged money growth (with no distinction between anticipated and unanticipated) and current government expenditure. The two models – the Barro and the Keynesian – are not nested, which means that one cannot be expressed as a restricted version of the other. For this reason, Pesaran used non-nested hypothesis testing procedures. These essentially test each hypothesis on the assumption that the alternative hypothesis is true. Pesaran was able to reject the Barro model on the assumption that the Keynesian model is true. However, he was not able to reject the Keynesian model under the assumption that the Barro model is true. By performing what he calls a 'proper test', Pesaran was able to reject the modified Barro model in favour of a Keynesian alternative, even when in some sense the Barro model 'conformed' to the data satisfactorily. Pesaran's point is that the Keynesian model 'conformed' even more closely. Of course, Pesaran's conclusion depends on his treatment of *FEDV*. Barro might argue that invalid assumptions about agents' information sets have introduced an 'error of measurement' into *DMR* which will weaken the conformity of his model to the data and therefore bias the test in favour of its rejection.

(c) Bean's test

In a further study of UK quarterly data over the period 1963(1)–1982(1), Bean (1984) found further evidence against the neutrality proposition. Bean's analysis involved three aggregate demand variables: the M1 definition of money, the £M3 definition and the three-month Treasury Bill Rate (TBR). The processes explaining the behaviour of these variables appeared to undergo structural breaks around 1972 (when the foreign exchange rates ceased to be strictly fixed) and 1976 (when monetary targets were officially announced). Bean exploited these breaks when identifying the effects of anticipated and unanticipated changes in each aggregate demand variable without the need for 'exclusion restrictions' (see chapter 3).

For M1 and TBR Bean found that he could reject the hypothesis that only the unanticipated component had real effects. Moreover, for these cases he found that the distinction between anticipated and unanticipated changes was unimportant in the sense that the coefficients on the anticipated and unanticipated terms were not significantly different from one another. However, only TBR was found to have a statistically significant effect on output. For £M3 Bean found that the coefficients on anticipated and unanticipated money growth were significantly different, but he found that both were not significantly different from zero. Bean's findings for the UK thus not only question the importance of the distinction between anticipated and unanticipated aggregate demand, but raise doubts about the importance of money supply in explanations of the business cycle. However, the monetary instrument TBR was found to have a significant effect on output. Similar conclusions have been obtained for the US in studies by Sims, to which we now turn.

(d) Sims's test

In an attempt to measure the impact of monetary growth on output, Sims (1972) estimated a set of 'vector autoregressions', or VAR's, using data for the US. In these VAR's a vector of variables (including real output and money) are regressed on their own lagged values over a 48-month horizon. Money is said to 'Granger-cause' output if its lagged values have explanatory power in the output equation conditional on the presence of lagged output itself in the equation. (For a discussion of Granger causality see Granger (1969) and Granger and Newbold (1977, ch. 7); for an example of the pitfalls of using the concept of Granger causality, see Mankiw (1986).) In this early study Sims found that 37 per cent of the forecast error in industrial production was explained by monetary surprises or innovations. He concluded that the monetary authorities could reduce the variability of real output by reducing the variability of monetary growth (for example, by following a constant growth rate rule).

However, Sims (1980) repeated the analysis but on this occasion he added the nominal interest rate to the VAR system. He now found that only 4 per cent of the forecast error in output was explained by money innovations. He concluded that 'some of the observed co-movements of industrial production and money stock are attributed to common responses to surprise changes in the interest rate', so that the 'imposition of a monetarist rule to make the quantity of money more predictable would have little real effect' (Sims, 1980, p. 253).

The VAR evidence presented by Sims suggested to some that money was unimportant in explaining output fluctuations, and that the Lucas and Barro models were 'blind alleys' in our attempt to understand business cycles. However, McCallum (1986, 1989) has challenged such an interpretation of the Sims results. McCallum argues that the monetary authority in the US (the Federal Reserve Bank) implements its policies by manipulating the rate of interest, and therefore interest innovations would reflect monetary policy surprises, with money stock innovations reflecting these policies together with changes in the other influences on money demand. 'In this case', argues McCallum, 'interest rate innovations would measure monetary policy surprises better than would money stock innovations' (McCallum, 1989, p. 35). The fact that money stock innovations have been found to be unimportant once allowance is made for interest rate innovations does not imply that monetary *policy* actions are unimportant for output. Indeed, quite the reverse is true, for Sims found that interest rates had a strong effect on output.

7.4 SUMMARY

In this chapter we have discussed some important criticisms of and notable extensions to the Lucas and Barro models which we described in chapter 6. In the first place, biases may arise in estimated coefficients if the process determining aggregate demand is not correctly specified in the sense that important influences on aggregate demand are omitted (influences that rational agents will be aware of). This problem is particularly serious for the tests performed by Lucas, in which he sought to show that countries experiencing a high variation in unanticipated aggregate demand will be characterized by lower coefficients linking unanticipated aggregate demand and output. If Lucas omitted important influences on nominal income growth – and it is very likely that he did – then we would expect to find an observed relationship between the variance of unanticipated aggregate demand and the influence of aggregate demand on output even when one does not exist in fact.

The Lucas and Barro models have been extended and their conclusions criticized by a number of researchers during the 1980s, and we have reviewed the most important in this chapter. Gordon specified a more complete model of nominal income growth and demonstrated that anticipated changes in it had real output effects in the US. Mishkin extended the lag on unanticipated money growth, nominal income growth and inflation, and also found that anticipated changes in aggregate demand (as measured by these three variables) had real output effects in the US economy. Pesaran argues that while the Barro model explained the historical data satisfactorily, the application of non-nested hypothesis-testing techniques revealed that it was generally less conformable to the data than an alternative 'Keynesian' model, in which the distinction between anticipated and unanticipated money growth is unimportant. Bean exploited structural breaks in the processes determining his chosen aggregate demand variables (M1, £M3 and the Treasury Bill Rate) in order to estimate the effect of anticipated and unanticipated changes in aggregate demand in the UK. He found that M1 and £M3 had no effect on real output, but that the Treasury Bill Rate – whether anticipated or otherwise – was significant in the output equation. Finally, Sims found that the money stock had a only a weak effect on output in the US once allowance was made for the contribution of nominal interest rates.

Therefore, by the end of the 1980s, there was a large body of empirical research which cast doubt on the force of the initial contributions of Lucas and Barro for the US, and Attfield, Demery and Duck for the UK. In the next chapter we shall see how these findings have led some to look for an explanation of business cycle fluctuations in *real* as opposed to *monetary* factors.

8

Real Business Cycle Theory

As chapter 7 has shown, the evidence relating to the model developed in chapter 4, in particular its predictions that fluctuations in real economic activity are caused largely by fluctuations in the unpredictable component of monetary growth or aggregate demand, has been very mixed. At the same time it has increasingly come to be seen as unrealistic to view imperfect information about the money supply as a major source of output fluctuations. After all, in modern economies information about the quantity of money is available within a very short period of time. As Barro has argued, 'if information about money and the general price level mattered much for economic decisions, people could expend relatively few resources to find out quickly about money and prices' (Barro, 1989, p. 2).

To Keynesian economists the mixed evidence mentioned above and the availability of information about money and prices pose no special problems: their models of the business cycle emphasize *imperfect competition* in either labour or product markets, or both, rather than *imperfect information*. But for economists working in the 'New Classical' tradition, one which assumes flexible prices, consistent optimization by all agents subject to constraints, and of course rational expectations, such evidence has prompted a search for alternative theories of the business cycle which maintain these core elements of the New Classical approach but which do not emphasize monetary factors. As a result, in recent years a body of theory has been developed which assigns a key role in the business cycle to 'real' factors such as changes in technology and preferences.

In this chapter we shall be presenting a simplified example of a real business cycle theory (RBC). Although this model lacks the complexity and generality of the models actually appearing in the literature, it is rich enough to illustrate the strengths and weaknesses of the real business cycle approach. But first we shall consider important developments in the empirical analysis of the business cycle, which have appeared to support the idea that monetary factors have only a minor role to play in accounting for output fluctuations.

8.1 THE NATURE OF ECONOMIC FLUCTUATIONS

(a) Trend and difference stationarity

We begin this review of recent empirical research into the nature of the business cycle – which was initiated by Nelson and Plosser (1982) – with a brief outline of two simple but very different models of economic fluctuations.

Until the early 1980s an accepted way of modelling output fluctuations could be summarized using the following equation:

$$y_t = y_0 + \gamma t + \epsilon_t \qquad (8.1)$$

where y_t is aggregate real output at time t, y_0 is output at time 0, t is an index of time, γ is a constant, and ϵ_t is a deviation around the time trend at time t, which is assumed to have a finite variance σ_ϵ^2.

In terms of the model developed in chapter 4 one could think of $y_0 + \gamma t$ as representing the growing natural level of output, and of ϵ_t as the deviation of output around that natural level due to monetary or aggregate demand fluctuations.

Now, ϵ_t could be a serially correlated variable, so that if output is above trend in any period it is likely to be above trend in subsequent periods (the 'persistence' feature of the business cycle). In order to focus on the central issues involved we shall begin by assuming that ϵ_t is a serially *independent* random variable with zero mean.

Imagine the economy described by equation (8.1) to be exactly on trend until period T, when it is subject to a positive shock (that is, $\epsilon_T > 0$). The shock only lasts for one period and in all subsequent periods ϵ_t is zero. The time path followed by the economy subject to this shock is set out graphically in figure 8.1. In this case

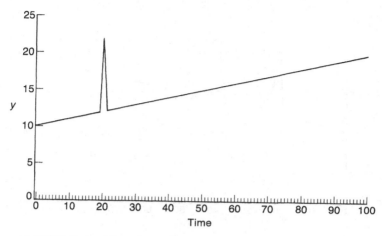

FIGURE 8.1   Trend-stationary process: no persistence.

the economy deviates from trend for only one period ($T = 20$) and then reverts to trend immediately in periods $T + 1$ and above. The economy's output is thus described as 'trend-reverting' or 'trend-stationary' (TS). What this means is that while output itself is *not* stationary, in other words its variance is not finite since equation (8.1) indicates that it is growing *ad infinitum*, the deviation around trend *is* stationary – its variance is constant by assumption.

This simple modelling of the cycle can be elaborated by assuming that the deviation around the trend follows some serial pattern. Consider the following alternative assumption about ϵ_t:

$$\epsilon_t = \kappa\epsilon_{t-1} + \zeta_t, \qquad -1 < \kappa < 1 \tag{8.2}$$

where ζ_t is a serially independent random variable.

In this case ϵ_t follows what is known as a first-order autoregressive process; that is, its value depends upon its own value lagged one period plus a serially independent random error. Again imagine the effect on output of a single positive shock ($\zeta_T > 0$). The dependence of ϵ_t on its lagged value will cause the deviation of output about its trend to be more drawn-out but, as is clear from figure 8.2, output is still trend-reverting or TS provided that κ is between -1 and 1. The *speed* of return to trend is affected by the value of κ (as the figure illustrates with adjustment faster for the smaller κ), but eventually the economy's output will return to its trend level.

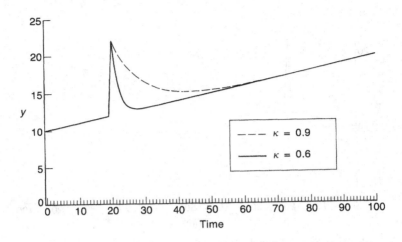

FIGURE 8.2 Trend-stationary process: with persistence.

This simple model illustrates a widely held view of output fluctuations. Output is seen as having a linear (or log–linear if y is measured in logarithms) trend from which it is continuously being perturbed but to which it will eventually return. Examples of its use are the empirical models of Barro (1978a) and Attfield, Demery and Duck (1981a), where output follows a trend but deviates around that trend through the effects of monetary surprises. These deviations are drawn-out (that is, the monetary surprise term appears with a number of lags) but the economy is seen as trend-reverting. An important assumption being made in these and similar studies is that the trend is unaffected by the transitory output deviations; that is, the parameter γ is a constant and is independent of ϵ_t.

An alternative way of modelling output is to assume that its *first difference* is stationary rather than its deviation around trend. In this case output is said to be difference-stationary (or DS). One example of a DS process for output is the 'random walk with drift', which can be written:

$$y_t = y_{t-1} + \mu + \omega_t \tag{8.3}$$

or, equivalently,

$$\Delta y_t = \mu + \omega_t \tag{8.4}$$

where μ (which is the mean change in y) is a constant; and ω_t is the deviation of Δy_t about its mean value which, for the random walk case, is a serially independent random variable.

In such a case output is said to have a 'unit root'. In a regression of output on its lagged value and a time trend we would expect the estimated coefficient on the lagged term to be unity, and that on the time trend to be zero. (If y is measured in logarithms then we can interpret Δy_t as the growth rate of y at the time t.) Imagine that ω_t has been zero for some time so that Δy_t has been a constant μ for each period; that is, $y_t = y_{t-1} + \mu$. Since y is simply increasing each period by μ, its path will be upward-sloping as shown in figure 8.3 (in which we have again assumed that output at time 1 is 10). Indeed, its path will look very much like the trend growth in figures 8.1 and 8.2, and if there were no shocks the two time profiles would be identical if $\mu = \gamma$.

Now imagine that at time T there is a positive shock to output, $\omega_T > 0$, and in the following period ω returns to and remains at zero. The output level at time T is the previous period's output (y_{T-1}) plus μ plus the shock term ω_T. The effect of this shock (imposed at $T = 20$) is shown graphically in figure 8.3. As in the case of the TS example above, the shock is assumed to be transitory, lasting for only one period, but in this case its effect on *future* values of y_t is very different. In period $T + 1$ output will equal its level in period T plus μ. This means it will resume its trajectory but now at a higher level, since output in period T has been subjected to a positive shock. In the random walk case, a single shock to output in period T will cause output in all future periods to rise by the value of that shock. In this case output does not return to its earlier trend (that is, it is not trend-reverting) but moves on to a higher level as a result of the shock.

As in the TS case we can generalize this process by relaxing the assumptions we have made about ω_t. Again assume that ω_t follows the process

$$\omega_t = \kappa\omega_{t-1} + \zeta_t, \qquad -1 < \kappa < 1 \tag{8.5}$$

In this case the transition to the new trend following a positive shock (that is, $\zeta_T > 0$) will be smoother, as is clear from figure 8.4. To ensure the same ultimate level of y_t as in figure 8.3 the initial shock (ζ_T) in the persistent case is one-tenth of the shock assumed in the no-persistence case. It is clear from figure 8.4 that

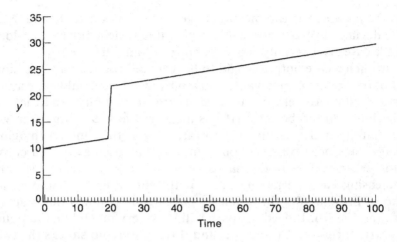

FIGURE 8.3   Difference stationary process: $\kappa = 0$.

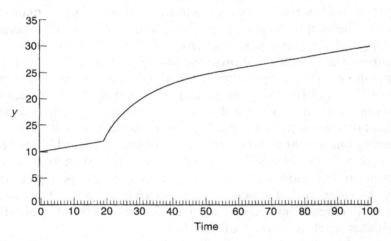

FIGURE 8.4   Difference stationary process: $\kappa = 0.9$.

the basic lesson from the random walk case carries over – a shock causes output to move onto a new trend.

An important question for the analysis of business cycles is: Which model best describes aggregate output fluctuations? If the TS class is best, then shocks to the economy are short-lived and transitory. On the other hand, if the DS class is best, shocks to output persist into the indefinite future. This is an important question, because if output fluctuations are primarily the result of monetary or aggregate demand shocks, that is if they are to be explained in terms of the model developed in chapter 4, one would expect them to be transitory. In such a model a monetary shock can cause output to deviate from its natural rate, but only temporarily: as agents correct their mistakes and as any propagation mechanism unwinds, output will move back to its natural level. So if output follows a DS process it suggests that the business cycle does not arise from monetary or other aggregate demand shocks. Shocks to real factors, on the other hand, such as spurts in technology, can have permanent effects: a sudden breakthrough in technology will not be reversed and can lead to a permanently higher level of output. For this reason evidence of a unit root in output is thought of as at least *prima facie* evidence for the existence of a real business cycle and against the existence of a monetary cycle.

(b) Tests of trend/difference stationarity

Tests which attempt to discriminate between the TS and DS proceses have been developed and applied by Nelson and Plosser (1982) and by Campbell and Mankiw (1987, 1989). In what follows we shall outline one of the approaches suggested by Campbell and Mankiw. We first write the DS process more generally as

$$\Delta y_t = \mu + B(L)\omega_t \tag{8.6}$$

where $B(L)$ is known as a polynominal in the lag operator L^j, defined as

$$B(L)\omega_t \equiv B_0\omega_t + B_1\omega_{t-1} + B_2\omega_{t-2} + B_3\omega_{t-3} + \ldots \tag{8.7}$$

where B_i are parameters; the lag operator L^j is defined by $L^j X_t \equiv X_{t-j}$ so that $L^0 X_t \equiv X_t$, $L^1 X_t \equiv X_{t-1}$ and so on. We shall measure ω_t in units such that $B_0 = 1$.

We write the TS process generally as

$$y_t = y_0 + \gamma t + \alpha(L)\epsilon_t \tag{8.8}$$

where, again, $\alpha(L)$ is a polynominal in the lag operator, defined by

$$\alpha(L)\epsilon_t \equiv \epsilon_t + \alpha_1\epsilon_{t-1} + \alpha_2\epsilon_{t-2} + \alpha_3\epsilon_{t-3} + \ldots \tag{8.9}$$

If we lag equation (8.8) by one period we obtain

$$y_{t-1} = y_0 + \gamma(t-1) + \alpha(L)\epsilon_{t-1} \tag{8.10}$$

and subtracting equation (8.10) from equation (8.8) we obtain

$$y_t - y_{t-1} \equiv \Delta y_t = \gamma + \alpha(L)\epsilon_t - \alpha(L)\epsilon_{t-1}$$

or

$$\Delta y_t = \gamma + (1 - L)\alpha(L)\epsilon_t = \gamma + A(L)\epsilon_t \tag{8.11}$$

where $A(L) \equiv (1 - L)\alpha(L)$ and where we define

$$A(L)\epsilon_t \equiv \epsilon_t + A_1\epsilon_{t-1} + A_2\epsilon_{t-2} + A_3\epsilon_{t-3} + \ldots$$

The TS process described in equation (8.11) looks very similar to the DS process given in equation (8.6). The key difference between the two lies in the two moving average error expressions, $B(L)\omega_t$ in the DS case and $A(L)\epsilon_t$ in the TS case. Since $B(L)\omega_t$ is an unrestricted moving average expression, that is the B_i's can take any value and there may be any number of lagged terms in ω present, it follows that there must be a restriction on $A(L)\epsilon_t$ that distinguishes the trend-reverting characteristic of equation (8.11) from the non-reverting characteristic of equation (8.6). We will now seek to identify the nature of this restriction.

First note that, in the long run, the TS process involves a return of output to its trend; that is, $y_t = y_0 + \gamma t$. To illustrate the nature of the restriction on $A(L)\epsilon_t$ we shall assume the following simple form for equation (8.8):

$$y_t = \gamma t + \epsilon_t + \alpha_1\epsilon_{t-1} \tag{8.12}$$

It follows that

$$\Delta y_t = \gamma + \epsilon_t + (\alpha_1 - 1)\epsilon_{t-1} - \alpha_1\epsilon_{t-2} \tag{8.13}$$

Setting $A_1 = (\alpha_1 - 1)$ and $A_2 = -\alpha_1$ we re-write equation (8.13) as

$$\Delta y_t = \gamma + \epsilon_t + A_1\epsilon_{t-1} + A_2\epsilon_{t-2}$$

or

$$y_t = y_{t-1} + \gamma + \epsilon_t + A_1\epsilon_{t-1} + A_2\epsilon_{t-2} \tag{8.14}$$

Lagging equation (8.14) by one period we obtain

$$y_{t-1} = y_{t-2} + \gamma + \epsilon_{t-1} + A_1\epsilon_{t-2} + A_2\epsilon_{t-3} \tag{8.15}$$

Equation (8.15) can be substituted in place of y_{t-1} in equation (8.14) to give

$$y_t = y_{t-2} + 2\gamma + \epsilon_t + (1 + A_1)\epsilon_{t-1} + (A_1 + A_2)\epsilon_{t-2} + A_2\epsilon_{t-3}$$
$$(8.16)$$

Equation (8.14) can be lagged twice and the resulting term substituted into equation (8.16), leaving a term in y_{t-3} on the right-hand side. This backward substitution for lagged terms in y can continue until we derive

$$y_t = y_{t-n} + \gamma n + \epsilon_t + (1 + A_1)\epsilon_{t-1} + (1 + A_1 + A_2)\epsilon_{t-2}$$
$$+ \ldots + (1 + A_1 + A_2)\epsilon_{t-n+1} + (A_1 + A_2)\epsilon_{t-n} + A_2\epsilon_{t-n-1}$$
$$(8.17)$$

If $t - n = 0$ (that is, the start of the period is indexed 0) and if ϵ_j are zero for all j, except $j = 1$, then equation (8.17) becomes

$$y_t = y_0 + \gamma t + (1 + A_1 + A_2)\epsilon_1 \qquad (8.18)$$

Equation (8.18) states that a shock at the start of the period, ϵ_1, will affect current output y_t if $(1 + A_1 + A_2)$ is non-zero. If the process is TS then we know by comparing equation (8.18) with the long-run solution ($y_t = y_0 + \gamma t$) that $(1 + A_1 + A_2)$ must be zero (that is, $\sum_0^2 A_j \equiv A(1) = 0$, recalling that $A_0 = 1$). This means that a shock at period 1 will have no effect on the level of output in period t if the process is TS. In our example the restriction on the sum of the A's is clearly satisfied for

$$\sum_0^2 A_j \equiv A(1) \equiv (1 + A_1 + A_2) = 1 + (\alpha_1 - 1) - \alpha_1 = 0$$

In order to test whether output is trend-reverting or otherwise, we can set up what is known as a *generic* function of the following form:

$$\Delta y_t = \varphi + C(L)\eta_t \qquad (8.19)$$

where $C(L)\eta_t \equiv \eta_t + C_1\eta_{t-1} + C_2\eta_{t-2} + C_3\eta_{t-3} + \ldots,$ η_t is a serially independent random shock, and φ is a constant.

If we found, when applying this equation to an economy's aggregate output data, that $\sum C_j \equiv C(1) = 0$, then output would be trend-reverting (that is, TS). Alternatively, if $C(1) \neq 0$, then output does not return to its trend. Moreover, $C(1)$ will give us a *measure* of the impact of a current shock to output (that is, η_t) on its long-run level. If the parameters of the moving average error process $C(L)\eta_t$ can be estimated it would then be possible to answer two related questions:

1 Is output trend-reverting; that is, is $C(1) = 0$?
2 If $C(1) \neq 0$, what is the long-term effect of a current shock to output; that is, what is the value of $C(1)$?

Campbell and Mankiw (1987, 1989) adopt the following method for measuring $C(1)$. They begin by estimating a general mixed autoregressive – moving-average (ARMA) model for Δy_t. This is referred to as ARMA(p, q), where p defines the lag length (or order) of the autoregressive component and q defines the lag length (or order) of the moving average error component. The ARMA (p, q) has the general form

$$\theta(L)\Delta y_t = \beta(L)\epsilon_t$$

where

$$\theta(L)\Delta y_t \equiv \Delta y_t - \theta_1\Delta y_{t-1} - \theta_2\Delta y_{t-2} - \theta_3\Delta y_{t-3} - \ldots$$
$$- \theta_p\Delta y_{t-p},$$

$$\beta(L)\epsilon_t \equiv \epsilon_t + \beta_1\epsilon_{t-1} + \beta_2\epsilon_{t-2} + \beta_3\epsilon_{t-3} + \ldots + \beta_q\epsilon_{t-q}$$

and ϵ is a serially independent random error.

To simplify the analysis we shall assume that an ARMA(1,2) fits the data on Δy_t best. For convenience we drop the intercept term and write this ARMA as

$$\Delta y_t = \theta\Delta y_{t-1} + \epsilon_t + \beta_1\epsilon_{t-1} + \beta_2\epsilon_{t-2} \qquad (8.20)$$

We also assume that $-1 < \theta < 1$, and that $-1 < (\beta_1 + \beta_2) < 1$.

Lagging equation (8.20) by one period and substituting the resulting expression for Δy_{t-1} in equation (8.20) we obtain

$$\Delta y_t = \theta(\theta\Delta y_{t-2} + \epsilon_{t-1} + \beta_1\epsilon_{t-2} + \beta_2\epsilon_{t-3}) + \epsilon_t + \beta_1\epsilon_{t-1}$$
$$+ \beta_2\epsilon_{t-2}$$

or

$$\Delta y_t = \theta^2\Delta y_{t-2} + \epsilon_t + (\theta + \beta_1)\epsilon_{t-1} + (\theta\beta_1 + \beta_2)\epsilon_{t-2} + \theta\beta_2\epsilon_{t-3}$$
$$\qquad (8.21)$$

Equation (8.20) can now be lagged twice and the resulting expression substituted for Δy_{t-2} in equation (8.21). After this substitution the expression for Δy_t will be

$$\Delta y_t = \theta^3\Delta y_{t-3} + \epsilon_t + (\theta + \beta_1)\epsilon_{t-1} + (\theta^2 + \theta\beta_1 + \beta_2)\epsilon_{t-2}$$
$$+ (\theta^2\beta_1 + \theta\beta_2)\epsilon_{t-3} + \theta^2\beta_2\epsilon_{t-4} \qquad (8.22)$$

Repeated substitutions of this type can be made until the coefficient on the lagged Δy term is approximately zero (because as n becomes larger, and with $-1 < \theta < 1$, $\theta^n \simeq 0$). As a result of this elimination of lagged Δy from the equation, Δy_t will be a function only of the current and lagged terms in ϵ. As is evident from equation (8.22), the coefficients on ϵ_t, ϵ_{t-1}, ϵ_{t-2}, $\ldots$, ϵ_{t-n-1} will be complicated functions of the underlying parameters θ, β_1 and β_2. This means that the ARMA(1,2) which best described the behaviour of output changes can be transformed into a moving-average error process like equation (8.19), but one with restrictions on the coefficients C_j, as these coefficients are now non-linear functions of the three ARMA parameters θ, β_1 and β_2.

Campbell and Mankiw (1987, 1989) selected the ARMA processes that best describe the time series data for a number of countries. Given the estimates that they obtained, Campbell and Mankiw calculated the sum of the coefficients in the restricted moving-average representation. This sum would then be an estimate of the 'persistence' of real output. Strictly speaking, the moving average representation is of infinite order but to gain some idea of the value of persistence (that is, $C(1) \equiv \Sigma C_j$) Campbell and Mankiw compute $C(1)$ over an 80-quarter horizon. Their results may be summarized as follows:

Country	ARMA(p, q)	$C(1)$
Canada	(1, 0)	1.15
France	(1, 2)	1.65
Germany	(2, 2)	1.00
Italy	(1, 0)	1.14
Japan	(1, 2)	3.67
UK	(0, 1)	0.82
US	(2, 2)	1.00

Most countries studied by Campbell and Mankiw were characterized by measures of persistence that exceed unity, with Japan indicating particularly pronounced persistence. The UK is the notable expection to the general pattern. However, it is sometimes hard to distinguish statistically between alternative ARMA specifications, and yet the measure of persistence can be sensitive to the particular ARMA selected. For example, Campbell and Mankiw calculate that with an ARMA(1, 2) or ARMA(2, 2) instead of an ARMA(0, 1) the measure of persistence in the UK is as low as 0.06, implying almost complete trend-reversion. However, the overall evidence presented by Campbell and Mankiw does suggest that for many countries current impulses to real output are likely to the long-lasting. It is this type of evidence which has led to the inference that output fluctuations must be real rather than monetary in character.

However, there are a number of weakness, both with the nature of the evidence and the inferences drawn from it. First, Christiano and Eichenbaum (1989) have recently argued that it is not possible to measure $C(1)$ with sufficient statistical precision to decide whether it is significantly different from zero (that is, it is not possible to test whether real income is TS or DS). They argue that our available data extends over too short a period for the required statistical accuracy and they conclude that 'one cannot discriminate, on the basis of postwar data, between the null hypothesis of trend and difference stationarity for US real GNP' (Christiano and Eichenbaum, 1989, p. 52). A similar observation had been made earlier by McCallum (1986).

Second, the studies we have cited have all assumed that there are no *breaks* in the underlying structures of both the TS or the DS processes. They have attempted to discover whether the behaviour of real GNP is best described by processes such as those of equations (8.6) (DS) and (8.8) (TS), where the trend growth rate (γ) in equation (8.8), and the drift term (μ) in equation (8.6) are constant throughout the period. Perron (1989) has suggested that the trend and drift terms in US real output were affected by the oil-price shocks of the 1970s. Once allowance is made for the impact of these shocks on the trend and drift terms, he found US output to be trend-reverting.

Finally, drawing inferences from these results about the nature of the business cycle is certainly not straightforward. It is not difficult to conceive of an economy in which aggregate demand or monetary shocks are the primary source of output fluctuations and which is also characterized by DS. A current aggregate demand shock can depress output in general and investment expenditure in particular. A lower level of investment implies lower capital accumulation and lower long-run growth. Historically, economists have focused on the short-run effects of changes in aggregate demand but there is no compelling reason to presuppose that the long-run effects of such changes are unimportant. Even if output does not revert to trend following a shock, it is not clear that this implies anything about the source of the disturbance. Indeed, we have already seen that in one important study of the effects of money on output in the US (Mishkin, 1982a,b) the measured effect of money on output spreads over five years. Similar long-lasting effects of monetary disturbances on output have been obtained from structural models of the US economy. Blanchard (1987), referring to dynamic simulations using the 1985 version of the D.R.I. model of the US economy, concludes that 'an increase in money of 1% increases GNP for about 3 to 4 years; it takes many more years for output to return to normal and only after long and slightly damped oscillations' (Blanchard, 1987, p. 12).

To summarize the discussion to date, we have seen how a careful time series analysis of output behaviour in several countries has given support to the view that fluctuations in aggregate output tend to be long-lasting and that output does not return to a deterministic trend. Although the findings from this research have yet to be exhaustively checked, they have suggested to some that fluctuations in output are not in the main attributable to changes in aggregate demand (caused, for example, by monetary shocks) and that economic analysis ought to turn to real changes in technology or tastes for explanations of the business cycle. In response to this, many economists in the New Classical tradition have developed theoretical models in which technology shocks are the primary source of output fluctuations, and it is to these models that we now turn.

8.2 REAL BUSINESS CYCLE THEORY

The aim of real business cycle theorists has been to develop a *theory* of fluctuations that can explain the major empirical regularities of the cycle while at the same time maintaining the following characteristically New Classical behavioural assumptions (see Hoover, 1988, for a useful discussion):

1 'Real' economic decisions – such as those on consumption and investment – are based on 'real' and not nominal or monetary factors. There is no 'money illusion'.

2 Agents are consistent and successful optimizers subject to the information they possess.

3 Agents make no systematic errors in evaluating their environment; that is, they form rational expectations.

The aim then is to construct model economies which mimic the main features of known business cycles and in which the primary source of output fluctuations are shocks to technology. We shall in this section outline a RBC model that provides a relatively simple example of the models that have appeared in the literature. The section draws heavily on McCallum (1989), and interested readers are referred to this reference for further details and a helpful discussion.

The model economy is assumed to be populated by a large number of *identical* economic agents (households, say) so that the behaviour of the aggregate economy can be modelled as if the economy consisted of a single or 'representative' agent. The aim here is avoid unnecessary detail and complexity arising from the need to aggregate over different individuals, and which will complicate the model and be of little or no value in aiding our understanding of *aggregate* or *macroeconomic* phenomena.

Even less realistically, we shall assume that the household lives for ever. This assumption may not be as unreasonable as it first appears. If we assume that the *present* household cares for the welfare of *future* generations (that is, the household is 'dynastic'), we can model the household's behaviour *as if* it lives for ever. In the analysis that follows we discount into the infinite future when we compute present values for such a household.

The representative consumer forms rational expectations and maximizes an expected lifetime utility function of the form

$$U = E_t\left[\sum_{j=0}^{\infty}\rho^j u(c_{t+j}, l_{t+j})\right] \tag{8.23}$$

where ρ is $1/[1 + r]$, and r is the (constant) rate at which agents discount the future; c_{t+j} is consumption at period $t + j$; $l_{t+j} \equiv (1 - n_{t+j})$ is leisure at period $t + j$; n_{t+j} is hours of work in period $t + j$, with the total time available for work or leisure each period normalized at 1.

According to equation (8.23) lifetime utility is assumed to be 'additively separable' over time, so that utility in any one period is independent of the utility enjoyed in any other period. Lifetime utility is simply the *sum* of utility enjoyed in each period. Of course, more utility in one period may mean less in another because the household will have limited lifetime resources or wealth, but there is no *direct* effect of utility in any one period on utility in any other.

To simplify the solution of the model we shall assume a specific functional form for equation (8.23). The following has been adopted in a number of contributions, including that of Long and Plosser (1983):

$$u(c_{t+j}, l_{t+j}) = \theta \log(c_{t+j}) + (1 - \theta)\log(l_{t+j})$$

so that

$$U = E_t\left[\sum_{j=0}^{\infty} \rho^j \{\theta \log(c_{t+j}) + (1 - \theta)\log(l_{t+j})\} \right] \tag{8.24}$$

Output in the model economy is determined by a production function of the form

$$y_t = z_t f(n_t, k_t) \tag{8.25}$$

where k is the capital stock, n_t is the quantity of labour employed, y_t is output, and z_t is a technology shock which has a mean value of 1. A favourable shock means a value for $z_t > 1$, and an unfavourable shock a value less than 1.

Again to help simplify the solution, we shall assume that equation (8.25) takes the following explicit Cobb–Douglas functional form:

$$y_t = z_t n_t^\alpha k_t^{1-\alpha} \tag{8.26}$$

Equilibrium requires that aggregate output equals aggregate demand; that is,

$$y_t = c_t + [k_{t+1} - (1 - \delta)k_t] \tag{8.27}$$

where δ is the rate of depreciation of capital, and $[k_{t+1} - (1 - \delta)k_t]$ is investment expenditure.

Again simplifying the model, we shall assume that all capital is written off within a year, so that the depreciation rate δ is equal to 1. Using this assumption and equating the right-hand sides of equations (8.26) and (8.27), we obtain

$$c_t = z_t n_t^\alpha k_t^{1-\alpha} - k_{t+1} \tag{8.28}$$

or, consumption is output less the current level of investment (k_{t+1}).

The problem for the household in the economy is to maximize its lifetime utility (equation (8.24)) subject to the constraint given by equation (8.28) and subject to some terminal condition concerning its final capital stock. For each period of its life, the household must decide how much to consume (c_t), how much to invest (k_t) and how much labour to supply (n_t) or, equivalently, how much leisure to take (l_t). In addition to equation (8.28), utility is maximized when the following conditions are satisfied (interested readers may check on the derivation of these conditions given in the appendix to this chapter):

$$\theta / c_t = \lambda_t, \tag{8.29}$$

$$(1 - \theta)/(1 - n_t) = \alpha \lambda_t z_t n_t^{\alpha - 1} k_t^{1 - \alpha}, \tag{8.30}$$

$$\lambda_t = (1 - \alpha) \rho E_t [\lambda_{t+1} (z_{t+1} n_{t+1}^{\alpha} k_{t+1}^{-\alpha})] \tag{8.31}$$

To solve for c_t and k_{t+1} (that is, current consumption and investment) we use the method of undetermined coefficients described in chapter 4. First we conjecture that there exist solutions of the following form:

$$c_t = \pi_{10} z_t k_t^{1-\alpha}, \qquad k_{t+1} = \pi_{20} z_t k_t^{1-\alpha}, \qquad n_t = n \quad (8.32\text{-}8.34)$$

where the π's are coefficients.

These equations state that in the conjectured solution the level of employment is constant and does not change when z_t changes, and that consumption and investment are specific functions of the current capital stock and the technology shock. Substituting equation (8.31) into equation (8.29), setting $E_t z_{t+1} = 1$ (that is, the expectation of z at period $t + 1$ is its mean) and using equations (8.33) and (8.34) we obtain

$$\pi_{20} = (1 - \alpha) \rho n^{\alpha} \tag{8.35}$$

Then using the constraint equation (8.28) together with the solution for π_{20} we also obtain

$$\pi_{10} = [1 - (1 - \alpha)\rho] n^{\alpha} \tag{8.36}$$

Thus the final solutions to the problem are:

$$c_t = [1 - (1 - \alpha)\rho] n^{\alpha} z_t k_t^{1-\alpha}, \qquad k_{t+1} = (1 - \alpha)\rho n^{\alpha} z_t k_t^{1-\alpha},$$

$$n_t = n \tag{8.37\text{-}8.39}$$

Taking logarithms of equation (8.38) gives

$$\log k_{t+1} = \phi_0 + (1 - \alpha)\log k_t + \log z_t \qquad (8.40)$$

where $\phi_0 = \log[(1 - \alpha)\rho n^{\alpha}]$.

McCallum (1989) argues that if $\log z_t = \beta \log z_{t-1} + \epsilon_t$ (that is, shocks in technology are serially correlated, with ϵ_t a white noise disturbance), then the logarithm of the capital stock will follow a *second-order* difference equation:

$$\log k_{t+1} = \phi_0(1 - \beta) + (1 - \alpha + \beta)\log k_t$$
$$- (1 - \alpha)\beta \log k_{t-1} + \epsilon_t \qquad (8.41)$$

Similarly, the logarithm of consumption will also follow a *second-order* difference equation:

$$\log c_t = \alpha(1 - \beta)\phi_1 + (1 - \alpha)(1 - \beta)\phi_0 + (1 - \alpha + \beta)\log c_{t-1}$$
$$- (1 - \alpha)\beta \log c_{t-2} + \epsilon_t \qquad (8.42)$$

where $\phi_1 = \log[\{1 - (1 - \alpha)\rho\}n^{\alpha}]$.

Thus if technology shocks follow a *first-order* autoregressive process (AR(1)), then capital stock (investment) and consumption will follow *second-order* autoregressive processes (AR(2)). 'This conclusion is of interest', argues McCallum, 'since *detrended* quarterly U.S. data series for the logs of various aggregate quantities are, in fact, reasonably well described by AR(2) models' (McCallum, 1989, p. 23).

There is another important feature of the model that makes it attractive, especially to economists in the New Classical tradition. The monetary business cycles of the sort we have described in earlier chapters required a *lower* real wage rate in booms in order to give higher employment and output, (see section 4.7(d)). According to monetary theories of the business cycle the real wage should move counter-cyclically. Defining the real wage (w_t) to be equal to the marginal product of labour:

$$w_t = \frac{dy_t}{dn} = \alpha z_t n^{\alpha - 1} k_t^{1 - \alpha} = \alpha(y_t/n) \qquad (8.43)$$

it is clear that according to our real business cycle model real wages move pro-cyclically. Due to the constancy of employment (n), a rise in output (arising from an increase in z_t) will raise the average and marginal productivity of labour and hence raise real wages. The observed cyclical patterns of real wages are closer to those implied by RBC than those of the monetary models of the business cycle.

The highly stylized model we have presented has ignored many interesting and important features of RBC models. However, our basic approach is similar to that adopted in more complex models; in other words, to develop a model economy that seeks to mimic the stylized features of business cycles. The simplified model also shares some of the weaknesses of the RBC approach with the more elaborate models.

First, we would expect specific sectors to be the main beneficiaries and losers following technology shocks, and it is hard to imagine a technology shock that will be enjoyed by all sectors of the economy simultaneously. In practice, however, business cycles are thought to affect *all* sectors of the economy (see Greenwald and Stiglitz (1988); however, Lilien (1982) provides some evidence for sectoral shifts in the business cycle).

Second, in order to explain the observed variation of aggregate output, the variance of z_t would need to be implausibly high. Citing a study by Jorgenson and Griliches (1967), McCallum argued that changes in factor inputs (such as labour and capital) accounted for 96.7 per cent of changes in output, with only 3.3 per cent accounted for (residually) by technology. If business cycles are dominated by changes in factor inputs, then theories of the cycle will need to explain the movements in such inputs. Technology shocks are simply not large enough to explain observed output fluctuations.

The development of RBC models is very much in its infancy, and its contribution to our understanding of business cycles has not been as thoroughly investigated as that of the monetary models we have discussed earlier. The theoretical developments do indicate the possibility that many movements in aggregate output may be due to fundamental shocks to technology that are inherently outside the control of the fiscal and monetary authorities. More importantly, the theories imply that there is no reason for macroeconomic stabilization policy, as economic agents are already acting purposefully and in their own interests. However, the Keynesian criticisms of the monetary models which we presented in chapter 4 apply equally to RBC models. Economists in the Keynesian tradition still see fluctuations as the effect of aggregate demand shocks in a world of fixed or sticky wages and prices.

8.3 SUMMARY

In this chapter we have outlined a theory of economic fluctuations that emphasizes the role of 'real' shocks to technology. We began by noting that recent empirical research has found that shocks to aggregate output tend to be long-lasting rather than trend-reverting, and this observation has led some economists to conclude that the impulses behind economic fluctuations are more likely to be 'real' in nature: for example, they may be the result of technology shocks or taste changes. The mediocre performance of many of the monetary models discussed in chapter 4 has further encouraged this view.

We developed a simplified model of the economy in which real technology shocks give rise to economic fluctuations similar in nature to those observed in practice. Macroeconomists in the New Classical tradition have been refining and extending such models in an attempt to provide a model economy that can account for the main features of observed business cycles. The development of these models is very much in its infancy, and they have not been subjected to the same degree of rigorous empirical testing as the monetary cycles discussed earlier in the book. The main weakness of the theories lies in the fact that in practice fluctuations in technology appear not to be substantial enough to explain the pronounced swings which we actually observe in economic activity.

SUGGESTIONS FOR FURTHER READING

The literature on real business cycles is relatively recent and, as a result, there are few general surveys. Eichenbaum and Singleton (1986) examine whether the empirical evidence for the US supports the view that the business cycle is not a monetary phenomenon (the reader may also find some of the discussion of this paper useful). McCallum (1986) presents a critical assessment of the evidence that output is not trend-reverting. Early examples of theoretical real business cycle models are found in Kydland and Prescott (1982) and Hansen (1985), but these references are somewhat technical in nature.

APPENDIX

The problem the household faces is the maximization of

$$U = E_t \left[\sum_{j=0}^{\infty} \rho^j \{\theta \log(c_{t+j}) + (1 - \theta)\log(l_{t+j})\} \right] \qquad (A.1)$$

subject to

$$c_t = z_t n_t^\alpha k_t^{1-\alpha} - k_{t+1} \qquad (A.2)$$

This may be written as

$$\underset{c,\, n,\, k}{\text{Max}} \; L = E_t \sum_{j=0}^{\infty} [\rho^j \{\theta \log(c_{t+j}) + (1 - \theta)\log(l_{t+j})\}$$

$$- \lambda_{t+j} \{c_{t+j} + k_{t+j+1} - z_{t+j} n_{t+j}^\alpha k_{t+j}^{1-\alpha}\}] \qquad (A.3)$$

where λ is the Lagrange multiplier.

Differentiating (A.3) with respect to c_t, l_t ($= 1 - n_t$), k_t (which appears as k_{t+1} in period $t + 1$) and setting the three derivatives equal to zero (first-order condition) gives

$$\theta/c_t = \lambda_t, \qquad (A.4)$$

$$(1 - \theta)/(1 - n_t) = \alpha \lambda_t z_t n_t^{\alpha-1} k_t^{1-\alpha}, \qquad (A.5)$$

$$\lambda_t = (1 - \alpha)\rho E_t [\lambda_{t+1}(z_{t+1} n_\alpha^{t+1} k_{t+1}^{-\alpha})] \qquad (A.6)$$

which are equations (8.29)–(8.31) of the text.

9

Rational Expectations and the Permanent-income Hypothesis

The rational expectations hypothesis has had an especially dramatic effect on research into the consumption function, in particular on research into the permanent-income hypothesis (or PIH) originally developed by Friedman (1957). In this chapter we outline PIH, explain some key implications of combining PIH and rational expectations, and discuss some of the empirical tests that have been made of the resulting joint rational expectations – permanent-income hypothesis, hereafter REPI.

9.1 THE PERMANENT-INCOME HYPOTHESIS

Imagine a representative individual who has, at the beginning of time period t, a certain stock of assets or *non-human wealth* such as government bonds and shares, the real value of which we shall denote by A_t. In addition to this stock of wealth the individual can be seen as having a stock of *human wealth*, the source of which is the income that the individual can earn by working, that is supplying labour, from the present until death or retirement. To show how this stream of current and future income can be viewed as a stock of human wealth we first denote the real value of the individual's labour income in period t by y_t, and assume that it is paid *at the end of period t*. In a world consisting of perfect capital markets, that is in which there are no barriers to an individual borrowing or lending at the same interest rate as everyone else, the amount that could be borrowed *at the beginning of period t* on the strength of y_t being received at the end of period t is $y_t/(1 + r)$, where r is the real rate of interest for borrowers and lenders, which is assumed to be measured so that a 5 per cent rate of interest implies that $r = 0.05$. (In what follows this rate is assumed to be *constant*.) The reason for this is that if, at the beginning of the period, the individual lent out at interest rate r a sum of money equal in a value to $y_t/(1 + r)$ its value at the end of the period would be $(1 + r)$ times $y_t/(1 + r)$; that is, y_t. Thus the amount y_t at the end of the period is in this sense equivalent to the amount $y_t/(1 + r)$ at the beginning of the period, and so $y_t/(1 + r)$ is termed the present value of y_t. If, as we shall assume, the discount rate for each individual, that is the rate of interest which he uses to work out what sum of income at the beginning of the period is for him equivalent to a given sum of income at the end of the period, is equal to r then the present value of y_t is $y_t/(1 + r)$.

By a similar argument the present value of income paid at the end of period $t + 1$, y_{t+1}, is $y_{t+1}/(1 + r)^2$, since this sum lent out at the beginning of period t would equal $y_{t+1}/(1 + r)$ at the end of period t; and *this* sum, if lent out at the beginning of period $t + 1$, would equal y_{t+1} at the end of period $t + 1$. In general, the present value of y_{t+i} is $y_{t+i}/(1 + r)^i$.

The sum of the present values of current and future real labour income is what we shall refer to as the stock of human wealth at time period t, H_t. It represents the amount the individual can borrow in period t against the income he expects to earn over the rest of his life. In what follows we shall assume that the value of real labour income in period t is known at the beginning of period t, but that all future values are not known and hence expectations have to be formed about them. It is this uncertainty which introduces expectations into the model. Formally, we write:

$$H_t = \sum_0^\infty \rho^{1+i} E_t y_{t+i} \tag{9.1}$$

where H_t is the real present value of current and expected future labour income, $\rho = 1/(1 + r)$, and $E_t y_t = y_t$.

In writing equation (9.1) we have assumed that the individual's planning horizon is infinite; that is, the summation runs from zero to infinity rather than from zero to the expected period of his death. This may seem odd but it greatly simplifies the analysis, and one way to rationalize it (as we did in chapter 8) is to imagine that each individual seeks to leave bequests to the next generation.

The present value of the individual's wealth can be seen as equal to the sum of non-human wealth, A_t, and human wealth, H_t. A central assumption of PIH is that there is diminishing marginal utility to consumption which implies that utility gained from a one-unit higher level of consumption in periods when income is unusually high is not sufficient to offset the loss in utility resulting from a one-unit lower level of consumption when income is unusually low. An implication of this is that given the value of their human and non-human wealth at time t individuals will gain most satisfaction from (and will therefore plan to carry out) *a constant* level of consumption from t onwards. This constant level of consumption from t onwards, it should be emphasized, is the level of consumption the individual *plans* at time t to carry out, given A_t and his view of H_t. In a subsequent period, say period $t + 1$, when new information may have caused him to change his estimate of his stock of wealth, the constant level of consumption he plans for $t + 1$ onwards will be different from the level planned at period t, but at each period the optimal plan involves specifying a *constant* level of consumption from the period onwards.

The problem the individual has to solve is: What is the maximum, constant level of consumption that he can carry out each period from t to infinity, given the value of $A_t + H_t$? The answer is $r|A_t + H_t|$; that is, the interest earned on his stock of wealth. This is the constant amount of his available resources which he can consume while preserving his stock of resources at their initial level. If he consumes any more than the interest earned from his stock of wealth, his stock of wealth will decline, eventually to zero, making positive consumption at some future date impossible; if he consumes any less, his wealth will gradually increase and hence he will not be consuming as much as he could. The sum that he can consume while preserving the value of his wealth, in other words $r|A_t + H_t|$, is called the individual's permanent income, y_t^p. PIH states that since y_t^p is the level of consumption that maximizes the individual's utility given the constraints imposed on him by his wealth, y_t^p will be his level of consumption. Formally, we can state PIH as

$$c_t = y_t^p = r\left[A_t + H_t\right] = r\left[A_t + \sum_0^\infty \rho^{1+i} E_t y_{t+i}\right] \tag{9.2}$$

where c_t is real consumption.

In this representation of PIH and in most of the rest of this chapter we shall ignore the possibility of any random error term on the right-hand side of equation (9.2); that is, we assume zero *transitory* consumption.

9.2 PIH AND RATIONAL EXPECTATIONS: HALL'S MODEL

Hall (1978) was one of the first to apply rational expectations to PIH and derive and test an unusual feature of the resulting model. To understand Hall's test it is helpful first to write in full some of the expressions in the summation term in equation (9.2):

$$c_t = rA_t + r\rho E_t y_t + r\rho^2 E_t y_{t+1} + r\rho^3 E_t y_{t+2} + r\rho^4 E_t y_{t+3}$$

$$+ r\rho^5 E_t y_{t+4} + \ldots \tag{9.3}$$

where '. . .' represents the further terms in the equation which, for expositional purposes, we omit.

Lagging equation (9.3) by one period gives

$$c_{t-1} = rA_{t-1} + r\rho E_{t-1} y_{t-1} + r\rho^2 E_{t-1} y_t + r\rho^3 E_{t-1} y_{t+1}$$

$$+ r\rho^4 E_{t-1} y_{t+2} + \ldots \tag{9.4}$$

Multiplying this by $1/\rho$ gives

$$(1/\rho)c_{t-1} = (1/\rho)rA_{t-1} + rE_{t-1} y_{t-1} + r\rho E_{t-1} y_t + r\rho^2 E_{t-1} y_{t+1}$$

$$+ r\rho^3 E_{t-1} y_{t+2} + \ldots \tag{9.5}$$

Subtracting equation (9.5) from (9.3) allows us to write

$$c_t - |1/\rho|c_{t-1} = rA_t - r(1/\rho)A_{t-1} - rE_{t-1} y_{t-1}$$

$$+ r\rho \sum_0^\infty \rho^i \Delta E_t y_{t+i} \tag{9.6}$$

where $\Delta E_t y_{t+i} \equiv E_t y_{t+i} - E_{t-1} y_{t+i}$, the change in expectation between period $t-1$ and t of the value of y_{t+i}.

Rearranging this slightly and recognizing that $1/\rho$ equals $1 + r$, we obtain

$$c_t - c_{t-1} = rc_{t-1} + rA_t - r(1/\rho)A_{t-1} - rE_{t-1} y_{t-1}$$

$$+ r\rho \sum_0^\infty \rho^i \Delta E_t y_{t+i} \tag{9.7}$$

Now, by definition, the value of assets as the beginning of period

t, A_t, equals to the value of assets at the beginning of period $t - 1$, A_{t-1}, plus income earned on those assets, rA_{t-1}, plus labour income in period $t - 1$, y_{t-1}, minus consumption in period $t - 1$, c_{t-1}. So we can write

$$A_t = (1 + r) A_{t-1} + y_{t-1} - c_{t-1} \tag{9.8}$$

and this can be rewritten to give

$$rc_{t-1} = r[y_{t-1} + (1/\rho)A_{t-1} - A_t] \tag{9.9}$$

Substituting this value for rc_{t-1} into equation (9.7) and noting that our assumption that $E_t y_t = y_t$ implies that $E_{t-1} y_{t-1} = y_{t-1}$, we obtain

$$c_t - c_{t-1} = r\rho \sum_0^\infty \rho^i \Delta E_t y_{t+i} \tag{9.10}$$

or

$$c_t = c_{t-1} + r\rho \sum_0^\infty \rho^i \Delta E_t y_{t+i} \tag{9.11}$$

Now, as we stressed in earlier chapters, it is a defining characteristic of a rational expectation of any variable that it uses all available information relevant to the behaviour of that variable. Therefore $E_{t-1} y_{t+i}$, the forecast of y_{t+i} made on the basis of information available in period $t - 1$, and $E_t y_{t+i}$, the forecast of y_{t+i} made on the basis of information available in period t, can only differ because of information which became available in period t and which was not available in period $t - 1$. This 'news' must have been unpredictable in period $t - 1$; otherwise one of the conditions for the rationality of the expectation would be violated. Therefore $\Delta E_t y_{t+i}$, the change in the expectation about y_{t+i}, must itself be unpredictable from any information available in period $t - 1$. This will be true for all values of i and hence will be true of the sum $\sum_0^\infty \rho^i \Delta E_t y_{t+i}$. It follows that since $r\rho$ is a constant we can replace $r\rho \sum_0^\infty \rho^i \Delta E_t y_{t+i}$ on the right-hand side of equations (9.10) and (9.11) with ω_t, a random error term with mean zero, and with the important characteristic that its value in any period t is wholly unpredictable from any information available in any earlier period. Thus:

$$c_t = c_{t-1} + \omega_t \quad \text{or equivalently} \quad \Delta c_t = \omega_t \tag{9.12, 9.13}$$

where $E_{t-1} \omega_t = 0$.

The combination of the permanent-income hypothesis and the rational expectations hypothesis has thus produced a surprisingly simple consumption function, one that explains current consumption by its own lagged value together with a random term. Consumption will follow what is called a 'random walk'.

The intuition behind this result is as follows: in period $t - 1$, given the information available, an individual sets consumption at c_{t-1}; that is, equal to his estimate of his permanent income in period $t - 1$. This decision takes full account of all information dated $t - 1$ and earlier. Since in period $t - 1$ he has consumed an amount equal to his permanent income, his stock of wealth in period t, if no *new* information about his future labour income has become available in period t, will be the same as it was at the beginning of $t - 1$, and so in period t his estimate of his permanent income will be unchanged and he will set consumption, c_t, at the same level as before, c_{t-1}. Only if *new* information becomes available between period $t - 1$ and t, for example that the individual has unexpectedly lost his job, will consumption change in period t. By definition, new information is unpredictable and so consumption differs from lagged consumption only by an unpredictable element.

Hall (1978) was the first to note this result and to argue from it that 'no variable apart from current consumption should be of any value in predicting future consumption' (p. 971).

9.3   TESTS OF HALL'S MODEL

One obvious but weak test of REPI would involve the estimation of the following:

$$c_t = \alpha + \beta c_{t-1} + \epsilon_t \tag{9.14}$$

Hall's model predicts that in the absence of transitory consumption the error term ϵ_t should be serially independent and the estimate of β should be close to unity. Examples of this weak test are Hall (1978) who, using quarterly US data for the period 1948–77, estimated β to be 1.011, and Daly and Hadjimatheou (1981) who, using UK quarterly data for the period 1964–79, estimated β to be 0.72 with a standard error of 0.25.

Although these estimates are close to unity as the Hall model predicts, the test is hardly an exacting one since, as Davidson and Hendry (1981) point out, other models of consumption may have the same implication. Another, and stronger, type of test, referred to as an orthogonality test, is to regress the change in consumption, Δc_t, on lagged variables and test the prediction of REPI that none of these laged variables should have any significance. Many studies of this form have been carried out. Of course, there are potentially an infinite number of lagged variables which might affect Δc_t and thereby refute REPI, so no single test which fails to refute REPI can be decisive: it may be that other lagged variables would have refuted REPI had they been tried. In fact, most studies of this type have found that while, as REPI suggests, lagged consumption, c_{t-1}, does account for a large amount of the movements in current consumption, c_t, other lagged variables exert a significant influence too. Hall (1978), for example, carried out this type of test and found that while lagged income had little predictive power for consumption, the recent change in the real value of the stock market did have a significant effect on current consumption. This latter result amounts to a rejection of REPI. Davidson and Hendry (1981) found, using UK data, that lagged income and a lagged measure of liquidity were significant influences on consumption even when lagged consumption was allowed for. Similarly, Daly and Hadjimatheou (1981) found on UK data that higher-order lags in consumption and income significantly influenced consumption. All in all, the results from this type of test suggest that while the simple REPI's random walk model of consumption accounts approximately for the actual behaviour of consumption, it nevertheless is strictly inconsistent with the data and on the basis of this evidence REPI would have to be rejected.

An alternative method of testing REPI which uses the Hall framework has been suggested by Flavin (1981) and applied by her to US data. The main features of this test can best be seen within the following simplified and modified version. Assume that the process determining labour income y_t can be adequately represented by the following:

$$y_t = \alpha_0 + \alpha_1 y_{t-1} + \epsilon_t \tag{9.15}$$

where the α's are coefficients and α_1 is presumed to be less than one in absolute value; ϵ is a serially independent zero mean random error.

If this is the process determining y_t and if the information set at period t includes y_t then we can write $E_t y_t = y_t = \alpha_0 + \alpha_1 y_{t-1} + \epsilon_t$. The expectation of y_t, formed on the basis of information available in period $t - 1$, does not include the error term ϵ_t but does include y_{t-1} and knowledge of the process. Since, from our assumptions about ϵ_t, the rational expectation at period $t - 1$ of the value of ϵ_t is zero, it follows that we can write $E_{t-1} y_t = \alpha_0 + \alpha_1 y_{t-1}$. The change in the expectation of y_t, $\Delta E_t y_t$, is therefore simply ϵ_t. By a similar but slightly more complex procedure we can derive the change in the expectation of any future value of y as a function purely of ϵ_t. We illustrate the procedure for the simple case $\Delta E_t y_{t+1}$.

By updating equation (9.15) by one period we have

$$y_{t+1} = \alpha_0 + \alpha_1 y_t + \epsilon_{t+1} \tag{9.16}$$

The information set at period t includes y_t and the α's, but not ϵ_{t+1}. From its assumed characteristics the best guess that can be made in period t about ϵ_{t+1} is that it will be zero. So we can write $E_t y_{t+1} = \alpha_0 + \alpha_1 y_t$. The information set at period $t - 1$ includes neither ϵ_t nor, of course, ϵ_{t+1}. So the expectation of y_{t+1} formed in period $t - 1$ will be $E_{t-1} y_{t+1} = \alpha_0 + \alpha_1 [\alpha_0 + \alpha_1 y_{t-1}]$. The change in expectation of y_{t+1} between periods $t - 1$ and t, $\Delta E_t y_{t+1}$, will therefore be $\alpha_1 \epsilon_t$. Similarly, $\Delta E_t y_{t+2}$ will be $\alpha_1^2 \epsilon_t$ (that is, α_1 squared times ϵ_t). In general, we can write

$$\Delta E_t y_{t+i} = \alpha_1^i \epsilon_t \tag{9.17}$$

From this, and equation (9.10), it follows that we can write

$$\Delta c_t = r\rho \sum_0^\infty \rho^i \alpha_1^i \epsilon_t \tag{9.18}$$

The term $r\rho \sum_0^\infty \rho^i \alpha_1^i \epsilon_t$ is really the revision to permanent income between period $t - 1$ and t. What equation (9.18) shows is that if labour income follows the process shown in equation (9.15) this revision is a function of the innovation in current measured labour income, ϵ_t. Thus the change in consumption will be a function of current income, or at least the 'innovation' in current income, ϵ_t. The amount by which consumption should change in response to a particular value for ϵ_t is given by equation (9.18). If consumption changes less than this amount, it is said to be 'excessively smooth' (see Campbell and Deaton (1989), who find evidence that

US consumption is excessively smooth).

To explain Flavin's test of equation (9.18) we first need to recognize that, since α_1 is absolutely less than one, the sum of the infinite series $\sum_0^\infty \rho^i \alpha_1^i$ can be written $1/(1 - \rho\alpha_1)$, which allows us to write

$$\Delta c_t = \varphi/(1 - \rho\alpha_1)\epsilon_t \qquad (9.19)$$

where $\varphi = r/(1 + r)$.

This equation, together with the equation defining the assumed process for y_t, gives a two-equation system with cross-equation restrictions imposed by REPI. This system, after substituting for ϵ_t in the equation for consumption, can be written as follows:

$$y_t = \alpha_0 + \alpha_1 y_{t-1} + \epsilon_t,$$

$$\Delta c_t = -\alpha_0 \varphi/(1 - \rho\alpha_1) + |\varphi/(1 - \rho\alpha_1)]y_t \\ - |\alpha_1 \varphi/(1 - \rho\alpha_1)]y_{t-1} \qquad (9.20)$$

The restricted nature of this system is apparent from the fact that there are five coefficients in the unrestricted version of equation (9.20), that is the two constants, the coefficients on y_{t-1} in both equations, and the coefficient on y_t in the Δc equation, but only two parameters, α_0 and α_1. (It is common practice in this literature to impose a plausible value for r, usually about 4 per cent per annum. As a result φ is not a parameter to be estimated – its value is determined by the imposed value of r. The reader can check that even if a prior value for φ were not imposed, equation (9.20) still imposes restrictions.) This restricted model could be compared with an unrestricted two-equation system:

$$y_t = \pi_0^* + \pi_1^* y_{t-1} + \epsilon_t^*, \qquad \Delta c_t = \pi_2^* + \pi_3^* y_t + \pi_4^* y_{t-1} \quad (9.21)$$

In fact Flavin, who incorporates a process for y_t which includes a larger number of lags than our equation (9.15), carries out a somewhat different test in which she includes in the consumption equation in the equivalent of equation (9.20) a series of additional terms in Δy_t and lags of Δy_t and tests for their joint significance. She also allows for an unrestricted constant term, μ, and an independent error term v_t, in the Δc_t equation. In terms of our simplified version her model is as follows:

$$y_t = \alpha_0 + \alpha_1 y_{t-1} + \epsilon_t,$$

$$\Delta c_t = \mu - \alpha_0 \varphi/(1 - \rho\alpha_1) + |\varphi/(1 - \rho\alpha_1)]y_t \\ - |\alpha_1 \varphi/(1 - \rho\alpha_1)]y_{t-1} + \beta_0 \Delta y_t + v_t \qquad (9.22)$$

Substituting for y_t in the second equation allows us to write the equation for Δc_t as

$$\Delta c_t = \mu^* + \beta_0[\alpha_1 - 1]y_{t-1} + \epsilon_{1t} \qquad (9.23)$$

where $\mu^* = \mu + \beta_0\alpha_0$, and $\epsilon_{1t} = [\beta_0 + \wp/(1 - \rho\alpha_1)]\epsilon_t + \nu_t$.

Flavin's test of REPI becomes then a test of the significance of β_0, the coefficient on lagged income in a regression of Δc_t. Thus Flavin's test is the same as the orthogonality tests described above, but one in which she concentrates on the role of lagged income.

Her findings, on US data, are that β_0 is not zero and that REPI can be therefore be rejected. Consumption appears to be 'excessively sensitive' to income; that is, consumption responds to changes in current income by an amount in excess of that which one would expect on the basis of REPI and the apparent process driving labour income.

One feature of Flavin's test is that she specifies a particular process for income: in her case the process consists essentially of a number of lagged values of income. Individuals may, as Flavin herself recognizes, have more information about their future labour income than is contained in lagged values of their income, and therefore the term $r\rho\sum_0^\infty \rho^i \alpha_1^i \epsilon_t$ may not be capturing the true change in permanent income. A recent idea put forward by Campbell (1987) suggests how we might get closer to a truer measure of the change in permanent income even though we do not actually observe it. This idea and the tests of REPI to which it has given rise are described in the next section.

9.4 SAVINGS AND REPI: CAMPBELL'S MODEL

Campbell (1987), Campbell and Clarida (1987) and Campbell and Deaton (1989) have developed the implications of REPI for the behaviour of savings, and used these implications as the basis of a test of REPI. The two testable implications which emerge from this work are: first, that if REPI is true then savings should exert a significant negative influence on the change in labour income; and, second, that REPI places restrictions on the coefficients in a two-equation system in which the change in labour income and savings are regressed on lagged labour income changes and lagged savings.

To understand these implications we need first to define savings, s_t, as the difference between the individual's total income (that is, labour income plus capital income) and consumption. Formally,

$$s_t \equiv y_t + rA_t - c_t \tag{9.24}$$

Using PIH, equation (9.2), we can substitute for c_t in equation (9.24) to obtain

$$s_t = y_t - r\rho \sum_0^\infty \rho^i E_t y_{t+i} \tag{9.25}$$

which can be written as

$$s_t = y_t - r/(1+r)y_t - r/(1+r)^2 E_t y_{t+1} - r/(1+r)^3 E_t y_{t+2}$$
$$- r/(1+r)^4 E_t y_{t+3} - r/(1+r)^5 E_t y_{t+4} - \ldots \tag{9.26}$$

Now the following are all definitionally true:

$$E_t y_{t+1} \equiv y_t + E_t \Delta y_{t+1},$$

$$E_t y_{t+2} \equiv y_t + E_t \Delta y_{t+1} + E_t \Delta y_{t+2},$$

$$E_t y_{t+3} \equiv y_t + E_t \Delta y_{t+1} + E_t \Delta y_{t+2} + E_t \Delta y_{t+3} \tag{9.27}$$

and so on.

These definitions follow from rationality: for example, what you expect the level of y to be in three periods time, $E_t y_{t+3}$, must equal what you know y to be this period, y_t, plus the amount you expect y to change next period, $E_t \Delta y_{t+1}$, plus the amount you expect y to change the period after that, $E_t \Delta y_{t+2}$, plus the amount you expect y to change the period after that, $E_t \Delta y_{t+3}$.

Using the definitions in equation (9.27) we can substitute for the expressions in $E_t y_{t+i}$ in equation (9.26) and write

$$s_t = y_t - r/(1+r)y_t - r/(1+r)^2(y_t + E_t \Delta y_{t+1})$$
$$- r/(1+r)^3(y_t + E_t \Delta y_{t+1} + E_t \Delta y_{t+2})$$
$$- r/(1+r)^4(y_t + E_t \Delta y_{t+1} + E_t \Delta y_{t+2} + E_t \Delta y_{t+3})$$
$$- \ldots \tag{9.28}$$

We can now collect up all the terms in y_t, all the terms in $E_t \Delta y_{t+1}$, all the terms in $E_t \Delta y_{t+2}$, and so on, and write

$$s_t = y_t - r/(1 + r)y_t - r/(1 + r)^2 \sum_0^\infty \rho^i y_t - r/(1 + r)^2 \sum_0^\infty \rho^i E_t \Delta y_{t+1}$$

$$- r/(1 + r)^3 \sum_0^\infty \rho^i E_t \Delta y_{t+2} - r/(1 + r)^4 \sum_0^\infty \rho^i E_t \Delta y_{t+3}$$

$$- r/(1 + r)^5 \sum_0^\infty \rho^i E_t \Delta y_{t+4} - \ldots \qquad (9.29)$$

Now, since ρ is defined as $1/(1 + r)$ the sum of the infinite series, $\sum_0^\infty \rho^i$ can be written $1/(1 - \rho)$ or, more simply, as $(1 + r)/r$. Therefore equation (9.29) can be written as

$$s_t = y_t - r/(1 + r)y_t - r/(1 + r)^2 [(1 + r)/r] y_t$$

$$- r/(1 + r)^2 [(1 + r)/r | E_t \Delta y_{t+1}$$

$$- r/(1 + r)^3 [(1 + r)/r] E_t \Delta y_{t+2}$$

$$- r/(1 + r)^4 [(1 + r)/r | E_t \Delta y_{t+3}$$

$$- r/(1 + r)^5 [(1 + r)/r] E_t \Delta y_{t+4}$$

$$- \ldots \qquad (9.30)$$

which, since the terms in y_t cancel out, can be written as

$$s_t = - \sum_1^\infty \rho^i E_t \Delta y_{t+i} \qquad (9.31)$$

This is what Campbell terms the 'savings for a rainy day' version of the permanent-income hypothesis. If the present value of expected future changes in labour income is negative, individuals will save in the current period; if the present value of expected future changes in labour income is positive, individuals will dissave in the currrent period. This implication for savings is clearly the result of the assumption of PIH that individuals desire to smooth out their consumption over their time horizon: they can do so by saving in anticipation of hard times and dissaving (that is, spending in excess of their current income) in anticipation of good ones.

The two implications of REPI mentioned earlier can be derived from equation (9.31); first, the implication that savings should exert a significant negative influence on the change in labour income. From equation (9.31) it follows that if an individual changes his view about the future course of his labour income then this will show up in a movement in current savings. Say, for example, that the individual obtains information in period t that the change in his labour income next period is going to be lower than he previously thought. Then equation (9.31) predicts that, if other things remain the same, this individual will increase his savings in period t. In aggregate then, a rise in current savings indicates that individuals in aggregate have revised downwards the present value of their expected future changes in labour income, and a fall in current aggregate savings indicates a revision upwards. If we, as outsiders, observe that individuals as a whole have increased their savings, it follows from REPI that we can infer that they have revised their view of their future labour income downwards, even though we may not directly observe the new information which has caused this revision.

Of course, each individual is likely to have a mass of information about the future course of his own labour income, of which it is impossible for an outsider to be fully aware. But, as Campbell's model shows, the behaviour of savings, which we *can* observe, signals the effects of this unobservable information to us. Furthermore, if expectations are rational then movements in *expectations* about the future change in labour income should be related to the true proccess governing the behaviour of the *actual* change in labour income. Thus movements in savings this period which signal changes in *expectations* about future labour income should also signal movements in *actual* future labour income. And therefore one would expect to find that lagged savings helps to predict current labour income. An econometrician estimating a regression of the current change in aggregate labour income on other variables is, according to REPI, therefore always likely to find that the inclusion of lagged aggregate savings improves the fit of his model. In Campbell's phrase, savings will have 'incremental explanatory power for future labour income'.

For example, in our simplified version of Flavin's model we assumed individuals predict labour income merely with reference to lagged income. Campbell's insight suggests that if individuals have any information at all other than lagged values of income which is useful for predicting current income then the inclusion of lagged savings, s_{t-1}, will improve the fit of the equation, and the coefficient estimated on s_{t-1} will be significant. Savings, if you like, is acting as a proxy for all the information which each individual has which is relevant to the future course of his labour income but which is unobservable to the econometrician or outside observer. In our example, we have assumed a very simple process for y_t, but however many other variables the econometrician includes in the regression of y_t, however complex he allows the process to become, he is unlikely thereby to capture all the information available to each individual.

It is therefore likely to be the case, if REPI is correct, that lagged savings will appear to exert a significant influence on the change in labour income. And since from equation (9.31) a rise in savings anticipates a fall in the present value of expected future changes in labour income, one would expect that savings exert a negative influence on the change in labour income. So, one test of REPI is to carry out a regression of Δy_t on a set of variables which conclude lagged savings and see if savings do exert a significant negative influence. We report on results of such tests later, but first we explain the second and more stringent test of REPI suggested by Campbell's framework.

This implication requires a little more mathematical manipulation. First, using equation (9.26), write

$$s_t = [1/(1 + r)] y_t - r/(1 + r)^2 E_t y_{t+1} - r/(1 + r)^3 E_t y_{t+2}$$
$$- r/(1 + r)^4 E_t y_{t+3} - r/(1 + r)^5 E_t y_{t+4} - \cdots \qquad (9.32)$$

Lagging this one period and multiplying the result by $(1 + r)$ gives:

$$(1 + r)s_{t-1} = y_{t-1} - r/(1 + r)E_{t-1} y_t - r/(1 + r)^2 E_{t-1} y_{t+1}$$
$$- r/(1 + r)^3 E_{t-1} y_{t+2} - r/(1 + r)^4 E_{t-1} y_{t+3} - \cdots \qquad (9.33)$$

On subtracting this from equation (9.32) we obtain

$$s_t - (1 + r)s_{t-1} = \Delta y_t - [r/(1 + r)] \sum_0^\infty \rho^i \Delta E_t y_{t+i} \qquad (9.34)$$

The last term in this expression is the sum of *revisions* to expectations, all of which must be unpredictable from information available in period $t - 1$. The whole term can therefore be replaced by a random, serially uncorrelated error term which is independent of any variable in period $t - 1$ or before. In fact, $s_t - (1 + r) s_{t-1} - \Delta y_t$ is, under our assumptions, identical to $- \Delta c_t$ and so from equation (9.13) we can denote this error term by $-\omega_t$. Therefore we can write

$$s_t - (1 + r)s_{t-1} - \Delta y_t = -\omega_t \qquad (9.35)$$

An implication of REPI is therefore that the variable $s_t - (1 + r) s_{t-1} - \Delta y_t$ should be independent of all variables known in period $t - 1$. One could therefore test REPI using the same sort of tests as we described above when explaining the Hall model: regressions of $s_t - (1 - r)s_{t-1} - \Delta y_t$ on lagged variables. REPI predicts that all the lagged variables should be insignificant. This is actually the form of the test which Campbell adopts.

An alternative way of testing REPI using Campbell's framework is to test the implied cross-equation restrictions on the coefficients of a vector autoregression (VAR) involving Δy_t and s_t; that is, a two-equation system in which Δy_t and s_t are regressed on lags of Δy and s. To show what these restrictions are we need to specify a process for the change in labour income. A point that we made when discussing Flavin's assumed process for labour income is that it was likely to omit information available to individuals but not observable to the econometrician. The analysis we have discussed above suggests that we can get round this problem to some extent by including lagged savings as an influence on Δy_t. To keep it relatively simple we shall assume that the process driving Δy_t can be captured by two lagged values of Δy_t itself and two lagged values of savings. Specifically, assume that

$$\Delta y_t = \alpha_0 + \alpha_1 \Delta y_{t-1} + \alpha_2 \Delta y_{t-2} + \beta_1 s_{t-1} + \beta_2 s_{t-2} + \xi_{1t} \quad (9.36)$$

where the α's and β's are coefficients and ξ_{1t} is a serially uncorrelated, zero mean random error term.

From equation (9.35) and this process for Δy_t we can deduce the following process for savings:

$$s_t = \alpha_0 + \alpha_1 \Delta y_{t-1} + \alpha_2 \Delta y_{t-2} + (1 + r + \beta_1)s_{t-1} + \beta_2 s_{t-2}$$
$$+ \xi_{2t} \quad (9.37)$$

where ξ_{2t} is another serially uncorrelated, zero mean random error term such that $\xi_{1t} - \xi_{2t}$ equals ω_t.

Equations (9.36) and (9.37) can be estimated jointly and the restrictions implied by REPI imposed. These are that the coefficients estimated on each variable should be the same in each equation except in the case of s_{t-1} where the coefficient in the savings equation should be larger by $1 + r$. (Strictly, the constants should be the same too but this restriction is often not imposed in practice.) An advantage of this form of the test is that one can at the same time test the first implication of REPI mentioned above that the coefficient (or sum of the coefficients) on lagged savings in the Δy_t equation should be significantly negative.

A number of tests have been made of REPI using Campbell's framework. They all show more or less the same thing: the first implication of REPI – that lagged savings should negatively influence the change in labour income – is confirmed; but the second implication – that the cross-equation restrictions implied by REPI on a VAR involving Δy_t and s_t should be valid – is rejected. Such are the findings reported in Campbell (1987) and Campbell and Deaton (1989) for the US, Campbell and Clarida (1987) for the UK and Canada, and Attfield, Demery and Duck (1990) for the UK.

9.5 SUMMARY AND RECENT DEVELOPMENTS

In summary, the combination of the rational expectations hypothesis and a simple version of the permanent-income hypothesis has produced a model of consumption which, while capturing some features of actual consumption behaviour – notably that lagged consumption influences current consumption and that lagged savings negatively influences the change in labour income – can nevertheless be rejected by standard statistical tests. In particular, the change in consumption does appear to be influenced, as REPI suggests it should not be, by past values of income and certain other variables.

This rejection of what is, of course, a joint hypothesis has begun to stimulate a considerable amount of new research. Most of this research involves modification of PIH part of the model rather than the rational expectations hypothesis. We conclude this chapter by briefly mentioning some of the lines that are currently being considered.

The first of these is a relaxation of the assumption on PIH that any individual can borrow to sustain his consumption at its permanent-income level when actual income is unusually low. Most individuals may feel that they are times 'liquidity constrained'; that is, they do not have the amount of assets readily convertible into money with which they need to sustain consumption when their current income is low, and they are unable to borrow enough to make up the deficiency. Many theoretical and empirical studies have considered the results of incorporating this idea into REPI with some success (they are surveyed in Hayashi, 1987). Another line of research distinguishes between the consumption of non-durables and durable goods (see, for example, Bernanke, 1984, 1985; Mankiw, 1985b). This distinction is likely to be important since PIH is really concerned with the flow of consumption *services* rather than consumption *expenditure*: some items which are classified as consumption expenditure are purchases of durable goods such as cars, refrigerators, televisions and so on. The values of these purchases themselves are not strictly consumption: one does not consume a television when one purchases it in the same sense that one consumes a glass of wine or a concert. It is really the flow of consumer services provided by the television which PIH is attempting to explain. The influence of lagged variables on the change in measured consumption expenditure may be due to expenditure on these items. Such expenditure is likely to be subject to costs of adjustment and therefore to appear to react more sluggishly than the simple REPI suggests. Again, this line of research shows some promise in reconciling REPI with the facts.

Other lines of research are the possibility that the real rate of interest may not, as we have assumed, be constant, and that there may be shifts in preferences which invalidate the simple version of REPI (see, for example, Hall, 1986; Wickens and Molana, 1984).

SUGGESTIONS FOR FURTHER READING

Lucas (1976) uses the consumption function as an illustration of his critique of econometric policy models. Hall's (1989) chapter in Barro (1989) provides a brief survey of the main theoretical and empirical work carried out on REPI, especially in the US. Attfield and Browning (1985) apply a rational expectations permanent-income model to a demand system. Mankiw and Shapiro (1985) show that Flavin's rejection of REPI may be due to her use of detrended data. West (1988) uses variance bounds techniques to test REPI. Another interesting area of research considers the fact that, while strictly REPI can be statistically rejected, the behaviour of aggregate consumption conforms reasonably closely to REPI's predictions. Cochrane (1989) introduces the idea of near-rationality to explain this.

10

Summary and Conclusions

10.1 THE RATIONAL EXPECTATIONS HYPOTHESIS

The rational expectations hypothesis has had an enormous impact on macroeconomics over the past 20 years. It has radically changed the way in which macroeconomic relationships are modelled; it has similarly changed views about macroeconomic policy; and it has led to a number of important developments in the estimation and testing of macroeconomic models.

Yet the hypothesis itself may, at first sight, appear innocuous. One way of viewing it is that it is merely a requirement for a model's internal consistency: models which incorporate expectations should assume that agents' expectations of a variable are formed in a way that is consistent with the way in which that variable is, according to the model, being determined. Alternatively, and more loosely, it can be viewed as an implication of a basic assumption of economics, that economic agents optimize subject to the constraints they face. Such an assumption implies that agents, when forming expectations of any variable that is important to them, will use the available information about the process determining that variable. Any other behaviour would be wasteful or suboptimal.

More concretely, why should agents ignore the stance of monetary policy when forming expectations about inflation, given the evidence about the role of monetary policy in determining inflation? Or, why should they ignore the role of the electoral cycle in influencing a government's fiscal policy, given the well-known tendency of fiscal policy to be more relaxed in the period running up to an election? In general, why should they form expectations about any variable in a way that is inconsistent with the process actually determining it?

At the very least, the rational expectations hypothesis, by asking these questions, has challenged other theories to answer them and has thereby raised the level of debate. The fact that it has done more than merely put other theories on the defensive is partly because these other theories have had difficulty in answering the questions posed, partly because of the pervasive influence of expectations within macroeconomics, and partly because of the assumption typically made in the rational expectations literature about the amount of information available to agents when forming expectations.

It is from this last assumption that the rational expectations hypothesis gains much of its power. In most areas in which rational expectations has been applied, the amount of information that agents possess about the process determining a variable is assumed to be at least equal to the amount of information available to the economic model-builder or to the econometrician testing the model. It is this which generates the typical rational expectation result that the predicted and predictable components of a process are identical, and that the forecasting error is the inherently unpredictable component.

This assumption about the amount of information that rational agents possess is obviously a very strong one and, some would say, a very unrealistic one. It has been justified on a number of grounds. First, a world in which expectations are rationally formed, but on the basis of a very restricted information set, would be very difficult to distinguish from a world in which expectations are not formed rationally. So, in order to make any distinctive, testable predictions, a strong assumption about the available information has to be made. Second, it is difficult to establish general principles about what information to exclude from or include in the information set. It is therefore difficult to know, in any particular application, what information should be excluded from the information set. (Indeed, as we have seen when discussing the role of saving in the consumption function, it may well be that economic agents possess *more* information than does the economic model-builder.) It is this inability to provide sound theoretical reasons for excluding information that has probably more than anything else led to the disuse of earlier theories of expectations formation. So, in applying rational expectations economists have, in the absence of any alternative, tended to assume that none of the information which they possess, or which their models suggest is important, is unavailable to agents. A third, related reason for this strong assumption is that presumably information relevant to a process will tend to become more rather than less widely known. Therefore, it is likely to become closer to, rather than further from, the truth to assume that the process determining a variable is known, and that the information available to agents is sufficient to allow them to forecast all but the inherently unpredictable component of that process.

This last sentence reinforces the view that rational expectations should be viewed as an *equilibrium* condition, whereas other methods of expectation formation cannot be. For if another method of forming expectations is assumed within an economic model, there must be some scope to change and improve that method, and the whole model is therefore not in full equilibrium. But once expectations are formed rationally this ceases to be the case: the whole model can then be in full equilibrium since there is no scope to improve on rational expectations.

With this in mind, rational expectations are most convincingly applied to phenomena which:

> . . . can be viewed as repeated instances of essentially similar events, [and where it is reasonable] to assume [that economic agents] have fairly stable arrangements for collecting and processing information, and that they utilise this information in forecasting the future in a stable way, free of systematic and easily correctable biases.
>
> (Lucas, 1977, p. 15)

For the same reason, the hypothesis is likely to be less useful in analysing events which are best viewed as unique, or at least cannot be seen as the result of a familiar process. Recent examples of such events are the oil-price shock in 1973, the abandonment of fixed exchange rates in the early 1970s, and the changeover in Eastern Europe from centrally planned to market-based economies.

10.2   POLICY IMPLICATIONS

The main impact of the rational expectations hypothesis on policy, or at least the theory of policy, is its implication that policies are likely to fail if, to be effective, they require that agents do not know or cannot discern the process actually determining those policies. For similar reasons, policies which work if agents understand them need to be credible; that is, agents have to be convinced that the policies announced will be pursued.

Initially, this message for policy was taken to imply that there was no role for government in stabilizing output, or at least that the government could not do so by linking its fiscal and monetary stance to the state of the economy. Instead, the government should announce its intentions about current and future fiscal and monetary policy, preferably by specifying what simple rules it intends to follow, and ensure that those rules are adhered to.

However, it soon became clear, as we have seen, that the ineffectiveness of government stabilization policy arose less from rational expectations itself and more from the model with which rational expectations was initially combined. Other models were developed which implied that government stabilization policy has a potential role even where expectations are rational, although the form that that stabilization policy takes may differ from the conventional Keynesian one. Furthermore, a number of empirical papers strongly questioned the strength of the evidence in favour of the proposition that government stabilization policy is likely to be ineffective.

At the same time, experiences such as the change in economic policy initiated by Mrs Thatcher in the UK in 1979 indicated that establishing credibility for policies was very difficult. The UK government elected in May 1979 announced what was called its Medium Term Financial Strategy (MTFS). A key element in this was a commitment to tighten both fiscal and monetary policy over the medium term. The subsequent sharp recession in the UK appeared to many to demonstrate that expectations had not been conditioned by the MTFS. Of course, it is always possible to argue, as the following quote from Minford (1980) shows, that the MTFS lacked credibility and that it was rational to believe that it would not be maintained but, as the quote also indicates, this illustrates a weakness in the rational expectations hypothesis; that is, it gives few guidelines about whether or not a policy change will be credible:

It is quite wrong to suggest that merely 'announcing intentions' will itself establish a credible strategy. The Rational Expectations view

of the economy has never made such a suggestion . . . The Rational
Expectations view does however assert that, once fully believed,
new policies will immediately condition expectations of inflation,
output growth etc. However, assessing the speed at which this
credibility will be attained is a highly uncertain matter.

(Minford, 1980, p. 131)

For all these reasons the rational expectations hypothesis has, as
yet, had much less impact on the actual conduct of policy than it
has had on macroeconomic modelling.

10.3   TESTS OF THE RATIONAL EXPECTATIONS HYPOTHESIS

A major feature of the rational expectations hypothesis is that it
imposes restrictions on what we should observe in the data. For
example, as we have seen in chapter 9, when combined with a simple version of the permanent-income hypothesis rational expectations implies that the first difference of consumption should be
uncorrelated with any lagged variable.

This characteristic of rational expectations has led to tests of
such restrictions becoming a much more prominent feature of
econometric research. However, a familiar problem with such tests
is that the restrictions are usually dependent upon the model with
which rational expectations are combined. Hence it is almost
always possible to 'explain away' the rejection of any restrictions
by arguing that the rest of the model, not rational expectations
itself, is at fault. Only if one is absolutely certain (and one never
really can be) about the model with which the rational expectations
hypothesis is combined can one really be sure about whether it is
the rational expectations hypothesis itself which is being tested. In
practice, if, in a variety of contexts, the restrictions implied by
rational expectations are rejected the hypothesis would be rejected.

The evidence on the rational expectations hypothesis in macroeconomics is still very mixed. The direct tests summarized in
chapter 3, or the tests of restrictions imposed by the hypothesis of
rational expectations on the foreign exchange market or bond
markets, also considered in chapter 3, provide at best only very
modest support for the hypothesis. The early work by Lucas and
Barro and others, considered in chapter 6, provides some support,
although this has been seriously challenged by studies such as those

surveyed in chapter 7. And there is some evidence in favour of rational expectations from the studies of the consumption function discussed in chapter 9, although once again the evidence is by no means clear-cut.

10.4 CONCLUSIONS

Despite this rather mixed evidence, rational expectations has undoubtedly become the standard way of modelling expectations in macroeconomics. Whatever the reason for this dominance, whether it is due to its own theoretical appeal or the absence of any theoretically attractive alternative, it is certainly true that there is hardly a branch of macroeconomic theory in which rational expectations has not been introduced and its implications explored; that its introduction has radically influenced the conduct of applied research in macroeconomics; and that for the moment it appears to have no serious rival.

References

Abel, A.B. and Mishkin, F.S. (1983) An integrated view of tests of rationality, market efficiency and the short run neutrality of monetary policy, *Journal of Monetary Economics*, 11, pp. 3–23.

Alberro, J. (1981) The Lucas hypothesis on the Phillips curve: further international evidence, *Journal of Monetary Economics*, 7, pp. 239–50.

Alogoskoufis, G. and Pissarides, C. A. (1983) A test of price sluggishness in the simple rational expectations model: UK 1950–1980, *Economic Journal*, 93, pp. 616–28.

Akerlof, G. and Yellen, G. (1985) A near-rational model of the business cycle with wage and price inertia, *Quarterly Journal of Economics*, 100, pp. 823–38.

Attfield, C.L.F. (1983) An analysis of the implications of omitting variables from the monetary growth equation in a model of real output and unanticipated money growth, *European Economic Review*, 23, pp. 281–90.

Attfield, C.L.F. and Browning, M.J. (1985) A differential demand system, rational expectations and the life cycle hypothesis, *Econometrica*, 53, pp. 31–48.

Attfield, C.L.F. and Duck, N.W. (1982) Tests of the rational expectations model of the term structure of UK interest rates, *Economics Letters*, 10, pp. 115–21.

Attfield, C.L.F. and Duck, N.W. (1983) The influence of unanticipated money growth on real output: some cross country estimates, *Journal of Money, Credit and Banking*, 15, pp. 442–54.

Attfield, C.L.F. and Duck, N.W. (1986) Distinguishing between rational expectations and 'Keynesian' models of the business cycle in the presence of a structural break in the money growth process, *Economics Letters*, 22, pp. 133–5.

Attfield, C.L.F., Demery, D. and Duck, N.W. (1981a) Unanticipated monetary growth, output and the price level: UK 1946–1977, *European Economic Review*, 16, pp. 367–85.

Attfield, C.L.F., Demery, D. and Duck, N.W. (1981b) A quarterly model of unanticipated monetary growth, output and the price level: UK 1963–1978, *Journal of Monetary Economics*, 8, pp. 331–50.

Attfield, C.L.F., Demery, D. and Duck, N.W. (1990) Saving and rational expectations: evidence for the UK, *Economic Journal*, forthcoming.

Baillie, R.T., Lippens, R.E. and McMahon, P.C. (1983) Testing rational expectations and efficiency in the foreign exchange market, *Econometrica*, 51, pp. 553–64.

Barro, R.J. (1976) Rational expectations and the role of monetary policy, *Journal of Monetary Economics*, 2, pp. 1–33.

Barro, R.J. (1977a) Unanticipated money growth and unemployment in the United States, *American Economic Review*, 67, pp. 101–15.

Barro, R.J. (1977b) Long term contracting, sticky prices, and monetary policy, *Journal of Monetary Economics*, 3, pp. 305–16.

Barro, R.J. (1978a) Unanticipated money, output and the price level in the United States, *Journal of Political Economy*, 86, pp. 549–80.

Barro, R.J. (1978b) A stochastic equilibrium model of an open economy under flexible exchange rates, *Quarterly Journal of Economics*, 92, pp. 149–64.

Barro, R.J. (1985) Recent developments in the theory of rules versus discretion, *Economic Journal*, Supplement, 96, pp. 23–37.

Barro, R.J. (1989) Introduction, in *Modern Business Cycle Theory* (Ed. R.J. Barro), Oxford, Basil Blackwell.

Barro, R.J. and Gordon, D.B. (1983) A positive theory of money policy in a natural rate model, *Journal of Political Economy*, 11, pp. 589–610.

Barro, R.J. and Grossman, H.I. (1971) A general equilibrium model of income and employment, *American Economic Review*, 61, pp. 82–93.

Barro, R.J. and Rush, M. (1980) Unanticipated money and economic activity, in *Rational Expectations and Economic Policy* (Ed. S. Fischer), Chicago, University of Chicago Press for National Bureau of Economic Research.

Bean, C. (1984) A little bit more evidence on the natural rate hypothesis from the UK, *European Economic Review*, 25, pp. 279–92.

Begg, D.K.H. (1982) *The Rational Expectations Revolution in Macroeconomics*, Oxford, Philip Allen.

Bernanke, B.S. (1984) Permanent income, liquidity, and expenditure on automobiles: evidence from panel data, *Quarterly Journal of Economics*, 99, pp. 587–614.

Bernanke, B.S. (1985) Adjustment costs, durables, and aggregate consumption, *Journal of Monetary Economics*, 15, pp. 41–68.

Bilson, J.F.O. (1981) The 'Speculative Efficiency' hypothesis, *Journal of Business*, 54, pp. 435–51.

Blanchard, O.J. (1987) Why does money affect output? A survey, National Bureau of Economic Research, Working Paper No. 2285; in *Handbook of Monetary Economics* (Eds B.M. Friedman and F. Hahn), North Holland, forthcoming.

Blinder, A.S. and Fischer, S. (1981) Inventories, rational expectations and the business cycle, *Journal of Monetary Economics*, 8, pp. 277–304.

Buiter, W.H. (1980), The economics of Dr Pangloss, *Economic Journal*, 90, pp. 34–50.

Buiter, W.H. (1983), Real effects of anticipated money: some problems of estimation and hypothesis testing, *Journal of Monetary Economics*, 11, pp. 207–24.

Cagan, P. (1956) The monetary dynamics of hyperinflation, in *Studies in the Quantity Theory of Money* (Ed. M. Friedman), Chicago, University of Chicago Press.

Calvo, G. and Rodriguez, C. (1977) A model of exchange rate determination under currency substitution and rational expectations, *Journal of Political Economy*, 84, pp. 617–25.

Campbell, J.Y. (1987) Does saving anticipate declining labour income? An alternative test of the permanent income hypothesis, *Econometrica*, 55, pp. 1249–73.

Campbell, J.Y. and Clarida, R.H. (1987) Household saving and permanent income in Canada and the United Kingdom, in *Economic Effects of the Government Budget* (Ed. E. Helpman et al.), Boston, MIT Press.

Campbell, J.Y. and Deaton, A. (1989) Why is consumption so smooth? *Review of Economic Studies*, 56, pp. 357–73.

Campbell, J.Y. and Mankiw, N.G. (1987) Are output fluctuations transitory?, *Quarterly Journal of Economics*, 102, pp. 857–80.

Campbell, J.Y. and Mankiw, N.G. (1989) International evidence on the persistence of economic fluctuations, *Journal of Monetary Economics*, 23, pp. 319–33.

Carlson, J.A. (1977) A study of price forecasts, *Annals of Economic and Social Measurement*, 6, pp. 27–56.

Carlton, D.W. (1986) The rigidity of prices, *American Economic Review*, 76, pp. 637–58.

Cecchetti, S. (1986) The frequency of price adjustments: a study of the newsstand prices of magazines, 1953 to 1979, *Journal of Econometrics*, 31, pp. 255–74.

Christiano, L.J. and Eichenbaum, M. (1989) Unit roots in real GNP: do we know and do we care?, National Bureau of Economic Research, mimeo.

Cochrane, J. H. (1989) The sensitivity of tests of the intertemporal allocation of consumption to near rational alternatives, *American Economic Review*, 79, pp. 319–37.

Cornell, B. (1977) Spot rates, forward rates and exchange market efficiency, *Journal of Financial Economics*, 5, pp. 55–66.

Cosset, J. C. (1984) On the presence of risk premiums in foreign exchange markets, *Journal of International Economics*, 16, pp. 139–54.

Cox, W. M. (1980) Unanticipated money, output and prices in the small open economy, *Journal of Monetary Economics*, 6, pp. 359–84.

Cramer, J. S. (1986) *Econometric Applications of Maximum Likelihood Methods*, Cambridge, Cambridge University Press.

Daly, V. and Hadjimatheou, G. (1981) Stochastic implications of the life cycle – permanent income hypothesis: evidence for the UK economy, *Journal of Political Economy*, 89, pp. 596–99.

Davidson, J. E. H. and Hendry, D. F. (1981) Interpreting econometric evidence: the behaviour of consumers' expenditure in the UK, *European Economic Review*, 16, pp. 177–92.

Demery, D. (1984) Aggregate demand rational expectations and real output: some new evidence for the UK 1963.2–1982.2, *Economic Journal*, 94, pp. 847–62.

Demery, D. and Duck, N. W. (1985) Inventories and monetary growth in the business cycle: some theoretical considerations and empirical results for the UK, *The Manchester School*, pp. 363–9.

Demery, D., Duck, N. W. and Musgrave, S. W. (1983) Price sluggishness in the UK: an alternative view, University of Bristol, Discussion Paper.

Demery, D., Duck, N. W. and Musgrave, S. W. (1984) Unanticipated money growth, output and employment in West Germany 1964–81, *Weltwirtschaftliches Archiv*, 120, pp. 244–55.

Dornbusch, R. (1976) Expectations and exchange rate dynamics, *Journal of Political Economy*, 84, pp. 1161–76.

Duck, N. W. (1983) The effects of uncertainty about the money supply process in a rational expectations macroeconomic model, *Scottish Journal of Political Economy*, 30, pp. 142–52.

Duck, N. W. (1984) Prices, output and the balance of payments in an open economy with rational expectations, *Journal of International Economics*, 16, pp. 59–78.

Duck, N. W. (1986) The influence of lagged unanticipated monetary growth on real output: a simple illustrative model, *Journal of Macroeconomics*, 8, pp. 183–92.

Edwards, S. (1983) Floating exchange rates, expectations and new information, *Journal of Monetary Economics*, 11, pp. 321–36.

Eichenbaum, M. and Singleton, K. J. (1986) Do equilibrium business cycle theories explain postwar US business cycles?, *NBER Macroeconomics Annual*, Cambridge, Massachusetts, MIT Press.

Fair, R.C. (1979) An analysis of the accuracy of four macroeconomic models, *Journal of Political Economy*, 87, pp. 701-18.

Fellner, W. (1980) The valid core of rationality hypotheses in the theory of expectations, *Journal of Money, Credit and Banking*, 12, pp. 736-87.

Figlewski, S. and Wachtel, P. (1981) The formation of inflationary expectations, *Review of Economics and Statistics*, 58, pp. 1-10.

Fischer, S. (1977) Long-term contracts, rational expectations and the optimal money supply rule, *Journal of Political Economy*, 85, pp. 191-205.

Flavin, M. (1981) The adjustment of consumption to changing expectations about future income, *Journal of Political Economy*, 89, pp. 974-1009.

Flemming, J.S. (1976) *Inflation*, Oxford, Oxford University Press.

Frenkel, J.A. (1981) Flexible exchange rates, prices and the role of 'News': lessons from the 1970's, *Journal of Political Economy*, 89, pp. 665-705.

Frenkel, J.A. and Razin, A. (1980) Stochastic prices and tests of efficiency of foreign exchange markets, *Economics Letters*, 6, pp. 165-70.

Friedman, B.M. (1979) Optimal expectations and the extreme information assumptions of rational expectations macromodels, *Journal of Monetary Economics*, 5, pp. 23-41.

Friedman, B.M. (1980) Survey evidence on the 'rationality' of interest rate expectations, *Journal of Monetary Economics*, 6, pp. 453-65.

Friedman, M. (1957) *A Theory of the Consumption Function*, Princeton, New Jersey, Princeton University Press for the National Bureau of Economic Research.

Friedman, M. (1959) *A Program for Monetary Stability*, New York, Fordham University Press.

Friedman, M. (1968) The role of monetary policy, *American Economic Review*, 58, pp. 1-17.

Friedman, M. and Friedman, R.D. (1980) *Free to Choose*, London, Secker and Warburg.

Friedman, M. and Schwartz, A.J. (1982) *Monetary Trends in the United States and the United Kingdom*, Chicago, University of Chicago Press.

Gordon, R.J. (1982) Price inertia and policy ineffectiveness in the United States, 1890-1980, *Journal of Political Economy*, 90, pp. 1087-117.

Granger, C.W.J. (1969) Investigating causal relations by econometric models and cross spectral methods, *Econometrica*, 37, pp. 424-38.

Granger, C.W.J. and Newbold, P. (1977) *Forecasting Time Series*, New York, Academic Press.

Gray, J.A. (1976) Wage indexation: a macroeconomic approach, *Journal of Monetary Economics*, 2, pp. 221-35.

Greenwald, B. C. and Stiglitz, J. E. (1988) Examining alternative macro-economic theories, *Brookings Papers*, 1, 207-60.

Hakkio, C. S. (1981) Expectations and the forward exchange rate, *International Economic Review*, 22, pp. 663-78.

Hall, R. E. (1978) Stochastic implications of the life cycle – permanent income hypothesis: theory and evidence, *Journal of Political Economy*, 86, pp. 971-87.

Hall, R. E. (1986) The role of consumption in economic fluctuations, in *The American Business Cycle: Continuity and Change* (Ed. R. J. Gordon), Chicago, University of Chicago Press, pp. 237-55.

Hall, R. E. (1989) Consumption, in *Modern Business Cycle Theory* (Ed. R. J. Barro), Oxford, Basil Blackwell, and Harvard, Harvard University Press.

Hansen, G. D. (1985) Indivisible labor and the business cycle, *Journal of Monetary Economics*, 16, pp. 309-27.

Hanson, J. A. (1980) The short-run relations between growth and inflation in Latin America, *American Economic Review*, 70, pp. 972-89.

Harvey, A. (1981) *The Econometric Analysis of Time Series*, Oxford, Philip Allen.

Hayashi, F. (1987) Tests for liquidity constraints: a critical survey and some new observations, in *Advances in Econometrics, Fifth World Congress* (Ed. T. Bewley), vol. 2, Cambridge, Cambridge University Press, pp. 91-120.

Hoffman, D. L. and Schmidt, P. (1981) Testing the restrictions implied by the rational expectations hypothesis, *Journal of Econometrics*, 15, pp. 265-87.

Hoover, K. D. (1988) *The New Classical Macroeconomics*, Oxford, Basil Blackwell.

Hudson, J. (1982) *Inflation: a Theoretical Survey and Synthesis*, London, George Allen & Unwin.

Johnston, J. (1984) *Econometric Methods*, Tokyo, McGraw-Hill.

Jorgenson, D. W. and Griliches, Z. (1967) The explanation of productivity change, *Review of Economic Studies*, 34, pp. 249-83.

Keynes, J. M. (1936) *The General Theory of Employment, Interest and Money*, London, Macmillan.

King, R. G. (1982) Monetary policy and the information content of prices, *Journal of Political Economy*, 90, pp. 247-77.

Kormendi, R. C. and Meguire, P. G. (1984) The real output effects of monetary shocks: cross country tests of rational expectations propositions, *Journal of Political Economy*, 92, pp. 875-908.

Koskela, E. and Viren, M. (1980) New international evidence on output inflation trade-offs: a note, *Economics Letters*, 6, pp. 233-9.

232   *References*

Kydland, F.E. and Prescott, E.C. (1977) Rules rather than discretion: the inconsistency of optimal plans, *Journal of Political Economy*, 85, pp. 473–91.

Kydland, F.E. and Prescott, E.C. (1982) Time to build and aggregate fluctuations, *Econometrica*, 50, pp. 1345–70.

Lawrence, C. (1983) Rational expectations, supply shocks and the stability of the inflation output trade-off: some time series evidence for the United Kingdom 1956–1977, *Journal of Monetary Economics*, 11, pp. 225–46.

Leiderman, L. (1980) Macroeconomic testing of the rational expectations and structural neutrality hypothesis for the United States, *Journal of Monetary Economics*, 6, pp. 69–82.

Lilien, D.M. (1982) Sectoral shifts and cyclical unemployment, *Journal of Political Economy*, 90, pp. 777–93.

Long, J.B. and Plosser, C.I. (1983) Real business cycles, *Journal of Political Economy*, 91, pp. 39–69.

Lovell, M.C. (1986) Tests of the rational expectations hypothesis, *American Economic Review*, 76, pp. 110–24.

Lucas, R.E. Jr. (1972) Expectations and the neutrality of money, *Journal of Economic Theory*, 4, pp. 103–24.

Lucas, R.E. Jr. (1973) Some international evidence on output–inflation trade offs, *American Economic Review*, 63, pp. 326–34.

Lucas, R.E. Jr. (1975) An equilibrium model of the business cycle, *Journal of Political Economy*, 83, pp. 1113–44.

Lucas, R.E. (1976) Econometric policy evaluation: a critique, in *Carnegie-Rochester Series on Public Policy* (Eds K. Brunner and A.H. Meltzer), vol. 1, Amsterdam, North Holland.

Lucas, R.E. Jr. (1977) Understanding business cycles, in *Stabilisation of the Domestic and International Economy* (Eds K. Brunner and A.H. Meltzer), Amsterdam, North Holland.

Lucas, R.E. Jr. (1987) *Models of Business Cycles*, Oxford, Blackwell.

Lucas, R.E. and Sargent, T.J. (1978) After Keynesian macroeconomics, in *After the Phillips Curve: Persistence of High Inflation and High Unemployment*, Federal Reserve Bank of Boston, Conference Series No. 19.

Lucas, R.E. and Sargent, T.J. (1981) *Rational Expectations and Econometric Practice*, Minneapolis, University of Minnesota Press.

McCallum, B.T. (1976) Rational expectations and the natural rate hypothesis: some consistent estimates, *Econometrica*, 44, pp. 43–52.

McCallum, B.T. (1977) Price level stickiness and the feasibility of monetary stabilisation policy under rational expectations, *Journal of Political Economy*, 85, pp. 627–34.

McCallum, B. T. (1978) Price level adjustments and the rational expectations approach to macroeconomic stabilisation policy, *Journal of Money, Credit and Banking*, 10, pp. 418–36.

McCallum, B. T. (1979) On the observational inequivalence of classical and Keynesian models, *Journal of Political Economy*, 87, pp. 395–402.

McCallum, B. T. (1980) Rational expectations and macroeconomic stabilisation policy, *Journal of Money, Credit and Banking*, 12, pp. 716–46.

McCallum, B. T. (1986) On 'real' and 'sticky price' theories of the business cycle, *Journal of Money, Credit and Banking*, 18, pp. 397–414.

McCallum, B. T. (1989) Real business cycle models, in *Modern Business Cycle Theory* (Ed. R. J. Barro), Oxford, Basil Blackwell.

Maddala, G. S. (1977) *Econometrics*, New York, McGraw-Hill.

Malinvaud, E. (1977) *The Theory of Unemployment Reconsidered*, Oxford, Basil Blackwell.

Mankiw, N. G. (1985a) Small menu costs and large business cycles: a macro-economic model of monopoly, *Quarterly Journal of Economics*, 100, pp. 529–39.

Mankiw, N. G. (1985b) Consumer durables and the real interest rate, *The Review of Economics and Statistics*, 67, pp. 353–62.

Mankiw, N. G. (1986) Comments, in *NBER Macroeconomics Annual*, Cambridge, Massachusetts, MIT Press, pp. 139–44.

Mankiw, N. G. and Shapiro, M. D. (1985) Trends, random walks, and tests of the permanent income hypothesis, *Journal of Monetary Economics*, 16, pp. 165–74.

Marini, G. (1985) Intertemporal substitution and the role of monetary policy, *Economic Journal*, 95, pp. 87–100.

Minford, P. (1980) *Memorandum on Monetary Policy*, No. 720, Memorandum in House of Commons, Treasury and Civil Service Committee.

Minford, P. and Peel, D. (1983) *Rational Expectations and the New Macroeconomics*, Oxford, Martin Robertson.

Mishkin, F. (1982a) Does anticipated monetary policy matter? An econometric investigation, *Journal of Political Economy*, 90, pp. 22–50.

Mishkin, F. (1982b) Does anticipated aggregate demand policy matter? *American Economic Review*, 72, pp. 788–802.

Muellbauer, J. and Portes, R. (1978) Macroeconomic models with quantity rationing, *Economic Journal*, 88, pp. 788–821.

Muth, J. F. (1960) Optimal properties of exponentially weighted forecasts, *Journal of the American Statistical Association*, 55, pp. 299–306.

Muth, J. F. (1961) Rational expectations and the theory of price movements, *Econometrica*, 29, pp. 315–35.

Muth, J.F. (1985) Short run forecasts of business activity, paper presented at the joint Pittsburgh Meetings of the Eastern Economics Association – International Society for Inventory Research.

Neary, J.P. and Stiglitz, J.E. (1983) Toward a reconstruction of Keynesian economics: Expectations and constrained equilibria, *Quarterly Journal of Economics*, 98, Supplement, pp. 199–228.

Nelson, C.R. and Plosser, C.I. (1982) Trends and random walks in macroeconomic time series, *Journal of Monetary Economics*, 10, pp. 139–62.

Okun, A. (1981) *Prices and Quantities: a Macroeconomic Analysis*, Washington, The Brookings Institution.

Parkin, M. (1986) The output inflation trade-off when prices are costly to change, *Journal of Political Economy*, 94, pp. 200–24.

Pearce, D.K. (1979) Comparing survey and rational measures of expected inflation, *Journal of Money, Credit and Banking*, 11, pp. 447–56.

Perron, P. (1989) The Great Crash, the oil price shock, and the unit root hypothesis, *Econometrica*, 57, pp. 1361–1401.

Pesando, J.E. (1975) A note on the rationality of the Livingston price expectations, *Journal of Political Economy*, 83, pp. 849–58.

Pesaran, M.H. (1982) A critique of the proposed tests of the natural rate – rational expectations hypothesis, *Economic Journal*, 92, pp. 529–54.

Pesaran, M.H. (1987) *The Limits to Rational Expectations*, Oxford, Basil Blackwell.

Phelps, E.S. (1967) Phillips curves, expectations of inflation and optimal unemployment over time, *Economica*, 34, pp. 254–81.

Phelps, E.S. (1970) The new microeconomics in employment and inflation theory, in *Microeconomic Foundations of Employment and Inflation Theory* (Eds E.S. Phelps et al), New York, Norton, pp. 1–27.

Phelps, E.S. and Taylor, J.B. (1977) The stabilising powers of monetary policy under rational expectations, *Journal of Political Economy*, 85, pp. 165–90.

Phillips, A.W. (1958) The relation between unemployment and the rate of change of money wage rates in the United Kingdom, 1861–1957, *Economica*, 25, pp. 283–99.

Revankar, N.S. (1980) Testing of the rational expectations hypothesis, *Econometrica*, 48, pp. 1347–64.

Rotemberg, J.J. (1982) Sticky prices in the United States, *Journal of Political Economy*, 90, pp. 1187–211.

Rotemberg, J.J. (1987) The new Keynesian microfoundations, in *NBER Macroeconomics Annual* (Ed. S. Fischer), Cambridge, Massachusetts, MIT Press.

Sargent, T. J. (1976a) The observational equivalence of natural and unnatural rate theories of macroeconomics, *Journal of Political Economy*, 84, pp. 631–40.

Sargent, T. J. (1976b) A classical macroeconometric model of the United States, *Journal of Political Economy*, 84, pp. 207–38.

Sargent, T. J. (1979) A note on maximum likelihood estimation of the rational expectations model of the term structure, *Journal of Monetary Economics*, 5, pp. 133–43.

Sargent, T. J. and Wallace, N. (1975) Rational expectations, the optimal monetary instrument and the optimal money supply rule, *Journal of Political Economy*, 83, pp. 241–54.

Shackle, G. L. S. (1958) *Time in Economics*, Amsterdam, North Holland.

Sheffrin, S. M. (1983) *Rational Expectations*, Cambridge, Cambridge University Press.

Shiller, R. J. (1978) Rational expectations and the dynamic structure of macroeconomic models, *Journal of Monetary Economics*, 4, pp. 1–44.

Shiller, R. J. (1980) Alternative tests of rational expectations models: the case of the term structure, National Bureau of Economic Research, working paper no. 563.

Siegel, J. J. (1972) Risk, interest rates and the forward exchange, *Quarterly Journal of Economics*, 86, pp. 303–9.

Sims, C. A. (1972) Money, income, and causality, *American Economic Review*, 62, pp. 540–52.

Sims, C. A. (1980) Comparisons of inter-war and post-war business cycles: monetarism reconsidered, *American Economic Review*, 70, pp. 250–7.

Solow, R. M. and Stiglitz, J. E. (1968) Output, employment and wages in the short run, *Quarterly Journal of Economics*, 82, pp. 537–60.

Taylor, J. B. (1979) Staggered wage setting in macroeconomic models, *American Economic Review Papers and Proceedings*, 69, pp. 108–13.

Turnovsky, S. J. (1970) Some empirical evidence on the formation of price expectations, *Journal of the American Statistical Association*, 65, pp. 1441–54.

Turnovsky, S. J. (1980) The choice of monetary instruments under alternative forms of price expectations, *The Manchester School*, 45, pp. 39–63.

Wallis, K. F. (1980) Econometric implications of the rational expectations hypothesis, *Econometrica*, 48, pp. 49–73.

Walters, A. A. (1971) Consistent expectations, distributed lags and the quantity theory, *Economic Journal*, 81, pp. 273–81.

Weiss, L. (1980) The role for active monetary policy in a rational expectations model, *Journal of Political Economy*, 88, pp. 221–33.

West, K.D. (1988) The insensitivity of consumption to news about income, *Journal of Monetary Economics*, 21, pp. 17–33.

Wickens, M.R. (1982) The efficient estimation of econometric models with rational expectations, *Review of Economic Studies*, 49, pp. 55–67.

Wickens, M.R. and Molana, H. (1984) Stochastic life cycle theory with varying interest rates and prices, *Economic Journal*, 94, pp. 133–47.

Wogin, G. (1980) Unemployment and monetary policy under rational expectations: some Canadian evidence, *Journal of Monetary Economics*, 6, pp. 59–68.

Author Index

Subject Index